CIVIL WAR

Other titles in the Perspectives in American Social History series

PERSPECTIVES IN
AMERICAN SOCIAL HISTORY

Civil War

People and Perspectives

Lisa Tendrich Frank, Editor
Peter C. Mancall, Series Editor

973.71
CIV

 A B C CLIO

Santa Barbara, California • Denver, Colorado • Oxford, England

Library of Congress Cataloging-in-Publication Data
Civil War: people and perspectives / Lisa Tendrich Frank, editor; Peter C. Mancall,
series editor.
    p. cm. — (Perspectives in American social history)
  Include bibliographical references and index.
  ISBN 978-1-59884-035-3 (hard copy : alk. paper) — ISBN 978-1-59884-036-0
(ebook) 1. United States—History—Civil War, 1861-1865—Social aspects.
I. Frank, Lisa Tendrich.
  E468.9.C475 2009
  973.7'1—dc22

                          2009014816

13   12   11   10   9   1   2   3   4   5

This book is also available on the World Wide Web as an e-book.
Visit www.abc-clio.com for details.

ABC-CLIO, LLC
130 Cremona Drive, P.O. Box 1911
Santa Barbara, California 93116-1911

This book is printed on acid-free paper ∞

Manufactured in the United States of America

For Noah

Contents

Series Introduction

Social history is, simply put, the study of past societies. More specifically, social historians attempt to describe societies in their totality, and hence often eschew analysis of politics and ideas. Though many social historians argue that it is impossible to understand how societies functioned without some consideration of the ways that politics worked on a daily basis or what ideas could be found circulating at any given time, they tend to pay little attention to the formal arenas of electoral politics or intellectual currents. In the United States, social historians have been engaged in describing components of the population that had earlier often escaped formal analysis, notably women, members of ethnic or cultural minorities, or those who had fewer economic opportunities than the elite.

Social history became a vibrant discipline in the United States after it had already gained enormous influence in Western Europe. In France, social history in its modern form emerged with the rising prominence of a group of scholars associated with the journal *Annales Economie, Societé, Civilisation* (or *Annales ESC* as it is known). In its pages and in a series of books from historians affiliated with the École des Hautes Études en Sciences Sociale in Paris, brilliant historians such as Marc Bloch, Jacques Le Goff, and Emanuel LeRoy Ladurie described seemingly every aspect of French society. Among the masterpieces of this historical reconstruction was Fernand Braudel's monumental study, *The Mediterranean and the Mediterranean World in the Age of Philip II*, published first in Paris in 1946 and in a revised edition in English in 1972. In this work Braudel argued that the only way to understand a place in its totality was to describe its environment, its social and economic structures, and its political systems. In Britain the emphasis of social historians has been less on questions of environment, per se, than in a description of human communities in all their complexities. For example, social historians there have taken advantage of that nation's remarkable local archives to reconstruct the history of the family and details of its rural past. Works such as Peter Laslett's *The World We Have Lost*, first printed in 1966, and the multiauthored *Agrarian History of England and Wales*, which began to appear in print in 1967, revealed that painstaking work could reveal the lives and habits of individuals who never previously attracted the interest of biographers, demographers, or most historians.

Social history in the United States gained a large following in the second half of the 20th century, especially during the 1960s and 1970s. Its development sprang from political, technical, and intellectual impulses deeply embedded in the culture of the modern university. The politics of civil rights and social reform fueled the passions of historians who strove to tell the stories of the underclass. They benefited from the adoption by historians of statistical analysis, which allowed scholars to trace where individuals lived, how often they moved, what kinds of jobs they took, and whether their economic status declined, stagnated, or improved over time. As history departments expanded, many who emerged from graduate schools focused their attention on groups previously ignored or marginalized. Women's history became a central concern among American historians, as did the history of African Americans, Native Americans, Latinos, and others. These historians pushed historical study in the United States farther away from the study of formal politics and intellectual trends. Though few Americanists could achieve the technical brilliance of some social historians in Europe, collectively they have been engaged in a vast act of description, with the goal of describing seemingly every facet of life from 1492 to the present.

The 16 volumes in this series together represent the continuing efforts of historians to describe American society. Most of the volumes focus on chronological areas, from the broad sweep of the colonial era to the more narrowly defined collections of essays on the eras of the Cold War, the baby boom, and America in the age of the Vietnam War. The series also includes entire volumes on the epochs that defined the nation, the American Revolution and the Civil War, as well as volumes dedicated to the process of westward expansion, women's rights, and African American history.

This social history series derives its strength from the talented editors of individual volumes. Each editor is an expert in his or her own field who selected and organized the contents of his or her volume. Editors solicited other experienced historians to write individual essays. Every volume contains first-rate analysis complemented by lively anecdotes designed to reveal the complex contours of specific historical moments. The many illustrations to be found in these volumes testify too to the recognition that any society can be understood not only by the texts that its participants produce but also by the images that they craft. Primary source documents in each volume will allow interested readers to pursue some specific topics in greater depth, and each volume contains a chronology to provide guidance to the flow of events over time. These tools—anecdotes, images, texts, and timelines—allow readers to gauge the inner workings of America in particular periods and yet also to glimpse connections between eras.

The articles in these volumes testify to the abundant strengths of historical scholarship in the United States in the early years of the 21st century. Despite the occasional academic contest that flares into public notice, or the self-serving cant of politicians who want to manipulate the nation's past for partisan ends—for example, in debates over the Second Amendment to the U.S. Constitution and what it means about potential limits to the rights of gun ownership—the articles here all reveal the vast increase in knowledge of the American past that has taken place over the previous half century. Social historians do not dominate history faculties in American colleges and universities, but no one could deny them a seat at the intellectual table. Without their efforts, intellectual, cultural, and political historians would be hard pressed to understand why certain ideas circulated when they did, why some religious movements prospered or foundered, how developments in fields such as medicine and engineering reflected larger concerns, and what shaped the world we inhabit.

Fernand Braudel and his colleagues envisioned entire laboratories of historians in which scholars working together would be able to produce *histoire totale*: total history. Historians today seek more humble goals for our collective enterprise. But as the richly textured essays in these volumes reveal, scholarly collaboration has in fact brought us much closer to that dream. These volumes do not and cannot include every aspect of American history. However, every page reveals something interesting or valuable about how American society functioned. Together, these books suggest the crucial necessity of stepping back to view the grand complexities of the past rather than pursuing narrower prospects and lesser goals.

Peter C. Mancall

Series Editor

Introduction

In the popular consciousness, wars are often mistakenly understood through the personalities of prominent military officers and national politicians. The American Civil War, fought between 1861 and 1865, is certainly no exception to this rule. Views of U.S. president Abraham Lincoln and Confederate president Jefferson Davis, as well as of such generals as Confederate Robert E. Lee and Union Ulysses S. Grant, have formed society's basic understanding of the war. Lee has become the embodiment of the South; Grant and Lincoln are seen as personifications of the North. For more than a generation, however, a new group of historians has challenged this traditional view of the Civil War by placing the experiences of nonelites at the center of the story. The results, many of which will be explored in this volume, have been revolutionary. Although adherents to the traditional approach continue to produce countless books and articles, social historians have forever changed the face of Civil War history. Few scholars can now deny the centrality of the African American and slave experience to the conflict, and increasingly the nation's popular culture has embraced images of common soldiers and civilian experiences. Although Lincoln, Lee, Grant, and Davis continue to attract attention, so too do female nurses like Clara Barton, slaves and abolitionists such as Frederick Douglass and Sojourner Truth, as well as countless individuals who participated in the conflict in various ways. Even more impressive, scholars have rescued the voices and experiences of myriad civilians, slaves, nurses, free blacks, soldiers, Indians, laundresses, factory workers, preachers, and immigrants. Although many of the findings and themes of the field of Civil War history have yet to shape the popular consciousness, the process of rewriting the past to include the greater population has already begun.

The War

The Civil War has long been recognized as a pivotal moment in the development of the fledgling American nation—a shared conviction that has led to most American universities using the Civil War as the dividing point in survey-level U.S. history courses. Before the war, localism shaped both the experiences of most Americans as well as their political outlooks. Most citizens identified with their families and local communities more than they did with their nation or even their states. In fact, the states' rights campaign that bolstered the secession movement of 1860–1861 had its roots in a long-standing belief in the legal and social importance, if not primacy, of the states over the nation. As Virginian Robert E. Lee notably commented with the prospect of secession looming: "If the Union is dissolved, I shall return to Virginia [and] share the fortune of my people" (Lee in Fellman 2003, 84). The four years of bloody internal strife ultimately allowed Americans to come together as a nation, even turning the United States from a plural noun to a singular entity. The Civil War destroyed and remade the geographic landscape, altered the social realities of national life, and forced Southerners and Northerners to come to grips with who they were and how they fit together as a nation. Over the course of the war's four years, approximately 2 percent of the American population was killed in battle. In addition to the more than 620,000 soldiers who died, unknown numbers of civilians lost their lives to stray bullets, hunger, exposure to the elements, and diseases. Those who did not die found their lives changed forever.

From the outset of the war, many Americans recognized, and others hoped, that the war would result in a social revolution. Most believed that the war and emancipation were intrinsically linked. When the war began in 1861, the U.S. population included 4 million slaves, or one-eighth of the population, and they were largely confined to the Confederate states. Although Lincoln repeatedly insisted that he lacked the constitutional authority to emancipate slaves, many Northerners and Southerners concluded otherwise. After all, he was a member of the newly formed Republican Party, which had the support of nearly all of the nation's most radical abolitionists. One correspondent for the *Anglo-African* wrote that after the presidential election, "he that is able to read this nation's destiny, can see and decipher the hand-writing upon the wall" (McPherson 1982, 11). Many Americans worried about Lincoln's intentions toward slavery— Southerners feared that he would abolish it and Northern abolitionists feared that he would not do enough to end it. Former slave and abolitionist lecturer Frederick Douglass felt that Lincoln's win would signify a move toward emancipation and "must and will be hailed as an anti-slavery triumph" (McPherson 1982, 8). The optimism and hope in abolitionist circles was more than matched by fears in the South over Lincoln's intentions toward their "peculiar institution" and a belief that his goal, stated or not, was to eradicate slavery. An article in the *Richmond Examiner*, for example, despaired that "a party founded on the single sentiment . . . of hatred of African slavery, is now the controlling power" (McPherson 1988, 232).

Despite their hopes and fears about the future of slavery, many Americans confidently believed that war could be avoided or ended quickly and that the nation could thereby avert any widespread social upheaval. The first battle of the war, which occurred shortly after 11 Southern states seceded from the Union and formed the Confederate States of America and just three months after the engagement at Fort Sumter, attracted onlookers who wanted to watch the war "game." Assuming that it would be a quick and bloodless military exercise, women and children sat up on the hills that surrounded the battlefield, which was 30 miles from Washington, to watch and to eat their picnics. However, the Battle of Bull Run, or Manassas, was a bloody and chaotic affair that overran the horrified spectators. In the aftermath, people in both the Union and Confederacy concluded that a protracted war was likely unavoidable. The four years that followed resulted in battles whose names—including Chickamauga, Gettysburg, Antietam, Shiloh, and Fredericksburg—have become synonymous with the resulting destruction, death, and heartbreak.

Although approximately 3 million men served as soldiers during the Civil War, most Americans were not in the military. The 29 million noncombatants may not have faced battle every day, but they faced their own wartime challenges as they simultaneously found ways to support their war efforts on the home fronts. The Civil War forced Union and Confederate civilians to deal with unprecedented shortages and daily hardships. Most Americans went without, or with significantly less, fresh meat and vegetables, new clothing, shoes, metal goods, or luxuries in general. Most Southerners lived with the effects of blockades, sieges, and warfare in and near their communities. Americans of all regions and races dealt with inflation, the influx of refugees to their homes or communities, life as refugees, the departure of men for the battlefield, and the uncertainty that accompanied the struggle. No community or family escaped the horrors of the war, as death became commonplace and mourning became widespread. For African Americans, the upheaval of the war resulted in opportunities to pursue and ultimately obtain their freedom. Although the contradictions of a slaveholding nation built on the ideals of freedom came to a head with the election of Republican Abraham Lincoln in 1860, emancipation was a slow process and one that brought its own anxieties across the nation. Even in Indian country, the status of blacks would be contested and then debated for decades to follow.

Traditional Histories of the Civil War

Early histories of the Civil War, and those that continue to follow this approach, focus on the masculine world of politics and war, highlighting the battles, commanders, and politicians, and ignoring the roles of common people in the conflict. Scholars focus on the movement of troops and the formal decisions that resulted in victories and defeats. At the same time, military commanders like Ulysses S. Grant, William T. Sherman, Robert E. Lee, and Thomas J. "Stonewall" Jackson are presented as exemplars of the attitudes of their regions and are given the credit for outcomes of battles and the war. Lee, for example, has been lionized as the quintessential Southern gentleman. Furthermore, he is given all of the credit for Confederate successes, and none of the blame for the ultimate defeat of his nation. Biographies of these commanders, as well as battle histories high-lighting their movements, shape understandings of the war and its pur-poses. Pulitzer Prize and National Book Award–winning writer Bruce Catton, for example, typified this approach to the Civil War in his writings during the 1950s. "Grant and Lee were in complete contrast, representing two diametrically opposed elements in American life. Grant was the mod-ern man emerging; beyond him, ready to come on the stage, was the great age of steel and machinery, of crowded cities and a restless burgeoning vitality" (Catton in Kennedy, Kennedy, and Aaron 2008, 213). Lee could not have been more different, according to Catton. He "might have ridden down from the old age of chivalry, lance in hand, silken banner fluttering over his head. Each man was the perfect champion of his causes, drawing both his strengths and his weaknesses from the people he led" (Catton in Kennedy, Kennedy, and Aaron 2008, 213).

Other scholars used political events, including elections, laws, and formal associations, as evidence of the attitudes of citizens. Facile assumptions—the Union could be understood through the abolitionist leaders or large planters exemplified the entire South—typified this approach. Consequently, the political figures who publicly vocalized the debates over slavery and secession received detailed examinations, whereas the populations who swayed their opinions got scant attention.

The prominent traditional view of the American Civil War has been augmented by the myth of the Lost Cause—a Confederate campaign to shape the public's understanding of the war that began long before Lee's surrender to Grant at Appomattox Court House in April 1865. The rhetoric of the Lost Cause holds that the Confederacy never had a chance against what is painted as a much stronger and better-prepared Northern military. Furthermore, the myth proclaims that the South should be revered for its valiant efforts and its ability to persevere as long as it did. Books published by Southern men and women in the immediate aftermath of the war pro-moted this view, as do many works published today. Furthermore, much of the Lost Cause has been repeated and spread through various works of fiction—most notably Margaret Mitchell's *Gone with the Wind* (1936). The best-selling novel won the Pulitzer Prize and, as a top-grossing movie in 1939, it won eight Oscar awards. The romanticized version of the Old South and the glory of Southern soldiers has infiltrated the hearts and minds of many. However, it blurs the truths of the war and the people who fought it.

The shortcomings of the traditional approach to the Civil War should be clear. The approach focuses almost exclusively on the experiences of rich over poor, white over black, native born over Native American, men over women, and officers over enlisted men. Although generals and presi-dents certainly helped shape the conflict, recent scholars have demon-strated that common people of various colors, ethnicities, classes, and sexes also shaped the war. The Civil War, in essence, was won and lost because of a combination of official policies and the willingness of individ-uals to follow those dictates.

The Chapters

The volume that follows offers a nuanced look at the experiences of the Civil War, an alternative to the top-down focus on elite white men and their policies. The lives, experiences, and perspectives of ordinary Americans are highlighted in *Civil War: People and Perspectives* through nine essays, a chronology, a glossary of basic Civil War terms, events, and people, as well as a collection of primary sources. The essays, all on various overlapping, but distinct themes, form the crux of the volume and allow readers insight into the lives of those people who lived the American Civil War. Essays examine in depth soldiers, civilians, women, children, immigrants, African Americans, Native Americans, members of religious minorities, and urbanites. Taken together, these essays reveal myriad interwoven experiences— a rich tapestry of experiences that combine to define the Civil War.

In Chapter 1, "'A Soldier's Life Is a Hard One at Best': Soldiers in the American Civil War," John M. Sacher examines the complex and wide-ranging motivations and experiences of Confederate and Union soldiers. Although many rushed to enlist at the outset of the war, they were not prepared for the realities of camp life during wartime. Additionally, as the war lengthened and the war aims expanded, soldiers on both sides had to adapt to new conditions and motivations. In Chapter 2, "When the Home Front Became a Battlefront: Civilians in Invaded and Occupied Areas," Antoinette G. van Zelm explores life for noncombatants. Civilians who came into contact with enemy soldiers all found their lives changed, but the types of changes invasion brought often depended upon a civilian's race, gender, and class. Whether facing military regiments or guerilla bands, civilians braced for hardships and danger. Lisa Tendrich Frank highlights the female experience in Chapter 3, "War on Two Fronts: Women during the Civil War." Frank explores how women both shaped and were shaped by the Civil War and wartime realities. Women did not, as traditional histories assume, stand on the sidelines for the war, but rather they played active roles as supporters, detractors, nurses, spies, soldiers, and workers. Karen A. Kehoe explores another marginalized group in Civil War studies in Chapter 4, "Children and the Civil War." The war not only affected children's circumstances at home, but also changed children's ways of playing as well as their schooling. In addition, Kehoe discusses children's roles in the conflict, which included making socks for the soldiers, raising money for the troops, and even participating in regiments as musicians. In Chapter 5, Fiona Deans Halloran highlights the experiences and contributions of immigrants to the war effort. "Patriotism, Preparation, and Reputation: Immigrants in Battle and on the Home Front in the American Civil War" examines the varying participation of immigrants in the Union and Confederacy. Although immigrants held leadership positions in the military, served as soldiers, nursed the wounded, and raised money for the troops, they were not immune from Nativist attitudes and often experienced discrimination. African Americans also dealt with discrimination and violence. Their wartime experiences and struggles are examined in Julie Holcomb's "From Enslaved to Liberators: African Americans and the Civil

War." In Chapter 6, Holcomb discusses how African Americans, North and South, made the war their own and how they affected its outcome. They pushed for emancipation, forced the hands of Union politicians and officers, and helped make the war into one over slavery. In Chapter 7, "The Longhouse Divided: Native Americans during the American Civil War," Andrew K. Frank demonstrates how Native Americans used the upheaval of civil war to their advantage. Although divided by loyalty and experiences, most Indians attempted to use the war to pursue tribal and personal ambitions. They settled old scores, pursued financial opportunities, and reshaped their relationship with federal and state governments while often participating in the Union or Confederate war efforts. Members of religious minorities lived on the outskirts of life, but still made the war their own, too. In Chapter 8, "Becoming American: Catholics, Jews, and Mormons during the American Civil War," Sarah K. Nytroe examines the wartime roles played by members of these groups as they tried to prove their loyalty to their nation in the face of society's questions about their commitment. Their perceived cultural differences did not prevent them from supporting, or opposing, their region's war efforts. Many fought in the Civil War armies, served as home front nurses, held government posts, and otherwise worked for the war. As Clinton Terry shows in Chapter 9, "The Urban Civil War," despite the nation's predominantly rural character, urban centers and their residents played pivotal roles in the Civil War. In addition to being the settings for draft and bread riots, cities in the North and South became places to rally troops and support, hiding places as well as gathering centers for spies, supply centers for the soldiers on the field, and shelters for refugees. This final chapter details the life experienced by many in the urban centers of the Confederacy and the Union.

Themes across Civil War History

Three themes in particular connect the essays in this volume and the social history of the Civil War. First, the authors illuminate the connections between the home front and the war front and between civilians and soldiers. Events throughout the Civil War demonstrate that neither can be considered independently of the other, but rather that events on the battlefront affected life on the home front, just as events on the home front shaped the battlefield. Second, these essays demonstrate the importance of including a diverse range of people in our understanding of the war because their varied personal experiences and rationales for their behavior often conflicted with official policies. Leaders may have determined the course of the war, but citizens supported or opposed those decisions for highly personal reasons. Third, these essays demonstrate how the war was an engine for social change as well as an opportunity for individuals and communities to pursue ambitions of their own. The remaking of the United States not only would allow more freedom for the freed slaves, but also would give shape to movements for change by women, Native Americans, workers, and others.

Home Front and War Front

The connection between home front and war front resulted in part from the geographic location of a war that was frequently fought in the backyards of civilians and in part from the various strains that enlisting 10 percent of the nation caused. Nowhere was this truer than in the Border States and other areas where guerilla warfare was rampant. One woman from the slaveholding and Unionist area around Baltimore recalled that "between the blue forces and the gray we were ground between two millstones of terror" (Bardaglio 2002, 321). In these areas, the Civil War did more than divide the nation; it divided towns and even households.

Whereas earlier historians have separated events on the home front from those on the battlefield, in reality, the Civil War blurred these lines. Battles took place in towns, cities, and on private farms. The Battle of Gettysburg, for example, literally took place on the farms of a small Pennsylvania town and townspeople hid in basements as the three-day battle ensued. As a result, civilians frequently became unwitting participants in the military side of the war. In Gettysburg, as elsewhere, civilians offered their services as nurses and cooks. In addition, private homes often became military headquarters or makeshift hospitals.

A vibrant interplay between soldiers and civilians further blurred the distinction between home front and war front, as soldiers marched through towns, impressed valuables, looted homes, and otherwise created havoc. In Indian Territory, for example, one agent reported that "everything which could be found, and which could be eaten by an Indian—every article of clothing that could be worn by men, women and children, and every article of bedding and blankets—was eagerly seized upon and carried away by" the enemy (McLoughlin 1993, 211). Near the end of the war, Philip Sheridan's campaign in Virginia's Shenandoah Valley and William T. Sherman's march through Georgia and the Carolinas destroyed any belief that soldiers and civilians could be separated. Sherman, for example, evacuated Atlanta and allowed "bummers" to ransack Confederate homes in the search for food and other wartime needs. As one woman recalled, "When they would say the Yankees were coming we would not know what to expect, whether someone would be killed, the house burned or what would happen, but there was one thing sure, they had to be fed" (Gardenhire 1939, 9).

As a result of the wartime destruction, suffering became common throughout the United States. Funerals were common, and anxiety enveloped loved ones who feared that they would lose husbands, sons, brothers, and sweethearts. Thousands of families became refugees, moving into the homes of distant friends and relatives to escape invading enemy troops or simply to pool their resources. Others moved for political purposes. Just as many Southern Unionists fled their homes to the safety of Northern communities, so did Creek Indians who wanted to maintain their neutrality or side with the Union. In addition, all Americans dealt with wartime shortages. In the South, the naval blockade, combined with the destructiveness and hunger of invading soldiers exacerbated dwindling supplies and left civilians with little food or supplies. With a lack of basic necessities, many civilians took out their frustrations on local governments and their neigh-bors. Bread riots, for example, erupted in several Southern cities in response to inflationary prices, while anger in New York City over the pros-pect of emancipation resulted in draft riots.

Even as they struggled to survive, many civilians sought to support the war in both tangible and psychological ways. From the outset of the war, soldiers' family members and communities helped outfit the troops, sent letters to support soldiers, and raised money for the well-being and care of wounded men. Many communities prepared meals for soldiers who passed through on their furloughs home. In addition, makeshift hospitals were formed in countless churches, homes, and public halls to nurse the wounded. As late as early 1865, Union and Confederate supporters held fund-raisers to support their respective causes.

Command and Consent

This volume illuminates the fallacy of assuming that a single set of experi-ences or a common rationale united people in the two warring nations. Although the election of 1860 and its abolitionist overtones certainly sparked the secession crisis, soldiers in both the North and South enlisted for reasons other than their political loyalties, Constitutional judgments, or attitudes about slavery. Many Confederate soldiers resented fighting to secure the property rights of elite Southerners. As one soldier complained, wealthier Southerners could get exemptions from the draft and were "living at home enjoying life because they have a few negroes" (Mitchell 1988, 160). Similarly, many Union soldiers fought despite their fears about emancipation. Some immigrants, like those who enlisted in the Irish Bri-gade, recognized that the war enabled them to demonstrate their patriotism and the loyalty of their ethnic community. This was especially important after the ascendance of the Republican Party—a political organization that enveloped many Nativist and anti-Catholic voices. Many community leaders advocated fighting in, and otherwise supporting, an Irish Catholic unit to soothe fears about their loyalties. Other soldiers fought for financial reasons or because of the pressures asserted by their communities, families, or friends.

Similar distinctions divided the wartime civilian populations in both the North and the South. Although war brought many people together, it could not erase deep-rooted differences. For example, in Atlanta, Georgia, a group of Unionists created a secret society so that they could support the United States from inside enemy territory. Secret Confederates formed similar ties behind Union lines. In some communities—especially in Border States and in Indian Territory—the war literally tore communities apart. Many Indian nations spent much of the war fighting against factions of their own people—reliving and refighting disputes that were often more than a generation old. This seemed to be particularly true among the Cher-okee, where the factions that predated removal in the 1830s continued to shape the Confederate-Unionist divide in the 1860s.

Social Changes

Finally, the war created opportunities for Americans of all walks of life to participate in the public sphere or to escape many of the confines that typically defined their lives. Many women, for example, found employment in munitions plants and in government offices. They also became nurses, helping transform a job that previously had been the domain of men into one seen as appropriate for women. Poor whites used their military service both for financial gain as well as to make claims for their civic importance. Native Americans similarly used the war to settle long-standing grievances and renegotiate their status with the U.S. government and with individual states. Even the daily lives of children were transformed by the war. They played increasingly militarized games, attended school less frequently, took on responsibilities that were once performed by fathers, and collected wartime items. Children were impressed into the informal and formal support systems that sustained both the Union and Confederate armies: they helped with fund-raisers, sewed flags and uniforms, became musicians for military units, and even lied about their ages to enlist.

The Civil War provided much of the capital necessary for the expansion of manufacturing and the transformation of urban life. The Confederacy and Union spent an estimated $5.2 billion during the war, and a lion's share of that amount went to the urban developers and factory owners who could outfit and supply the armies. Both armies created supply depots, built railroads, encouraged shipbuilding, and funded armories. However, Union besiegement, occupation of, and destruction of many Southern cities exacerbated the differences between the North and South by the war's end. Southern cities, which had not had the power, population, or industry of their Northern counterparts before the war, were left even further behind as a result of destruction caused during the Civil War.

The greatest and most lasting changes inspired by the war took place for the nation's African American population. These changes began at the start of the war. In the Sea Islands off the coast of South Carolina, African Americans obtained de facto freedom early in the war as their masters and overseers fled to safer terrain. The social transformation that ensued was remarkable. Former slaves divided up their property, organized the land into family plots, began to educate their children, and otherwise restructured society without the "guidance" of their former masters. Other African Americans enlisted in the Union Army, attempting to get on "the road to Responsibility; Competency; and an honorable Citizenship" (Berlin, Reidy, and Rowland 1982, 712). Frederick Douglass, for example, concluded that the enlistment of black soldiers would secure many of the ambitions of the abolitionists.

> Let the black man get upon his person the brass letters "U.S."; let him get an eagle on his button, and a musket on his shoulder and bullets in his pocket, and there is no power on earth which can deny that he has earned the right to citizenship in the United States. (Douglass as quoted in Litwack 1980, 72)

Conclusion

In recent years, social historians have transformed our understanding of the American Civil War. Although generals and politicians continue to attract the attention of scholars and the general public, historians increasingly embrace the stories of common soldiers, civilians, African Americans, European immigrants, Native Americans, and other social groups. By prioritizing the experiences and influences of the masses and telling the story from the bottom up, these scholars have demonstrated that there was no single experience in the Civil War. They have emphasized how the war enveloped and transformed the entire nation. This volume illuminates these modern findings and demonstrates the revolutionary nature of the war.

Lisa Tendrich Frank

References and Further Reading

Ayers, Edward L. 2003. *In the Presence of Mine Enemies: War in the Heart of America, 1859–1863*. New York: W. W. Norton and Company.

Bardaglio, Peter. 1992. "The Children of the Jubilee: African American Childhood in Wartime." In *Divided Houses: Gender and the Civil War*, edited by Catherine Clinton and Nina Silber, 213–229. New York: Oxford University Press.

Bardaglio, Peter. 2002. "On the Border: White Children in Maryland." In *The War Was You and Me: Civilians in the American Civil War*, edited by Joan E. Cashin, 313–331. Princeton, NJ: Princeton University Press.

Berlin, Ira, Joseph P. Reidy, and Leslie S. Rowland, eds. 1982. *Freedom: A Documentary History of Emancipation, 1861–1867. Series II: The Black Military Experience*. New York: Cambridge University Press.

Blair, William. 1998. *Virginia's Private War: Feeding Body and Soul in the Confederacy, 1861–1865*. New York: Oxford University Press.

Cashin, Joan E., ed. 2002. *The War Was You and Me: Civilians in the American Civil War*. Princeton, NJ: Princeton University Press.

Clinton, Catherine, and Nina Silber, eds. 1992. *Divided Houses: Gender and the Civil War*. New York: Oxford University Press.

Clinton, Catherine, and Nina Silber, eds. 2006. *Battle Scars: Gender and Sexuality in the American Civil War*. New York: Oxford University Press.

Faust, Drew Gilpin. 1996. *Mothers of Invention: Women of the Slaveholding South in the American Civil War*. Chapel Hill: University of North Carolina Press.

Faust, Drew Gilpin. 2008. *This Republic of Suffering: Death and the American Civil War*. New York: Alfred A. Knopf.

Fellman, Michael. 2003. *The Making of Robert E. Lee*. New York: Random House.

Gardenhire, Kibbie Tinsley Williams. 1939. Tennessee State Library and Archives, Nashville.

Kennedy, X. J., Dorothy M. Kennedy, and Jane E. Aaron, eds. 2008. *The Brief Bedford Reader*. New York: Macmillan.

Lawson, Melinda. 2002. *Patriot Fires: Forging a New American Nationalism in the Civil War North*. Lawrence: University Press of Kansas.

Litwack, Leon F. 1980. *Been in the Storm So Long: The Aftermath of Slavery*. New York: Vintage Books.

Manning, Chandra. 2007. *What This Cruel War Was Over: Soldiers, Slavery, and the Civil War*. New York: Knopf.

Marten, James. 1998. *The Children's Civil War*. Chapel Hill: University of North Carolina Press.

McLoughlin, William Gerald. 1993. *After the Trail of Tears: The Cherokees Struggle for Sovereignty, 1839–1880*. Chapel Hill: University of North Carolina.

McPherson, James M. 1982. *The Negro's Civil War: How American Negroes Felt and Acted during the War for the Union*. Urbana: University of Illinois Press.

McPherson, James M. 1988. *Battle Cry of Freedom: The Civil War Era*. New York: Ballantine Books.

McPherson, James M. 1997. *For Cause and Comrades: Why Men Fought in the Civil War*. New York: Oxford University Press.

Mitchell, Reid. 1988. *Civil War Soldiers*. New York: Viking Press.

Paludan, Phillip S. 1988. *A People's Contest: The Union and Civil War, 1861–1865*. Lawrence: University Press of Kansas.

Roark, James L. 1977. *Masters Without Slaves: Southern Planters in the Civil War and Reconstruction*. New York: W. W. Norton.

Taylor, Amy Murrell. 2005. *The Divided Family in Civil War America*. Chapel Hill: University of North Carolina Press.

Whites, LeeAnn. 1995. *The Civil War as a Crisis in Gender, Augusta, Georgia, 1860–1890*. Athens: University of Georgia Press.

About the Editor and Contributors

Andrew K. Frank is associate professor of history at Florida State University. He is the author of *Creeks and Southerners: Biculturalism on the Early American Frontier* (University of Nebraska, 2005) and *The Routledge Historical Atlas of the American South* (Routledge, 1999). He is currently writing *The Second Conquest: Indians, Settlers and Slaves on the Florida Frontier*.

Lisa Tendrich Frank is an independent scholar who has taught courses in the American Civil War and women's history at universities around the country. She received her doctorate from the University of Florida in 2001. She is the editor of *Women in the American Civil War* (ABC-CLIO, 2008), and is the author of several articles on women and the Civil War. She is currently writing a book on the experiences of Confederate women during Sherman's March through Georgia and the Carolinas. She lives in Tallahassee, Florida.

Fiona Deans Halloran is assistant professor of American history at Eastern Kentucky University. She received her doctorate in 2005 from the University of California–Los Angeles, where she wrote a dissertation on the American political cartoonist Thomas Nast. Halloran currently is revising that manuscript for publication as a book and continues to work with political cartooning, American popular culture, and the history of the Civil War era.

Julie Holcomb is a doctoral candidate in history at the University of Texas at Arlington. Her dissertation focuses on the transatlantic free produce and antislavery movements. A certified archivist, Holcomb served as the College and Special Collections Archivist at Navarro College before being named director in 2004. Her book *Southern Sons, Northern Soldiers: The Remley Brothers and the 22nd Iowa* was published by Northern Illinois University Press in 2004.

Karen A. Kehoe is assistant professor of history at St. Vincent College in Latrobe, Pennsylvania, where she teaches courses in early U.S. history. She received her doctorate from Marquette University in 2003 and studies and writes about women and musicians during the era of the American Civil War.

Sarah K. Nytroe received her doctorate in history from Boston College. She has written articles on Catholic women and the U.S. Sanitary Commission for *Women in the American Civil War* (ABC-CLIO, 2008). Her scholarship focuses on American religious history and the 19th-century United States.

John M. Sacher is assistant professor of history at the University of Central Florida. He received his doctorate from Louisiana State University in 1999. He is the author of *A Perfect War of Politics: Parties, Politicians, and Democracy in Louisiana, 1824–1861* (Louisiana State University Press, 2003), which won the 2003 Kemper and Leila Williams Prize for best book on Louisiana history. He is currently researching a book on Confederate conscription.

Clinton W. Terry is assistant professor of history and assistant dean at Mercer University. He received his bachelor of arts degree from Ohio State and his doctorate from the University of Cincinnati. He is currently writing a book on Cincinnati during the Civil War.

Antoinette G. van Zelm is the historian for the Tennessee Civil War National Heritage Area, a partnership unit of the National Park Service that is administered by the Center for Historic Preservation at Middle Tennessee State University. She received her doctorate from the College of William & Mary. Her publications have appeared in *Virginia Cavalcade, Negotiating Boundaries of Southern Womanhood, A History of Tennessee Arts, The Encyclopedia of Emancipation and Abolition*, and *Women in the American Civil War*. Van Zelm is active in the Southern Association for Women Historians and serves as book review editor for the association.

Chronology

December 1833 The American Anti-Slavery Society forms in Philadelphia.

July 1840 Abby Kelly is elected to the board of the American Anti-Slavery Society. Subsequent debate over the role of women in the abolitionist movement results in some members forming a separate American and Foreign Anti-Slavery Society. William Lloyd Garrison remains with the American Anti-Slavery Society.

July 1848 Lucretia Mott, Elizabeth Cady Stanton, and other supporters of women's rights hold a convention at Seneca Falls, New York, and issue a "Declaration of Sentiments."

1850 Allan Pinkerton opens a detective agency in Chicago.

September 1850 President Millard Fillmore signs a series of bills that became known as the Compromise of 1850.

May 1851 Former slave Sojourner Truth delivers her "Ain't I a Woman?" speech at a women's rights convention in Akron, Ohio.

June 1851 Washington-based abolitionist newspaper, *The National Era*, begins publishing in serial form Harriet Beecher Stowe's *Uncle Tom's Cabin; or, Life Among the Lowly*.

December 1851 The first American Young Men's Christian Association (YMCA) opens in Boston, Massachusetts.

March 1852 *Uncle Tom's Cabin; or, Life Among the Lowly* is published in book form.

April 1853 Former slave Harriet Tubman begins working on the Underground Railroad to bring other slaves to freedom.

May 1854 Congress passes the Kansas-Nebraska Act. Escalating violence in Kansas begins between proslavery and antislavery settlers in the territory and continues until Kansas' admission to the Union as a free state in January 1861. This violence is referred to as "Bleeding Kansas."

June 1854 The first YMCA opens in Buffalo, New York.

April 1856 The first bridge to span the Mississippi River opens.

May 1856 Massachusetts senator Charles Sumner delivers his "Crime Against Kansas" speech.

John Brown and his sons kill five proslavery men during a raid on Pottowatomie Creek.

November 1856 Proslavery democrat James Buchanan is elected as the fifteenth president of the United States.

March 1857 The Supreme Court makes its *Dred Scott v. Sanford* ruling.

May 1857 Elizabeth and Emily Blackwell open the New York Infirmary for Women and Children.

August 1857 Widespread financial panic and economic depression begin with the failure of the New York branch of the Ohio Life Insurance and Trust Company.

June 1858 Abraham Lincoln delivers his "House Divided" speech.

August 1858 The first transatlantic telegraph cable is completed. It breaks after a few weeks of operation.

Abraham Lincoln and Stephen A. Douglas engage in their first debate in Ottawa, Illinois.

October 1858 A fancy dry-goods store, opened by R. H. Macy in New York City, will become one of the nation's first department stores.

Lightweight sewing machines by Isaac Singer become available for family use.

Abraham Lincoln and Stephen A. Douglas engage in their final debate in Alton, Illinois.

April 1859 Machinist and blacksmith union workers meet in Philadelphia and call for an eight-hour workday.

October 1859 Abolitionist John Brown leads a raid on the federal arsenal at Harpers Ferry, Virginia (now West Virginia), hoping to initiate a slave rebellion.

December 1859 John Brown is executed in Charlestown, Virginia, after being found guilty of murder, treason, and attempting to incite a slave insurrection.

February 1860 Jefferson Davis asks the Senate to pass slave codes for the territories.

March 1860 Approximately 6,000 shoemakers stage a protest march in Lynn, Massachusetts, for union recognition and higher wages. At least 800 women join their male colleagues in the strike.

April 1860 Mail service between Missouri and California, via the Pony Express, begins.

The Democratic Party splits over slavery.

Anna Dickinson delivers "The Rights and Wrongs of Women" at a Quaker meeting.

May 1860 Former members of the Whig and American Parties create the Constitutional Union Party.

October 1860 Hoping to train a ministry for the Episcopalian Church and prevent the influence of abolitionism, Leonidas Polk founds the University of the South at Sewanee, Tennessee.

November 1860 Abraham Lincoln is elected president of the United States.

December 1860 South Carolina secedes from the Union.

The Crittenden Compromise, which upholds the Compromise of 1850, is enacted.

January 1861 Kansas is admitted to the Union under its antislavery constitution.

Mississippi, Florida, Alabama, Georgia, and Louisiana secede from the Union.

Harriet Jacobs [Linda Brent] publishes *Incidents in the Life of a Slave Girl.*

February 1861 Texas secedes.

The seceded states hold convention in Montgomery, Alabama, where they adopt a Confederate Constitution and elect Jefferson Davis to be president of the Confederate States of America.

The Confederacy inaugurates Jefferson Davis as its president.

Former president John Tyler chairs a peace convention in Washington, DC.

March 1861 Abraham Lincoln is inaugurated as president of the United States.

April 1861 Confederates fire upon and capture Fort Sumter in South Carolina. Lincoln declares that an insurrection exists, calls for 75,000 soldiers to put it down, and orders a naval blockade of Confederate seaports.

Virginia secedes.

Lincoln orders all civilian employees within the executive branch to take a Loyalty Oath.

Riots erupt in Baltimore, Maryland.

New York City women form the Women's Central Association of Relief.

Dorothea Dix is appointed superintendent of female nurses for the Union Army.

May 1861 Arkansas and North Carolina secede.

Dorothea Dix organizes the first military hospitals in the United States.

Congress creates the Department of Agriculture.

June 1861 The Women's Central Association of Relief is sanctioned by Lincoln and it becomes the U.S. Sanitary Commission.

After speaking at a pro-Union rally, Sojourner Truth is arrested for breaking a state law that prohibited African Americans from entering Indiana.

Mary Ann Bickerdyke begins her work at Union hospitals.

Western counties in Virginia secede from the state and form West Virginia.

July 1861 Congress authorizes the enlistment of 500,000 soldiers and passes the Crittenden Resolution, which declares that the United States was waging war to reunify the nation rather than to eliminate or restrict slavery.

The Confederate and Union armies face each other for the first time at the Battle of Bull Run (Manassas) in Virginia.

The U.S. Congress passes the Crittenden Resolution, affirming that the war will be fought to preserve the Union and not to end slavery.

August 1861 Lincoln declares the Confederate states to be in a state of insurrection.

Congress passes the first Confiscation Act.

Congress passes the first federal income tax.

The U.S. Secret Service arrests and imprisons Rose O'Neal Greenhow for spying on behalf of the Confederacy.

Anna Ella Carroll publishes *Reply to the Speech of Honorable John C. Breckinridge*.

September 1861 Sally Louisa Tompkins becomes a commissioned Confederate officer to keep Robertson Hospital open in Richmond, Virginia.

Reverend L. C. Lockwood opens a Sunday school for freed slaves at Fortress Monroe, Virginia.

The American Missionary Association opens the first school for freedpeople.

October 1861 The first transcontinental telegraph line is completed.

Abraham Lincoln suspends the writ of habeas corpus.

Charlotte Forten goes to Port Royal, South Carolina, to work as a teacher for recently freed African Americans.

November 1861 General Winfield Scott resigns his post as head of the U.S. Army. Lincoln appoints George B. McClellan to replace him.

The YMCA establishes the U.S. Christian Commission.

January 1862 The first federal income tax (3 percent of income more than $800) goes into effect.

The Port Royal Experiment begins on the Union occupied Sea Islands in South Carolina.

The Union's first ironclad steamer (the *Monitor*) is launched in Long Island, New York.

February 1862 Jefferson Davis suspends the writ of habeas corpus.

Julia Ward Howe publishes "The Battle Hymn of the Republic" in *Atlantic Monthly*.

March 1862 Lincoln recommends that Congress compensate slave owners in states that accept gradual abolition.

The Confederate ironclad *Merrimac* and Union ironclad *Monitor* fight to a draw.

The Peninsular Campaign begins.

The U.S. Congress passes the Impressment Act.

To begin the work of educating freedpeople, teachers and superintendents sail from New York to Port Royal, South Carolina.

April 1862 The Battle of Shiloh takes place.

Forces commanded by Admiral David Farragut capture New Orleans, Louisiana.

Congress abolishes slavery in the District of Columbia.

The Confederacy passes its first Conscription Act.

May 1862 The U.S. Congress enacts the Homestead Act, providing for settlement of the west.

Delegates from pro-Union western counties of Virginia officially vote to secede from Virginia and create the state of West Virginia.

Union general Benjamin Butler takes command of occupied New Orleans, Louisiana. Butler issues his General Order Number 28, the "Woman Order."

Without approval, Union general David Hunter frees slaves in Georgia, South Carolina, and Florida. Lincoln revokes the order.

While working for the Confederate Navy, slave Robert Smalls navigates the *Planter* from Charleston Harbor, South Carolina, and into Union lines where he surrenders it.

June 1862 Virginian Robert E. Lee assumes command of the Confederate Army.

July 1862 The U.S. Congress passes the second Confiscation Act.

The U.S. Congress issues the Ironclad Oath. It requires all federal, civil, and military officials to pledge allegiance to the U.S. Constitution.

Lee and McClellan face each other at The Seven Days' Battle.

General Henry Halleck takes control of the Union Army.

The U.S. Congress passes the Pacific Railway Act.

Confederate spy Belle Boyd is imprisoned at the Old Capitol Prison.

The U.S. Congress passes the Morrill Land Grant Act, giving states federal lands on which to establish colleges.

U.S. general Ulysses S. Grant chooses Colonel John Eaton to run the Freedmen's Bureau in Arkansas.

Abraham Lincoln signs the Second Confiscation Act, freeing slaves that escape behind Union lines.

August 1862 When their government annuity is delayed, the Santee Sioux, led by Little Crow, revolt in Minnesota.

Confederate soldiers defeat the Union Army at the Second Battle of Bull Run (Manassas) in Virginia.

September 1862 Lee's Army of Northern Virginia invades the North. The deadliest day of fighting occurs when 26,000 soldiers die at the Battle at Antietam in Maryland.

Lincoln issues a preliminary Emancipation Proclamation.

Laura M. Towne establishes a school for freedmen and freedwomen on St. Helena Island, South Carolina.

An explosion at the Allegheny Arsenal kills 78 workers, mostly young women and girls.

October 1862 Jefferson Davis amends the draft law, exempting those who own 20 or more slaves.

Southerners organize the Protestant Episcopal Church of the Confederate States of America.

November 1862 General Ambrose E. Burnside replaces McClellan as Commander of the Union's Army of the Potomac.

December 1862 Confederates defeat Union forces at the Battle of Fredericksburg.

In Minnesota, 38 leaders of a Sioux uprising are executed.

Ulysses S. Grant issues General Order Number 11, which expels Jews from his area of operation, in the hopes of ending war profiteering. He revokes his order after a few weeks.

Louisa May Alcott begins work at Union Hospital in Washington, D.C.

January 1863 Lincoln's Emancipation Proclamation goes into effect.

General Joseph Hooker replaces Ambrose Burnside.

Union general Ulysses S. Grant takes control of the Army of the West.

Recruitment begins for the Massachusetts Fifty-fourth Infantry Regiment, the nation's first African American regiment.

February 1863 The U.S. Congress passes the National Banking Act, creating a national banking system.

March 1863 The National Academy of Sciences is incorporated.

The Habeas Corpus Act gives the government the authority to imprison an individual indefinitely without charging that person.

An explosion at an ordnance lab in Richmond, Virginia, kills 34 women.

Women in Salisbury, North Carolina, riot in response to their shortage of salt and flour.

The U.S. Congress passes the Conscription Act.

April 1863 Women in Richmond, Virginia, engage in a bread riot to protest the wartime shortages.

The Battle of Chancellorsville begins.

Confederate Mary Francis Battle is arrested for spying.

The Union's policy of conscription goes into effect.

May 1863 Lee defeats Hooker at Chancellorsville.

The National Women's Loyal League meets for the first time.

Louisa May Alcott begins to publish in serial form her *Hospital Sketches*.

Fanny Kemble publishes her *Journal of a Residence on a Georgian Plantation* while in England; it is published in the United States that July.

Union spy Pauline Cushman is captured.

Confederate general Thomas "Stonewall" Jackson dies in Virginia from complications from friendly fire.

June 1863 General Ambrose Burnside orders the anti-Lincoln *Chicago Times* to close its doors; Lincoln overrules the order three days later.

Lee again invades the North as he heads into Pennsylvania.

General George G. Meade becomes the Union commander of the Army of the Potomac.

Residents of Vicksburg, Mississippi, evacuate to nearby caves to avoid Union shelling.

Western Virginia becomes West Virginia and is admitted to the union. West Virginia's new state constitution establishes public schools for African Americans.

July 1863 The Union Army defeats Lee at the Battle of Gettysburg.

Union forces under Grant capture Vicksburg and take control of the Mississippi River.

The Battle of Honey Springs takes place in Indian Territory.

The Fifty-fourth Massachusetts, the Union's first African American regiment, suffers heavy casualties at Battery Wagner, South Carolina.

Draft riots in New York City expose home front frustrations and result in the wounding and deaths of approximately 1,000 people. Similar riots occur in Boston, Massachusetts, Holmes County, Ohio, and elsewhere across the Union.

August 1863 Confederate William C. Quantrill and 450 supporters raid Lawrence, Kansas.

September 1863 Confederates win the Battle of Chickamauga.

Union troops capture Little Rock, Arkansas.

October 1863 Lincoln calls for a national day of thanksgiving to be held in November.

Grant takes control of all operations in the western theater.

The U.S. Sanitary Commission holds one of its most successful sanitary fairs in Chicago.

November 1863 Lincoln delivers the "Gettysburg Address" at the dedication of a national cemetery near the battlefield in Pennsylvania.

Grant repels the Confederate siege at Chattanooga, Tennessee.

January 1864 Jefferson Davis enacts a conscription law that requires the enlistment into the Confederate Army of all white males between the ages of 18 and 45.

February 1864 Confederates win the Battle of Olustee in Florida.

The National Women's Loyal League presents Congress with a petition demanding the abolition of slavery.

Rebecca Lee becomes the first African American woman to earn a medical doctorate.

March 1864 Grant takes control of all the armies of the United States and General William T. Sherman assumes control of Union forces in the west.

Women protest for peace in High Point, North Carolina.

April 1864 The U.S. Sanitary Commission holds a three-week fund-raising fair in New York that raises $1 million.

A bread riot erupts in Savannah, Georgia.

Nathan Bedford Forrest and his Confederate cavalry capture Fort Pillow, Tennessee. They murder African American soldiers who are trying to surrender.

May 1864 Union troops under Grant's command fight Confederate forces led by Lee at the Battles of the Wilderness and Spotsylvania.

Sherman advances toward Atlanta and the Army of the Tennessee.

The U.S. Congress passes the Wade-Davis Bill, requiring that the majority of white male citizens in each rebel state take an oath of allegiance to the United States and that each state adopt a constitution acceptable to the president and Congress before it can be readmitted to the Union.

Montana becomes a territory separate from the Idaho Territory.

June 1864 Confederates win the Battle of Cold Harbor.

Grant begins a nine-month siege of Petersburg, Virginia.

The U.S. Congress passes an Internal Revenue Act that increases income tax rates and raises taxes on some items.

A national cemetery is established at Arlington.

July 1864 Sherman forcefully evacuates female workers and their families from the textile mill town of Roswell, Georgia.

September 1864 Sherman captures Atlanta and issues Special Field Order Number 67, evacuating the city of all civilians. The order primarily affects the city's women and children.

Frustrations lead to bread riots in Mobile, Alabama.

October 1864 Union general Philip H. Sheridan defeats Jubal Early's Confederate troops in the Shenandoah Valley.

Nevada becomes the 36th state.

November 1864 Lincoln is reelected as president, defeating McClellan.

Sherman burns Atlanta and begins his March to the Sea.

December 1864 Salmon P. Chase becomes Chief Justice of the Supreme Court.

General George H. Thomas defeats the Army of the Tennessee.

Sherman captures Savannah, Georgia.

January 1865 Freed slaves obtain control of the Sea Islands between Jacksonville, Florida and Charleston, South Carolina when Sherman issues Special Field Order Number 15.

Sherman marches through South Carolina, destroying much of Charleston, Columbia, and the surrounding areas.

Before Sherman arrives, the women of Columbia, South Carolina, hold the Confederacy's largest fund-raising bazaar.

February 1865 In Hampton Roads, Virginia, Confederate peace commissioners meet with Abraham Lincoln and U.S. Secretary of State William Seward.

Sherman captures Columbia, South Carolina.

African American Julia C. Collins begins publishing "The Curse of Caste; or, The Slave Bride" as a serial in the *Christian Recorder*, a weekly newspaper run by the African Methodist Episcopal Church.

March 1865 Grant defeats Lee at the Battle of Petersburg.

Jefferson Davis signs a bill that allows African American enlistment in the Confederate Army.

Congress creates the Freedmen's Bureau to help former slaves in their transition to freedom.

Clara Barton establishes the Office of Correspondence with Friends of the Missing Men of the United States Army.

April 1865 Confederate forces evacuate from Richmond, Virginia.

Lee surrenders his Confederate forces to Grant at Appomattox Court House, Virginia.

John Wilkes Booth assassinates President Lincoln at Ford's Theater in Washington, D.C.

Joseph E. Johnston surrenders his Confederate forces to Sherman at Durham Station, North Carolina.

Andrew Johnson becomes president of the United States.

May 1865 General O. O. Howard becomes head of the Freedman's Bureau.

Northerners celebrate with a victory parade down Pennsylvania Avenue in Washington, D.C.

General Edmund Kirby-Smith surrenders his troops to General E. S. Canby in New Orleans, Louisiana.

July 1865 Four convicted conspirators—Mary Surratt, David E. Herold, Lewis Paine, and George A. Atzerodt—are hanged for their involvement in the plot to assassinate Lincoln. Four others are given prison sentences for their roles.

August 1865 A convention in Jackson, Mississippi, repeals secession and outlaws slavery.

October 1865 A convention in Savannah, Georgia, repeals secession and outlaws slavery.

November 1865 Mississippi passes the first Black Code. Other Southern states follow with their own restrictive codes.

Mark Twain publishes *The Celebrated Jumping Frog of Calaveras County*.

December 1865 Congress ratifies the Thirteenth Amendment, abolishing slavery.

The Ku Klux Klan forms in Pulaski, Tennessee.

March 1866 Congress enacts the Civil Rights Act of 1866.

April 1866 President Andrew Johnson ends the "insurrection" with a proclamation of peace.

May 1866 Susan B. Anthony and Elizabeth Cady Stanton organize the Eleventh National Women's Rights Convention in New York City.

Jefferson Davis is indicted for treason against the United States.

June 1866 Congress approves the Fourteenth Amendment, guaranteeing citizenship rights to all men born and naturalized in the United States.

July 1866 A race riot erupts in New Orleans.

Despite President Andrew Johnson's veto, the U.S. Congress passes the Freedmen's Bureau bill.

March 1867 Republican Thaddeus Stevens proposes freedpeople receive 40-acre plots of land. Congress votes down this plan.

Congress enacts the Reconstruction Acts, dividing the South into five militarily controlled districts.

Congress passes the Tenure of Office Act, requiring Senate approval before the president can dismiss a cabinet member.

July 1867 The Ladies Memorial Association unveils the first monument to the Confederate dead in Cheraw, South Carolina.

July 1868 The Fourteenth Amendment is ratified. It grants citizenship to all men born or naturalized in the United States. The amendment introduces the term "male" to the Constitution.

November 1868 Ulysses S. Grant is elected president.

February 1869 Congress passes the Fifteenth Amendment, which prevents states from denying voters the right to vote on the basis of race, color, or previous condition.

May 1869 Susan B. Anthony and Elizabeth Cady Stanton establish the National Woman Suffrage Association.

Lucy Stone founds the American Woman Suffrage Association.

December 1869 Wyoming passes the first women's suffrage law in the United States.

April 1871 Congress passes the Civil Rights Act of 1871, also known as the Ku Klux Klan Act.

June 1872 Congress abolishes the Freedman's Bureau.

March 1875 The U.S. Supreme Court, in *Miner v. Happersett*, concludes that citizenship does not guarantee suffrage.

The Civil Rights Act of 1875 guarantees that African Americans receive equal treatment in public facilities.

November 1876 Rutherford B. Hayes is elected president.

April 1877 Hayes orders the last federal troops to leave South Carolina, and Reconstruction comes to a formal end.

May 1881 Former Civil War nurse Clara Barton forms the American Association of the Red Cross.

September 1894 The United Daughters of the Confederacy is formed.

"A Soldier's Life Is a Hard One at Best": Soldiers in the American Civil War

1

John M. Sacher

I n the aftermath of the Confederate attack on Fort Sumter on April 12, 1861, President Abraham Lincoln asked for 75,000 90-day volunteers to suppress the rebellion. The following month, the Confederate Congress authorized President Jefferson Davis to accept as many volunteers as he felt necessary to repel the Union invasion. In the wake of these calls, young men from both the North and the South, not wanting to miss any of the action, rushed to join the war effort. Ultimately, the combination of volunteering and drafts produced armies whose numbers would have seemed inconceivable in 1861. At that point, 16,000 men served in the U.S. army. By the end of the Civil War, approximately 3 million men—slightly more than 2 million Billy Yanks in the Union Army and slightly fewer than 1 million Johnny Rebs in the Confederate Army—had donned uniforms. In the North, 35 percent of the white, male military-age population served, while in the South an even greater percentage of eligible soldiers, possibly as high as 61 percent, participated in the contest. These men, even if they possessed some prior militia experience, generally were not professional soldiers but were instead volunteers representing a cross-section of American society. For most of them, military service lasted longer and included greater hardships than they could have conceived at the outset of the Civil War.

The Call to Join

In the summer of 1861, a patriotic fervor swept across the entire nation with units forming faster than their respective armies could supply or employ

NOTE: Chapter title quoted in Joiner, Gary D., Marilyn S. Joiner, and Clifton D. Cardin, eds. *No Pardons to Ask, nor Apologies to Make: The Journal of William Henry King, Gray's 28th Louisiana Infantry Regiment* (Knoxville: University of Tennessee Press, 2006), 19.

Samuel Rush Watkins (1839–1901)

Convinced that the South and North were separate civilizations, Sam Watkins, a single 21-year-old Tennessean, eagerly enlisted in the Confederate Army in the summer of 1861. Although Watkins entered the war expecting excitement and worried that he might miss all of the action, he soon found that for "webfoots"—his term for privates—the Civil War did not bring glory. Instead, for a meager salary of $11 per month, it brought suffering and death. Of the 120 men who enlisted in Company H of the First Tennessee Infantry Regiment, only Watkins and six others remained at the war's conclusion.

Watkins's company participated in many major battles, including Shiloh, Chickamauga, and the Atlanta campaign. Yet, as a webfoot, Watkins had no sense of the strategic significance of these campaigns, and he acknowledged that in battle he never had a sense of anything outside his immediate surroundings. Instead, he described battles as a blur of sights and sounds with survival his main goal. Rather than focusing on his Yankee foes, Watson spent much more time combating a fiercer enemy—hunger. With his stomach perpetually empty, Watson repeatedly resorted to foraging, including stealing from civilians.

them. Unlike soldiers in later wars, Civil War volunteers joined companies composed almost entirely of men from their own community. Throughout the summer, Northern and Southern enlistment operated similarly. Signs, newspaper advertisements, and word of mouth publicized meetings. At these events, local dignitaries and sometimes aged veterans would publicly call on men to sign up for the local company. Preachers exhorted men to join the ranks, and single women provided an additional impetus by declaring that they would only marry soldiers. Peer pressure and appeals to masculinity helped propel men into the service. Approximately a week or two later, a second public ceremony would be held during which politicians and newly minted officers would give speeches to the town's new military company, and this oratory would be followed by a picnic or dance. Generally, the highlight of the day occurred when the locality's women presented the company with a flag that they had sewn. These flags reminded soldiers that they fought not just for themselves, but also for an entire community. Army organization generally reinforced this community identification as 10 local companies—ideally with 100 men each—from the same state combined to form a regiment, which then received a designation such as the Twentieth Maine or the Eleventh Alabama.

Many factors motivated men to volunteer. In the rage militaire of 1861, some men joined the army because their friends were enlisting, because of community pressure, or because of a desire for excitement beyond the bounds of their community. Most Civil War soldiers, however, enlisted because of sincerely held ideological beliefs. Ironically, Northern and Southern soldiers who reflected on their enlistment shared common motivations: to preserve their liberty, their self-government, and the heritage of the American Revolution. An Illinois soldier recognized this common sentiment and admitted to his wife that "they are fighting for the same

Throughout his four years in the army, Watkins's greatest complaint was that a private was simply an automaton who had no choice but to follow orders simply because men of a higher rank issued them. When these orders were not followed, privates were punished. Regarding this mistreatment, Watson heaped particular criticism on General Braxton Bragg, whom he considered to be a martinet with no feelings for his men. In contrast, Watkins had nothing but praise for Bragg's successor, Joseph E. Johnston, who demonstrated a much greater concern for common soldiers' well-being. Watkins's despair over soldiers' dehumanization reached a crescendo with the passage of a Confederate conscription law in April 1862. He contended that the war might as well have ended at that point, as all the pride associated with military service had disappeared. Nevertheless, Watkins remained in the army until the war ended, demonstrating that a webfoot could simultaneously disparage his leaders and remain committed to the Confederate cause.

thing that we are, *Liberty*" (Shannon 1947, 25). Although both sides used similar language and considered themselves true Americans, Confederate and Union volunteers ascribed vastly different meanings to American ideals. Confederates placed themselves in the role of the nation's founding fathers, who, according to Southern interpretation, in 1776 had thrown off the yoke of an oppressive British government and established a nation dedicated both to states' rights and the preservation of slavery. A Georgia soldier succinctly contended, "We will have to fight like Washington did" (Hagan in Robertson 1988, 9). To preserve their rights, these ancestors had rebelled, and Confederates saw themselves as following this precedent. In their eyes, Republican president Abraham Lincoln represented a modern-day King George III, threatening to destroy Southern liberty. Liberty was held sacrosanct, for its opposite was slavery. As men who lived in a slave society, Confederate soldiers knew what it meant to be denied one's liberty, and they frequently vowed not to become slaves to the North.

Union soldiers saw themselves preserving the heritage of the founding fathers. In their view, these leaders had established a perpetual republic, which Southern secession threatened to undermine. If Northerners allowed Southern states to secede, the Union would crumble, and the world's greatest republican experiment would fail. Lincoln's election had been constitutional, and consequently Southern secession set the precedent that any state that disagreed with the federal government could flee the Union, a surefire formula for anarchy and destruction of the Union that would negate the handiwork of their ancestors.

Although both sides spoke of liberty, the motives of Johnny Reb and Billy Yank did not precisely coincide. To win the war, the Union Army had to invade the Confederacy, and thus Southerners had the added incentive of literally fighting for their homes and, according to a Louisiana corporal, "driving the envading host of tyrants from our soil" (Lee in McPherson 1994, 11). They also repeated Confederate president Jefferson Davis's contention that they did not desire to conquer any territory, but just wanted to be left alone. In contrast to these defensive goals, a minority of Northern soldiers wished to wage a war for the abolition of slavery. Nevertheless, in 1861, most Northern soldiers did not enlist to fight slavery; instead, they focused on preserving the Union. Although Southern soldiers could unite in their desire to defend slavery, the slavery issue proved divisive for Union soldiers who initially could not agree on whether emancipation would aid or hamper their efforts to restore the Union. Only in the aftermath of the January 1863 Emancipation Proclamation and Lincoln's emphasis on abolishing slavery as a way to help end the war did most Northern soldiers accept emancipation as a goal.

Camp Life

Regardless of their motivation to enter the army, most volunteers had an overly romantic picture of combat and eagerly sought to enter into battle or as they phrased it, "see the elephant." If men desired to participate in a grand battle immediately, they quickly became disabused of this notion as they discovered that soldiers spent more time in camp than on the battlefield. At first, camp provided its own excitement, for many men had never been so far from home before, nor had they ever met so many new acquaintances their age. Soldiers, especially Northerners, took the opportunity to

Engineers of the 8th New York State Militia, 1861. (*National Archives*)

have their pictures taken, most likely for the first time in their lives. A camp's early thrills soon disappeared as men settled into the monotony of army life. According to one Yankee's sarcastic description of a typical day at a camp of instruction, "The first thing in the morning is drill, then drill, then drill again. Then drill, drill, a little more drill. Then drill, and lastly drill. Between drills, we drill and sometimes stop to eat a little and have roll-call" (Robertson 1988, 48). Officers intended drills to prepare men for marching and fighting as a unit and to ensure that soldiers would follow orders during combat. Although the armies drilled to improve their cohesion in battle, they spent surprisingly little time practicing tactics or even shooting at targets.

Not only could drilling be dull—and frustrating for those who did not know left from right—but it also meant following orders. If volunteers on both sides fought for their own liberty, they quickly discovered that preserving their liberty in the long run meant sacrificing it in the short run. Soldiers had lived in societies that preached equality, independence, and a democracy of white men. When entering the army, volunteers did not easily give up their democratic leanings, and they initially followed them by electing their officers. Yet an army operated from the top down, and officers, whether appointed or elected, gave orders that had to be followed rather than debated. Soldiers in both armies united in their repeated complaints about officers who abused their power. Southerners had an easy reference point for men who lacked independence and were subject to the orders of another—slaves. These white men resented treatments that smacked of slavery, such as having to wake up to the sound of a horn at 5:00 A.M., facing corporal punishment for violating orders, and having to carry a pass to leave camp. Northern volunteers also recognized that officers' treatment of their men had a parallel with the South's peculiar institution, with one succinctly noting, "yesterday a freeman—today a slave" (Geer in Mitchell 1988, 58).

Despite these complaints, there was more to camp life than sacrificing one's independence and drilling all day. Soldiers had a significant amount of free time, and they took advantage of it. As young men asserting their masculinity, they enjoyed such sports as racing, boxing, and baseball, which saw its popularity grow as a result of the Civil War. Additionally, responsible young men attended religious meetings or wrote letters home, with the typical thousand-man regiment sending out hundreds of letters per day. Others spent their time running camp newspapers or participating in debating societies. More commonly, they sang many of the songs that have become synonymous with the Civil War, including "John Brown's Body," the "Battle Cry of Freedom," "Home Sweet Home," "When Johnny Comes Marching Home," and "When This Cruel War Is Over." Young men with free time, however, did not limit themselves to engaging in worthwhile endeavors. Some soldiers showed their maturity by practicing self-restraint, but others enjoyed the opportunity to practice the masculine vices of drinking, gambling, and visiting prostitutes.

In camp, Billy Yanks and Johnny Rebs alike discovered that military service not only struck at their autonomy, but it also struck at their health. In addition to introducing soldiers to new diversions, camp life introduced them to unfamiliar microbes. Soldiers, especially those from small, isolated

Frederick M. Osborne (1845–1923)

Although Frederick Osborne did not fight in as many famous battles as Samuel Watkins did, many of his fellow soldiers would have recognized his Civil War experience as more typical. In the summer of 1861, Osborne, a 16-year-old boy from Salem, Massachusetts, enlisted in the town's Union Drill Club, which soon became Company F of the Massachusetts Twenty-third Regiment. Osborne started the conflict auspiciously, participating in one of the Union's early victories, a successful amphibious assault on Roanoke Island, North Carolina, in February 1862. Despite spending four hours wading through waist-high water in a swamp, Osborne emerged in high spirits. This brief battle, however, represented the peak of Osborne's military career.

After Roanoke Island, Osborne's unit served mainly in a garrison function in North Carolina, building bridges, patrolling the eastern part of the state, and serving as a police force. Through letters, Osborne and his family kept in close touch, with Osborne surprisingly worried that they sent him too many packages. At one point, he sent part of a package back home to his mother, for he felt that he already

communities, lacked immunity to many common maladies. Additionally, in 1861, volunteers did not face a medical screening before enlistment and as many as 25 percent of the men, according to a Union government report, should have been rejected as unfit for duty. Compounding this error, officers chose campsites based on strategic rather than health considerations, and widespread ignorance regarding the transmission of diseases led soldiers to drink polluted water, place latrines in bad locations, and practice poor sanitation and personal hygiene habits. Soldiers multiplied these mistakes by eating a diet deficient in vitamins and minerals. Epidemics of measles, mumps, and chicken pox debilitated many units in the early weeks at their camps of instruction. Many units lost more than one-third of their soldiers before entering into combat. The average regiment at Shiloh in April 1862 contained only 560 men rather than the 1,000 originally recruited. More deadly diseases, including malaria, typhoid fever, and dysentery, decimated the ranks, with the Union Army reporting more than 1 million cases of malaria alone. The ever-increasing presence of fleas, lice, mosquitoes, flies, and other pests further exacerbated the problem. Overall, soldiers justly feared these diseases for they killed many more men than combat did. Of the 360,000 total Union deaths, an estimated 250,000 stemmed from disease, with dysentery alone killing 57,265. Poor Confederate recordkeeping makes it impossible to know how many Southern soldiers died in this manner, but some historians estimate that as many as three-fourths of the 260,000 Confederate deaths resulted from disease.

In considering their health, soldiers justly blamed their rations, which they regarded as inferior in terms of both quantity and quality, with the absence of vegetables being the most significant detriment to their health. In both armies, men generally ate in a "mess" with three to eight of their comrades. Northern soldiers subsisted primarily on coffee, bacon, and half-had far too much to carry. Nevertheless, that rebuff did not mean that Osborne begrudged all items from home. He often made specific requests regarding clothing, especially footwear, which he needed. In return, he sent several photographs of himself home.

Though Osborne did not experience too many hunger pangs, he did suffer from both chronic dysentery and a severe knee injury that ultimately forced him out of his regiment and into the nonfighting Invalid Corps. Osborne was not alone in his inability to serve in the Massachusetts 23rd. In 1864,

when the unit entered its most significant military engagement at Drury's Bluff, Virginia, only 226 men out of its original 1,000-man contingent took part. In his letters home, Osborne stoically did not complain about his health. He reserved his carping for the way the army treated enlisted men and for shirkers who dodged the draft. Having enlisted for three years, Osborne declined to accept a furlough and a bonus to reenlist and instead mustered out of the army on September 28, 1864.

inch thick crackers called hardtack, although they often referred to the latter by more creative names such as "sheet iron cracker," "tooth duller," or "worm castle." Army regulations specified beans, rice, and potatoes, but these foods were less prevalent. Initially, the Confederate Army stipulated that it would supply the same rations as the Union Army. This goal quickly proved unobtainable, and by the spring of 1862, the army had reduced the standard ration, and it would reduce it again in 1864. Confederates lived on cornbread and pickled beef and considered captured Yankee coffee to be a luxury. Occasionally, Johnny Rebs cooked their meat and cornbread together in grease to form a concoction they termed "cush." Living in a land of plenty, Southern soldiers' diets worsened as the war dragged onward, primarily because their army's supply system collapsed. In both armies, soldiers on the march or in combat received less food than those in camp with soldiers in besieged garrisons, such as Confederates in Vicksburg and Port Hudson in 1863, who were compelled to eat boiled weeds and, in rare cases, mules and rats.

Both sides tried to find ways to supplement their inferior diets. Some soldiers received food from home, and others purchased food from sutlers, civilians who followed the army selling a variety of goods to soldiers. Sutlers' exorbitant prices, however, made them extremely unpopular and made their wares inaccessible to many. Foraging represented the most common way that both Union and Confederate soldiers augmented their diets. Foraging ranged from picking berries and nuts to stealing chickens and hogs to taking food at gunpoint. Later in the war, soldiers from both sides expanded the pillaging aspect of foraging. Union soldiers had come to see taking the war to Southern civilians as a method of defeating the Confederacy, and consequently, the interests of their stomachs and their nation coincided. In contrast, Confederates felt that they deserved the full support of Southern civilians and that this support should include access to civilian food supplies.

Heading Off to Battle

When not in camp, soldiers spent much of their time marching. During a soldier's first march, he generally "simmered down," meaning that he shed his excess baggage, including overcoats, blankets from home, and other luxuries. A soldier might have started the war carrying as much as 80 pounds of material, but by the time of Sherman's March to the Sea in late 1864, Union soldiers had reduced their load to the essentials— a rifled musket, a bayonet, 80 rounds of ammunition, a haversack with a blanket, a canteen, a tin cup, a knife, and possibly playing cards or some paper and a pencil or ink. Regardless of their load, soldiers on the march suffered. They often wore ill-fitting or worn-out shoes, and occasionally Confederates lacked any shoes at all. When it was wet, their water-logged and muddy packs were even heavier than usual, and infantry men had to help move wagons stuck in the mud. When it was hot and dry, marchers suffered from thirst and from dust kicked up by thousands of tramping feet. A Union Army of 100,000 men could be accompanied by 2,500 wagons, 35,000 animals, and 600 tons of supplies. Armies on the march clogged roads ill-equipped to handle this volume of traffic. Given the choice, soldiers preferred to be at the head of these columns. The lead units got their choice of campsites at the end of the day, did not swallow as much dust, and arrived at the destination many hours before troops bringing up the rear. When Civil War armies moved, they moved slowly, averaging only approximately 2.5 miles per hour, although when necessary, units could move much faster. Most famously, in its 1862 Shenandoah Valley Campaign, Stonewall Jackson's "foot cavalry" marched 650 miles and fought five battles in less than two months.

Witnesses to a march would have quickly perceived that there was nothing uniform about soldiers' uniforms. In 1861, the same local women who had sewn a company's battle flag often made their uniforms as well. Wealth, the color of available cloth, and personal taste dictated early uniform choices with men wearing green, yellow, or red in addition to the stereotypical blue and gray. At the outset of the war, even the wearing of blue or gray did not necessarily identify one as a Union or Confederate soldier. In July 1861, in the smoke and confusion of the battle of Bull Run, Union soldiers mistakenly opened fire on a gray-clad unit from Wisconsin and allowed blue-clad Virginians to approach their lines unmolested. Similar battle flags added to the confusion and led to the Confederacy's adoption of what is today considered the Rebel flag. The following month at Wilson's Creek in Missouri, Union troops allowed gray-uniformed Louisiana soldiers to almost overrun their positions because they mistook their attackers for an Iowa unit that also wore gray. Not until early 1862, after several incidents like these, did the Union Army adopt the standard dark blue coat and light blue pants that are most commonly associated with its forces. With the Union blockading textile imports from England, the South never truly succeeded in cladding all of its soldiers in gray. In reality, butternut, a yellowish brown dye made primarily from walnut hulls, was a more common sight among Confederates than gray. Even some degree of uniformity, however, did not guarantee that a uniform fit well, and complaints, especially regarding shoes, abounded. Tattered Confederates could not always even rely on their government to provide adequate clothing and instead used clothing sent from home, acquired by their state governments, purchased from their fellow troops, or pilfered from dead Yankees to supplement their official uniforms.

Ultimately, all of this training and marching led to combat. Here, soldiers used the discipline that they had learned in drill to face the enemy. Generally, the attack involved either a frontal assault or an effort to flank—go around the left or right end of their lines—the enemy. These traditional tactics had become superseded by equipment, particularly the employment of rifling, which represented a major advancement in both accuracy and distance over the traditional musket. The musket, the mainstay of pre–Civil War armies, had an effective range of 80 to 100 yards. Rifling its barrel and using a new bullet, the minié ball, increased the range to approximately 400 yards. A soldier loaded the gun through its muzzle and with practice could fire three shots in a minute, although in the stress of combat one shot per minute was more common. The North, with a greater industrial might, quickly armed its soldiers with Springfield rifles, eventually producing more than 2 million of these guns. Southerners more commonly relied on Enfield rifles imported from England and used Springfield rifles taken from Union soldiers.

Not only did defenders wield rifles, they also increasingly fired from trenches or behind fortifications. In 1861, many officers believed that digging in was cowardly, and Robert E. Lee earned the derisive nickname, "The King of Spades," for ordering his troops to entrench. As the war progressed, opposition to entrenching disappeared, and the extent of these earthworks steadily increased, culminating in the Petersburg campaign of 1864–1865, in which armies constructed elaborate networks of trenches, presaging the trench warfare of World War I. Attacks against defenders protected by walls or trenches became heroic failures, with Pickett's charge on the third day of Gettysburg representing the classic folly of a head-on attack. Of the estimated 12,500 Confederates who charged three-quarters of a mile alongside Pickett, 54 percent (almost 7,000 men) were killed, wounded, or captured. Although both attackers and defenders possessed bayonets, they were much more likely to use them to heat their dinner than to stab their enemy, with only 0.4 percent of all Civil War casualties resulting from bayonet wounds.

For the ordinary soldier, whether charging or defending, the battlefield contained a bewildering and frightening array of sights and sounds. Soldiers repeatedly contended that one had to face battle to understand it. In attempting to explain their participation in battle, most soldiers would agree with a North Carolinian's succinct assertion, "I can't describe a battle to you" (McPherson 1997, 12). Based on their accounts, even participating in a battle did not ensure knowledge of what had happened. Limited visibility negated both comprehension and much of the distance advantage provided by the new rifles. Civil War soldiers generally did not fight in open fields but in forests or forest clearings. Not only did trees hinder one's vision, but also during battles smoke was ubiquitous. Thus, soldiers might not have exaggerated in claiming to have fought entire battles without ever seeing their opponents. Instead, men fired where they suspected the enemy stood, where they saw muzzle-bursts, or where they heard the enemy. With most battles fought in the summer months, soldiers, in addition to having limited vision, suffered from heat and thirst. Additionally, they recounted hearing a great number of deafening and disorienting sounds, including artillery shells bursting, drums and bugle calls, bullets whizzing by, cursing, wounded men crying out in pain, and, when Confederates attacked, the infamous rebel yell.

The rebel yell represented one way that Confederates boosted their courage during terrifying battles. Civil War soldiers viewed battles as a test of their manhood, and they expected themselves and their comrades to act bravely. When time permitted, officers offered an inspirational speech before the battle during which they stressed the importance of the war and appealed to the soldiers' manhood. To fortify their nerves, some soldiers prayed while others drank alcohol. The charge, where men had to hold their fire until ordered to do so, represented a supreme test of this courage. All units contained men who shirked their duty during battle by feigning illness, intentionally straggling behind the unit, volunteering to take wounded comrades to the rear, or simply running from the fight. Civil War soldiers castigated those who "showed the white feather" and abandoned their comrades. Most men, however, did not forsake their duties. Instead, they retained their courage because they felt the cause, their reputation, or their fellow soldiers, whom they literally stood elbow to elbow with, should not be let down. That did not mean that men relished combat, and after having "seen the elephant" once, few expressed an eagerness to see it again soon.

Not all soldiers emerged from combat unscathed. Despite the confusion of battle, some shots hit their mark. When struck by a minié ball, a man's suffering had only just begun. Wounded soldiers were expected to maintain their courage, but this proved difficult as they lay, possibly in excruciating pain, for hours and perhaps even for a day or two before being attended to. The screams of the wounded and smells of the dead helped create a situation that horrified the eyes, ears, and noses of witnesses to the carnage. Civil War ambulances, generally two- or four-wheeled wagons, provided men a bumpy and painful trip to the field hospitals. There, the wounded encountered overwhelmed Civil War doctors, who had a reputation for being quacks who did more harm than good. In reality, these doctors did the best they could to treat the wounded, but they lacked both the medical knowledge and the technological expertise to provide much relief. Neither army had any hospital system in place when the war began, and neither ever possessed a sufficient number of doctors, although the Union with 11,000 surgeons was better off than the Confederates with

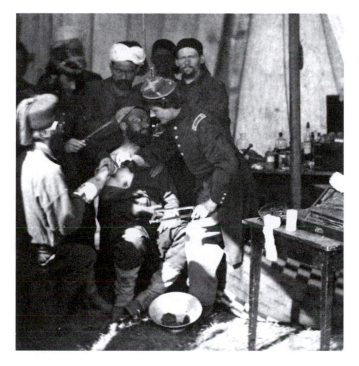

A surgeon at a field hospital prepares to amputate the arm of a wounded soldier (1861). (*Library of Congress*)

only 2,600 surgeons. At Gettysburg, where inundated Union doctors faced more wounded men than they could handle, they first divided the men into two categories: those they had a chance to save and those they did not, offering no treatment to the latter group.

For soldiers, receiving treatment frequently meant simply more pain. Doctors employed unsanitary equipment, often not wiping the blood off of knives as they moved from patient to patient, and hospitals were infested with flies and maggots. Infections from both these unsanitary procedures and from minié balls, which generally carried bits of clothing and hair into the body, were common. For arm and leg wounds, amputation, often without anesthesia or with whiskey serving in its place, represented the most common procedure, with Union doctors alone amputating more than 30,000 arms and legs. In contrast, wounds to the torso generally meant death. If a soldier survived a field hospital, he might be sent to a more permanent hospital, most commonly in the North or South's respective capital cities for recovery, if he was lucky, or for a slower death, if he was not so lucky. Overall, 18 percent of wounded Confederates and 14 percent of wounded Yankee soldiers died.

Demographics

Although the exact figures are impossible to discover, approximately 3 million men fought in the Civil War. Most soldiers served in the infantry—80 percent in the North and 75 percent in the South—with smaller percentages joining the cavalry or artillery. Although few of these men had experience in the U.S. Army, which included only 16,000 men in 1860, many had served in local militia organizations, which varied from well-trained units to glorified social clubs. Most soldiers volunteered, although both the Confederacy and the Union resorted to conscription when the pipeline of volunteers dried up. The majority of these men were literate, native-born, white Protestants. Approximately 30 percent were married. Soldiers in both armies were most likely in their early to mid-20s at the time of their enlistment, with Confederates slightly older than their Union counterparts. They averaged between five feet five inches and five feet nine inches in height and were of slight build, which, because of their inadequate diets, became slighter over the course of the war. Not all soldiers, however, shared these traits. The Union Army in particular housed a diverse array of soldiers. Approximately 200,000 Germans and 150,000 Irish fought for the Union, often in regiments consisting almost entirely of members of their ethnic group. Foreigners also served in the Confederate ranks, but because the South had not attracted many immigrants during the 1850s, they numbered fewer than 100,000 men.

Additionally, after the Emancipation Proclamation made the Civil War a war to end slavery as well as to restore the Union, more than 180,000 African Americans, mainly former slaves, volunteered for the Union Army. They battled both for their race's emancipation and to demonstrate their worth to society. From the beginning of the war, Frederick Douglass, the most prominent African American in the 19th-century United States, had recognized that the Civil War would become a war to end slavery. He also asserted that for African Americans getting "upon his person the brass letters, U.S. . . . and a musket on his shoulder" (McPherson 1988, 564) would contribute to gaining rights in both the North and the South. Serving as the U.S. Colored Troops, African Americans did not immediately gain much respect or many rights. Instead, they served under white officers in otherwise completely segregated units, initially received lower pay than white troops, and were assigned to a disproportionate amount of fatigue duty. Their performance at battles such as Port Hudson and the assault on Battery Wagner, led by the 54th Massachusetts, the most famous African American unit in the war, contributed to an equalization of pay and ultimately to the ending of slavery and the granting of citizenship rights in the Thirteenth, Fourteenth, and Fifteenth Amendments.

Although African Americans in the army may have earned themselves some respect from Northerners, white Southern soldiers viewed them in a much different light. The Confederacy refused to recognize armed blacks as representing anything other than a slave revolt, and thus, they threatened to enslave all captured African Americans and to execute their white officers. Though these threats were not officially carried out, they played a part in stopping the exchange of prisoners of war. Also, they contributed to the attitude that led some Southern soldiers to provide no quarter to African American troops. In addition, evidence indicates that in some battles, particularly the Confederate assault on Fort Pillow (Tennessee) in April 1864 and the Battle of the Crater (Petersburg, Virginia) in July 1864, Confederate soldiers killed African Americans who had attempted to surrender. These executions led to Union retaliation as "remember Fort Pillow" became a battle cry for many units regardless of their racial composition.

The Draft and Desertion

Some African Americans as well as foreign- and native-born men volunteered, but others entered the ranks through the operation of the Union and Confederate drafts. The outnumbered Confederacy needed every man it could get into its ranks, and consequently, it adopted conscription in April 1862 with the Union following suit in March 1863. Soldiers already in the army endorsed the draft as a means to make service in the war more equitable, but they expressed skepticism regarding the fighting ability of men forced into the army. The precise impact that conscription had on the size of Civil War armies is debatable. For instance, incomplete records indicate that of the 776,000 Union men drafted, only 46,000 shouldered weapons. Yet the Union draft could still be considered a success as a stimulus to volunteering. Avoiding the stigma of being branded as a conscript, a volunteer often had a greater choice of units and, if he played his cards right, could receive local, state, and federal bounties totaling as high as $1,000 (at a time when the average worker earned $460 a year). Conscription did not affect all citizens equally, and many Northern and Southern soldiers concurred that the exemptions in their respective drafts had made the conflict into a rich man's war but a poor man's fight. Both sides provided means for legally avoiding the draft, which, in the North, included the long-standing military tradition of providing a substitute in one's place or the payment of a $300 commutation fee. The South also allowed for substitutes and exempted men in key occupations—generally those judged essential for the war or for society. Most controversially, the Confederacy exempted one man for each plantation comprising 20 or more slaves, leading a Johnny Reb to voice the common complaint that the poor had to bear the burden of fighting, while the rich were "living at home enjoying life because they have a few negroes" (Mitchell 1988, 160).

Nevertheless, despite these class-based exemptions, evidence regarding the assertion that the conflict represented a poor man's fight is not entirely clear-cut. Unquestionably, farmers accounted for the largest group in both armies, and some of these men undoubtedly resented the idea that their wealthier neighbors had found ways to avoid military service. Studies of the Union Army indicate that white-collared workers were slightly underrepresented in the army, but this can be explained by the relative youth of the soldiers. In fact, more likely laborers, the group most often associated with the lower class, and immigrants did not serve in numbers corresponding to their presence in society. In the South, evidence indicates that slaveholders actually served at a rate higher than their percentage of the population would indicate, and of the 30,000 men eligible to gain exemption based on the "20-negro law," only 4,000 to 5,000 did so—a figure that represented only 3 percent of all men who obtained exemptions. Regardless of the precise figures, many common soldiers retained the perception that this conflict was a rich man's war and poor man's fight, and they continued to begrudge the message sent by these class-based privileges.

For angry soldiers who could not legally avoid service, desertion offered a possible escape route. Again, figures are imprecise, but estimates contend that 200,000 Northerners and 100,000 Southerners deserted. On both sides, substitutes, draftees, and those enlisting simply to earn a bounty—"bounty jumpers"—were considered the most likely to desert. Desertion hurt the Confederacy more than the Union, for the Confederate total represented a higher percentage of its army, and with a smaller pool of potential soldiers, they were less easily replaced. Partially owing to the effects of desertion, Confederate War Department figures in 1865 depict an army with the strength of almost 360,000 men on paper but with only 160,000 present for duty. Given the perceived hopelessness of the cause, however, this speaks as much to the dedication of those who remained as it does to the infidelity of those who deserted. A few deserters headed toward enemy lines, but home communities represented a far more likely destination. Receiving plaintive appeals depicting starvation and other privations on the home front, some Confederate soldiers concluded that the army had abandoned them, that the Confederacy was doomed to failure, and that they could better protect their families by returning home rather than by remaining on the front lines. By 1865, the destitution on the home front and the inability of the Confederate government to provide for soldiers' families led one North Carolina private to conclude that for most people on the home front, "desertion *now* is not *dishonorable*" (Robertson 1988, 136). Poorer soldiers also justified their decision to desert with the "rich man's war, poor man's fight" complaint, contending that if their slaveholding neighbors could remain at home, then they should not have to risk their lives for the cause either. Aware that news from home could contribute to desertion, Confederate officials requested that women use their influence to persuade their soldier-relatives to stay in the army, and some women did remind their kinfolk that allegations of cowardice would damage their family as much or even more than material deprivation.

Both armies used a combination of the carrot and the stick to solve the desertion problem. Promises of amnesty mixed with threats of punishment succeeded in returning at least 80,000 Union and 21,000 Confederate deserters to the ranks. Deserters and others who violated military rules risked punishment if caught. Penalties varied based both on the offense, with some of the most common infractions being insubordination, drunkenness, theft, and absence without leave, and on the whim of the officer in charge. Nevertheless, for soldiers in both armies, the punishments increased in severity over the course of the war. These could include public humiliations such as having one's head shaved or having to wear a placard describing one's crime to more painful treatments. Convicted soldiers could be forced to wear a ball and chain or a barrel or ride a saw horse for hours. Being bucked and gagged—which meant having a bayonet inserted in one's mouth, being put into a seated position with one's knees drawn to

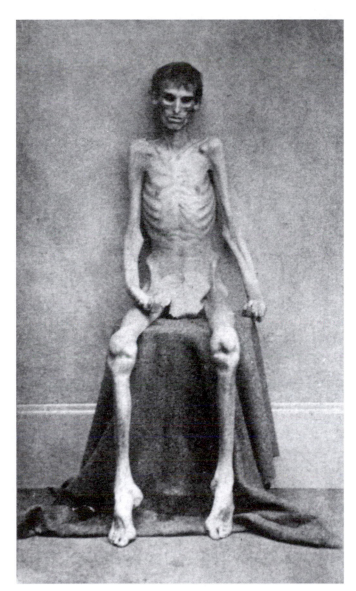

Prisoners of war behind Confederate lines suffered from a general lack of food and other basic necessities. This emaciated Union soldier eventually obtained his freedom. (*Library of Congress*)

one's chest, having a stick run between the legs, and then having one's arms placed beneath the stick and one's hands tied in front of the legs produced terrible cramping and pain over a number of hours. Other men could be hung by their thumbs, branded, face hard labor, or in the most extreme cases, face execution. Of the 267 Union soldiers executed during the Civil War, 147 had been convicted of desertion. Confederate records do not provide a total number of executions, but circumstantial evidence indicates that the South executed more men than the North. In addition to the men executed, other men sentenced to die received last-minute reprieves as a reminder not to repeat their crimes. With punishments designed to deter soldiers from repeating their comrades' mistakes, commanders compelled soldiers to either witness or participate in these public affairs.

Punishments inflicted by one's own army paled in comparison to some of the treatment of prisoners of war. More than 400,000 soldiers—slightly more than 200,000 Confederates and slightly less than 200,000 Union men—headed to prison camps. In the early part of the war, these stays could be tolerable and brief as the Union and Confederacy regularly exchanged prisoners. If the numbers to be exchanged were not equivalent, men could be paroled until an official exchange occurred. When the Confederacy announced that it would not treat black soldiers as prisoners of war, the North ended the exchange program in 1863. This cessation contributed to prison overcrowding, most infamously at the Confederate prison camp in Andersonville, Georgia. At one point, 33,000 Union soldiers there lived in a 26-acre enclosure meant to hold only 10,000 men. The combination of overcrowding, lack of shelter, inadequate food, poor sanitation, and guards with itchy trigger fingers led to the death of almost 30 percent of the inmates. Soldiers who survived emerged in horrible physical condition, and undoubtedly the publication of pictures of these survivors added fuel to Northern hostility and contributed to the postwar execution of the camp's commandant, Henry Wirz, the only man executed for war crimes during the Civil War.

Confederates countered complaints about their prisons with the assertion that Southern prison problems resulted from the collapse in the Confederate supply system but that poor treatment in Union prisons resulted from malice. The Union did reduce the rations in their prison camps 25 percent in response to reports of the conditions in the South, but the overall conditions in Northern prisoner-of-war camps did not descend to Southern depths—only 12 percent of Southern prisoners in the North died in contrast to the 15.5 percent of Northern prisoners of war who perished. Nonetheless, the closeness of those figures and the deaths of 25 percent of the Confederates housed at a camp in Elmira, New York, demonstrate that the South did not have a monopoly on prisoner mistreatment.

Despite these prison atrocities, the Civil War still can be described as a brother's war. This phrase has many meanings. In some cases, relatives joined opposing sides. Even President Lincoln saw four of his brothers-in-law take up arms for the Confederacy. Additionally, with the Union serving as a family writ large, Southern secession metaphorically represented the splitting up of a family. Also, soldiers, particularly since they had come from the same community and often had relatives in their unit, saw their comrades as a band of brothers. This solidarity, which historians have termed small-unit cohesion, helped them maintain their commitment to their respective causes. Finally, Civil War soldiers often viewed their supposed enemies as brothers. They shared not only a common language, culture, and religion, but also faced similar experiences, which forged a common bond between Union and Confederate troops. On occasion, opposing troops dined together, and most soldiers adhered to a gentleman's agreement not to shoot men on picket duty. Overall, these men recognized that, as soldiers, they shared an attachment that united them in a way that civilians and even most officers could not understand. By the time of the Confederacy's defeat in 1865, Billy Yanks and Johnny Rebs, in four years of fighting, had grown accustomed to similar hardships such as poor food and terrible medical care, had together seen the elephant at places such as Shiloh, Antietam, and Gettysburg, and they had persevered.

References and Further Reading

Joiner, Gary D., Marilyn S. Joiner, and Clifton D. Cardin, eds. *No Pardons to Ask, nor Apologies to Make: The Journal of William Henry King, Gray's 28th Louisiana Infantry Regiment.* Knoxville: University of Tennessee Press, 2006.

Logue, Larry M. 1996. *To Appomattox and Beyond: The Civil War Soldier in War and Peace.* Chicago: Ivan R. Dee.

McPherson, James M. 1988. *Battle Cry of Freedom: The Civil War Era.* New York: Ballantine Books.

McPherson, James M. 1997. *For Cause and Comrades: Why Men Fought in the Civil War.* New York: Oxford University Press.

Mitchell, Reid. 1988. *Civil War Soldiers.* New York: Penguin Books.

Robertson, James I., Jr. 1988. *Soldiers: Blue and Gray.* Columbia: University of South Carolina Press.

Shannon, Fred A., ed. 1947. *The Civil War Letters of Sergeant Onley Andrus.* Urbana: University of Illinois Press.

Wiley, Bell Irvin. 1943/1994. *The Life of Johnny Reb: The Common Soldier of the Confederacy.* Baton Rouge: Louisiana State University Press.

Wiley, Bell Irvin. 1952/1994. *The Life of Billy Yank: The Common Soldier of the Union.* Baton Rouge: Louisiana State University Press.

When the Home Front Became a Battlefront: Civilians in Invaded and Occupied Areas

2

Antoinette G. van Zelm

C ivilians who lived in occupied or invaded territory experienced the Civil War firsthand. For at least a few moments, they shared some of the fear and exhilaration that accompanied soldiers into battle. Most civilians would never forget the day the war came to their front door. Beyond understanding that they were living through a momentous event in their lives, civilians had varied reactions to invasion and occupation. Age, sex, color, socioeconomic status, political inclination, and war-weariness influenced how individuals responded as the home front became a battlefront.

The Consequences of Union Occupation

Most of the civilians who experienced invasion and occupation lived in the Confederacy. For most of the white residents of the South, the invading enemy was the Union Army. These civilians deeply resented the coming of Union forces. Still, a significant minority of white Southerners were Unionists and welcomed the Yankees. Most of the Confederacy's black residents, slave and free, cheered the arrival of Union troops as well.

Residents of the Border States, who were sharply divided over the war, also experienced occupation by Union forces throughout the conflict. Incursions by Confederate troops took place occasionally and had the support of Southern sympathizers in these areas. Northerners in towns like Gettysburg, Pennsylvania, and Sharpsburg, Maryland, also experienced invasion by Confederate forces.

Invasion and occupation by Union troops presented Southern civilians with both challenges and opportunities. With the threat of invasion came the difficult decision of whether to stay or go. Confederate supporters had to choose whether to remain at home and try to protect their property or to leave home and become refugees deeper within the Confederacy. With

Charlotte Forten Grimké (1837–1914)

A teacher on the South Carolina Sea Islands during the Civil War, Charlotte Forten helped former slaves make the transition to freedom. Born in Philadelphia, Pennsylvania, in 1837 to a prominent black family, Forten attended school and then taught in Salem, Massachusetts, before the war. Her family advocated the abolition of slavery and racial equality.

Sponsored by the Port Royal Relief Association, Forten began teaching on St. Helena Island, South Carolina, in October 1862. She was the first black teacher on the island and one of the first in all of the Union-occupied areas. She taught children of all ages to read, write, spell, and do math. She also gave lessons in history, highlighting the lives of abolitionist John Brown and Haitian revolutionary Touissaint L'Ouverture. Like other teachers of the former slaves, Forten also provided moral instruction and practical advice to adults.

While on the Sea Islands, Forten developed a genuine care and concern for the ex-slaves. She was moved by their generosity and loved their stirring spirituals. As did many of the well-educated Northerners with whom she worked, Forten occasionally expressed a patronizing attitude toward the former slaves.

While on St. Helena, Forten became friends with fellow teacher Laura Towne, as well as with Union colonel Thomas Wentworth Higginson, commander of the First South Carolina Volunteers, a regiment of black soldiers recruited on the Sea Islands. Forten and the unit's surgeon, Dr. Seth Rogers, shared a love of literature and the outdoors.

Forten kept a diary while on the Sea Islands and drew on these journals to publish descriptions of her experiences in the *Liberator* and the *Atlantic Monthly* during the war. Chronic respiratory illness and the death of her father prompted Forten to move back to the North in 1864. She remained involved in

invasion came the dire prospect of witnessing the carnage of battle or even getting caught in the crossfire. The arrival of Union troops signaled freedom for many enslaved civilians, who took advantage of the opportunity to leave slavery behind.

Occupation brought new rules and regulations governing everyday life, and Union authorities eventually tightened these restrictions to clamp down on Confederate civilians' active support for the Rebel war effort. Perhaps most significant, occupying troops looked to civilians to provide them with food and shelter. The occupiers generally took what they needed, leaving Confederate supporters and even many Unionists with significant grievances against the Yankee troops.

Relatively little Confederate territory came under Union control in 1861. The land held by the Yankees existed on the fringes of the Confederacy and consisted mostly of western Virginia and coastal islands along the shores of Virginia, North Carolina, South Carolina, and Georgia. In these areas, local civilians became guinea pigs, as the army and government officials worked out the policies and procedures that would guide the early years of occupation.

Charlotte Forten Grimké was a free-born African American activist who fought for the abolition of slavery and later for the education of African Americans. (*Photographs and Prints Division, Schomburg Center for Research in Black Culture, The New York Public Library, Astor, Lennox and Tilden Foundations*)

the transition to freedom, however, serving as secretary of the Teachers Committee of the New England Branch of the Freedmen's Union Commission for six years and then returning to South Carolina to teach for a year at the Colonel Robert Gould Shaw Memorial School in Charleston.

In 1878, Forten married Francis Grimké, a Presbyterian minister and former slave. The Grimkés shared a vibrant political, religious, cultural, and intellectual life in Washington, D.C., until Charlotte Forten Grimké's death in 1914.

Perhaps inevitable in a war fought over the issue of the expansion of slavery, some of the first residents of the Confederacy to live under occupation forces in large numbers were slaves themselves. When Union troops invaded Port Royal Sound along the South Carolina coast in November 1861, most white residents of the Sea Islands fled to the mainland. Most of the local slaves stayed behind; many of them refused to become refugees with their owners, and some paid a high price when they were beaten or even killed. One contemporary estimate held that close to 10,000 slaves lived on the Sea Islands at the time of the Union invasion. These slaves were soon joined by others, who were escaping the lowcountry plantations of the mainland. One slave family left a Savannah River rice plantation during the night. The grandmother of the family successfully steered them to a federal gunboat. "'My God! are we free?'" she exclaimed when her family's boat touched the Union vessel (Schwalm 1997, 95).

Late in 1861 and early in 1862, another key group of civilians to live under Union occupation within the Confederacy began to arrive. Northern teachers came to areas of coastal Virginia, North Carolina, South Carolina, Georgia, and Florida to assist the former slaves living under Union occupation.

These teachers, most of whom were unmarried women from the New England states, performed varied tasks. Sponsored by secular and religious societies, the teachers did much more than give lessons in reading, writing, and arithmetic. They also provided moral instruction, medical care, sewing lessons, and advice on conduct, dress, child care, and household organization. In addition, these Northerners distributed donated clothes among the ex-slaves and supervised black field workers on occupied plantations. By war's end, there would be about 900 such teachers working in the former Confederacy.

As President Abraham Lincoln sought to shore up support in the Border States in 1861 and early 1862, Union troops occupied areas of Maryland, Missouri, and Kentucky. While Unionists welcomed the Yankees with flag presentations and other demonstrations of support, Confederate partisans expressed their disdain for the occupiers. In Maryland, for example, tensions quickly arose between civilians and Union troops. In Baltimore, where there was considerable secessionist sentiment, the Union Army attempted unsuccessfully to stifle Confederate support. Not allowed to display Confederate flags or banners, residents found other ways to demonstrate their loyalties. Women wore ribbons and bows that reflected their leanings. Similarly, girls clothed themselves and their dolls in Confederate colors. Defiantly, on July 4, 1861, about 70 boys who supported the Confederacy went to a Union encampment and paraded around with a homemade Confederate flag.

Beginning in February 1862, the Union Army began to take over significant pieces of the Confederacy, particularly in the Western theater of the war. By spring, the Union would claim the cities of Nashville and Memphis, Tennessee, and surrounding regions; Norfolk and areas of southeastern Virginia; and New Orleans and Baton Rouge, Louisiana. Also in Union hands were footholds in coastal Virginia, North Carolina, South Carolina, Georgia, and Florida, as well as parts of northern Alabama, Arkansas, northern Mississippi, and northern Virginia. The anticipated arrival of Union troops provoked turmoil, fear, and uncertainty within the Confederacy. John McCline, an enslaved boy who lived outside of Nashville during the war, later described the evacuation of Tennessee's capital by the Confederates in February 1862: "The fact that they seemed so frightened and helpless left us under the impression that the yankee was an exceedingly dangerous foe" (Furman 1998, 43). Indeed, even before they laid eyes on any Yankee troops, many Confederate supporters viewed them as a depraved bunch. As sectional tensions had mounted during the antebellum period, people in the North and those in the South adopted severely distorted and highly stereotypical views of each other. In the minds of many Southerners, Northerners were greedy, worldly, selfish, and ruthless.

Southern Civilians and the Union Army

Before civilians saw the Yankees, they usually heard them coming. The bellow of artillery and the rumble of wagon trains signaled the arrival of Union troops for the residents of invaded areas. Families who lived near the battle front also heard the sounds of maiming and death—the movement of ambulances and the cries of the dying, wounded, and sick. Many civilians could not quite believe what they were hearing. John C. Spence

Like many families across the war-torn South, this family fled with their prized possessions loaded on a cart to live as refugees in places that they hoped would prove safe. (*National Archives*)

of Murfreesboro, Tennessee, described his neighbors as "never once dreaming that they should ever hear the roar of cannon, the rattle of muskets, or the groans of the dying" (Spence 1993, 10).

As Union forces captured Confederate territory in 1862, more and more civilians came face to face with the horrors of war. In battle zones, the distinction between soldier and civilian often disintegrated. Townspeople in Murfreesboro found themselves in the line of fire on July 13, 1862, when Confederate colonel Nathan Bedford Forrest's cavalry attacked the occupation forces. A young girl was shot in the face. Several major battles with horrific numbers of casualties took place in 1862, particularly late in the year. The bloody reality of the war came home to all civilians, North and South, but perhaps especially to those who witnessed the carnage. The mind-numbing death and destruction at Shiloh, Antietam, Fredericksburg, and Stones River shocked and saddened civilians. Makeshift hospitals sprang up everywhere as severely wounded men overwhelmed the communities near these battlefields. Civilians helped care for the wounded in homes, schools, churches, hotels, stores, and public buildings. Marylanders who lived in and near the town of Sharpsburg did their best to cope with what would be the bloodiest day of the entire war, with 22,719 casualties at the Battle of Antietam on September 17, 1862.

In 1861 and most of 1862, Union troops took a relatively lenient stance toward the civilians in occupied areas. President Lincoln and many other Northerners believed that most residents of the South had simply been duped by their slaveholding leaders into supporting the Confederacy and that, with benevolent treatment, these everyday citizens would soon change their allegiance.

Despite the relative leniency of early occupation, Confederate supporters chafed under Yankee rule. They resented the sounds of the occupation troops, from drilling to shouting and drinking. Union troops sometimes rang bells in occupied towns to signal Union victory; the prospect of such an eventuality prompted residents of Charleston, South Carolina, to send their bells inland to Columbia. Many Confederate civilians did not shy away from letting the Yankees know what they thought of them. Confederate supporters in New Orleans rained down insults on Union troops when they entered the city in May 1862. Residents shared with the soldiers their fervent hope that the yellow fever would soon take many of the occupiers away to what they saw as deserved early graves. Murfreesboro, Tennessee, resident Mattie Ready vocally defended the Confederate cause to Union officers who occupied the town. Ready's outspoken defense of Kentucky cavalryman John Hunt Morgan to Yankee officers in the summer of 1862 got back to Morgan, and the two were married that December.

To the chagrin of Confederate supporters, romances between Union occupiers and Confederate women developed occasionally as well. Women who fraternized with Union troops did so knowing that they would likely be ostracized and threatened by family members and neighbors.

Because of the battle front's unrelenting demand for Confederate soldiers, the Southern home front increasingly became a female world. Women thus played an important role in the reception of Yankee troops in occupied areas. Union general Benjamin Butler quickly recognized this in New Orleans. Butler, whose hard-line policies governing civilian life in the Crescent City in 1862 presaged the adoption of harsher occupation terms throughout the occupied South, issued his infamous General Order Number 28 to stifle the vitriol directed at Union troops by Confederate women. Butler's order stated that women who insulted Union officers and soldiers would be treated as prostitutes. Although Butler's threat succeeded in making life more comfortable for his troops, he became a pariah among Confederate Southerners, who called him "Beast" Butler. His rigid control of civilian life prompted numerous complaints to his superiors, and President Lincoln replaced him late in 1862.

Although the harshness of Butler's rule stands out among occupied territory in the first few years of the war, Confederate supporters in all Union-held areas found themselves being governed by an alien authority that intended to regulate some of their activities. Tensions arose between civilians and Union occupiers, for example, over the payment of taxes, the confiscation of land, and the oath of allegiance, which was required of civilians who wanted to carry on their businesses or professions.

Because President Lincoln wanted commerce and agriculture to continue on a limited basis in Union-occupied territory, he encouraged Congress to pass laws to allow for the use of lands within Union-held areas. In June 1862, Congress instituted a real estate tax for residents of occupied areas. U.S. officials could confiscate the lands of planters who could not pay their taxes. The next month, Congress passed the Second Confiscation Act, which authorized federal troops to confiscate and make use of property that was being used to support the Confederacy, as well as the property of Confederate officers, officials, and active supporters.

The U.S. Treasury Department oversaw the leasing of abandoned and confiscated land within the Confederacy. The land could be leased to Northerners, loyal Southerners, and individuals of dubious loyalty who partnered with Unionists. At the same time, the Union military wanted to use some of the lands within occupied areas to support the occupation forces. Consequently, land confiscation not only resulted in friction between occupiers and civilians but also among the occupiers themselves.

As the number of Union forces in occupied areas of the Confederacy rose to more than 350,000 by mid-1862, civilians found their farms, plantations, and homes subject to the army's voracious appetite for food and supplies. Both Confederates and Unionists lost goods and property to the Union Army during the war. Some property was confiscated officially, some was taken unofficially, and some was destroyed simply for the sake of destruction. Troops not infrequently took more than they needed; some looted simply to get revenge on secessionists or for amusement. On the Hoggatt family plantation near Nashville in 1862, Union troops who were camped nearby killed livestock and dismantled rail fences for firewood. John McCline, a slave on the plantation, saw his owner and the plantation's overseer begging the soldiers to spare the animals, but their pleas fell on deaf ears until a general arrived on the scene. Mr. Hoggatt assured the soldiers he was a Unionist, but his slave doubted that they believed this.

Civilians very often had to fulfill the basic need of the ever-growing Union occupation forces for food. Kibbie Gardenhire, who was a young girl in rural Middle Tennessee during the war, perhaps summed it up best when she recalled in her memoir: "When they would say the Yankees were coming we would not know what to expect, whether someone would be killed, the house burned or what would happen, but there was one thing sure, they had to be fed" (Gardenhire, "Memoir," 9).

Relations between occupying troops and civilians deteriorated as 1862 progressed. Confederate successes on the battlefield emboldened Southerners who opposed Yankee rule. Many residents of occupied Tennessee, for example, believed that the Confederate Army might reclaim their state. This hope fueled civilian resistance. Residents of occupied areas smuggled, spied, and adopted guerilla warfare tactics.

Military reversals for the Union in the second half of 1862, along with continued resistance to Yankee occupation by Confederate civilians, hardened soldiers against the Confederacy and all of its inhabitants. In December 1862, the bloody Battle of Fredericksburg in Virginia was accompanied by the looting of civilians' houses and the destruction of their personal property by Union troops. Soldiers helped themselves to books, bedding, china, clothing, furniture, children's toys, food, paintings, silver, glasses, and musical instruments. What the troops did not use or keep they destroyed, littering the streets with civilians' possessions. One resident of the town reported, "I can tell you much better what they left, than what they destroyed" (Rable 2002b, 100). Such callous behavior by Union troops enraged civilians and Confederate soldiers. The Union soldiers' actions only fed Confederate civilians' negative views of Yankees. Some of the Union forces themselves were appalled and saddened by the sack of the town. Others among the invaders sought to justify their actions, in part by blaming the Rebels for initiating the war in the first place.

Newfound Freedom for Slaves

The tangible loss of provisions and personal property angered Confederate civilians in occupied areas, but the presence of Union troops wreaked havoc in other ways as well. Tensions rose within households and between neighbors. Kate Carney of Murfreesboro, Tennessee, wrote in her diary of the disquiet generated by Yankee occupation. Slaveholders were growing increasingly distrustful of their slaves, she noted, and personal antagonisms were breaking out between former friends.

Slaveholders' distrust of their slaves was well-justified, especially as the war progressed. The disruption of the war and the arrival of Union troops served as a catalyst for the South's slaves, causing them to reconsider their position and their options. On occupied Craney Island near Norfolk, Virginia, an escaped slave named Nancy told missionary Lucy Chase that she had been content in her relationship with her mistress—until the Union Army got close. The demise of slavery came about because slaves like Nancy took advantage of the new developments taking place around them to claim their freedom.

The lives of slaves changed dramatically just with the threat of invasion by Union troops. Some slave owners simply sold their slaves, for fear of getting nothing in return for such valuable investments. Others moved their slaves south or to interior areas of the Confederacy. Some slaves also became refugees with their owners, often moving more than once in the course of the war.

Accustomed to watching and listening closely, slaves immediately perceived changes ushered in by the war. The bondpeople noticed the anxiety of their owners and the disruption of everyday routines. They listened for the approach of Union troops and quickly learned the location of Union camps. Some slaves began celebrating as soon as they knew that Union troops were nearby. Others waited until they actually saw the Yankees in person.

Slaves had to decide whether to break for Union lines and the unknown or to stay put and see how the war played out. U.S. policy toward escaped slaves evolved as the war progressed. In August 1861, Congress passed the First Confiscation Act, which allowed for the confiscation of slaves working for the Confederacy. The Second Confiscation Act of July 1862 declared free all slaves who entered Union lines and who had been owned by Confederate masters. That same month, the Militia Act freed the mothers, wives, and children of men who had left their Confederate owners and joined the Union forces. The Preliminary Emancipation

Proclamation, issued in September 1862, and the final version of January 1863 mandated the enforcement of the Second Confiscation Act by military personnel.

Slave owners tried various tactics to discourage their slaves from leaving to join Union forces. John McCline's mistress gave the slaves on her plantation near Nashville Confederate money, perhaps to counter the blankets and clothing the Union troops were distributing to her slaves. Slave women on the plantation were also working for the soldiers on their own time and receiving pay in return. Susie King Taylor, who was a young slave in Savannah, Georgia, when the war broke out, recalled: "The whites would tell their colored people not to go to the Yankees, for they would harness them to carts and make them pull the carts around, in place of horses" (Taylor 1904/1968, 7). Taylor's grandmother assured her that these were just scare tactics. Taylor soon escaped to St. Catherine Island with her uncle's family. Like Taylor, many slaves who escaped to Union lines traveled in family groups. Those who left home as individuals tended to be young men. A simple invitation by a passing Union soldier to come up North and be free convinced young John McCline to leave slavery behind near Nashville in December 1862.

Escaping to Union lines could be dangerous. Fanny Wright, who became a regimental laundress, lost a child to a sniper's bullet when escaping to Union lines at Port Royal, off the South Carolina coast. En route to St. Simon's Island off the Georgia coast on a Union gunboat in 1862, Susie King Taylor remembered hiding between decks when a slave owner sailed up looking for his bondpeople.

Even within Union lines, safety was not ensured. Particularly early in the war, slave owners often showed up at Union camps to claim their former slaves. Taylor recalled that the ex-slaves on St. Simon's stuck close to their quarters, for fear of being captured by former slave owners. In Kentucky, one teenage female slave disguised herself as a soldier to evade her owner when he came looking for her. The Union soldiers for whom she cooked helped her in this ruse. In many other cases, the Union military was not so welcoming. Some Union officers helped Unionist slaveholders reclaim their escaped slaves.

Obviously, slaves who successfully escaped to Union territory wanted to be free. They also sought to avoid some of the trauma associated with the Confederate home front during wartime, including the breakup of families as owners moved slaves around, raids by hungry troops, and hunger as shortages mounted within the Confederacy by late in 1862.

Important developments in 1863 influenced civilian life in Union occupied areas. Perhaps most significant, the Union Army began to enlist and heavily recruit black soldiers. This turning point encouraged more slaves to escape, particularly young men but also entire families. In 1863, Yankee rule also became more oppressive for Confederate supporters who lived in occupied areas. Authorities replaced the conciliatory policy of the early war years by stricter controls and far less tolerance for expressions of dissent.

As the recruitment of black soldiers and the capture of additional Confederate territory increased the number of slaves escaping to Union lines, the Union military found itself unprepared to deal with the number of refugees. Some commanders simply refused to let women and children into camp. In one of the most notorious instances of egregious behavior against the families of black soldiers, military authorities at Camp Nelson, Kentucky, expelled about 400 women and children during bitterly cold weather in November 1864. Although the families were allowed to return several days later, many died or became chronically ill. As late as 1865, soldiers in the Sixtieth U.S. Colored Infantry, stationed in Helena, Arkansas, had to get permission from their company commanders for their wives to join them.

Families of black soldiers received some assistance with basic necessities from Union military officials in occupied areas. In December 1863, for example, General Benjamin Butler issued General Order Number 46 requiring that black soldiers mustered into units in the Department of Virginia and North Carolina receive certificates of subsistence for their families to bring to Union officials. Referring to Butler's order, Ann Sumner of Portsmouth, Virginia, wrote to the general in February 1864 and told him that she was having trouble getting officials to supply her with some much-needed wood.

Authorities were reluctant to give too much aid. They feared encouraging dependence, and most believed that ex-slave women should work to help support their families. Many slave women who had escaped got relief work in Union-occupied towns and at Union encampments. Many such women worked as cooks and washerwomen. Others did basic custodial work, sewed for the men, or sold them baked goods. With the formation of black regiments, black women found additional opportunities. Women who worked for black regiments could take on more responsibility than black women who worked for white regiments. At the Benton Barracks Hospital in St. Louis, Missouri, for example, black women worked as nurses in the hospital's black ward. Susie King Taylor, officially a regimental laundress for the Thirty-third U.S. Colored Troops, nursed, taught, and even cleaned guns.

Other ex-slave women worked as field hands on lands confiscated by the federal government. Some of the newly freed began their own businesses, including hotels, groceries, and brothels. Others, responding to the eagerness for education among former slaves of all ages, learned enough to become teachers themselves. The famous Harriet Tubman, who served as a Union spy and nurse at Beaufort, South Carolina, during the war, set up a wash-house where women could learn to wash and gain some independence.

Some escaped slaves initially lived in contraband camps, which were temporary settlements in occupied areas. In these camps, the ex-slaves lived in tents, shanties, abandoned houses, cabins, former barracks, and lean-tos. Contraband camps quickly became overcrowded; exposure to the elements and poor sanitary conditions led to high rates of disease and death. Consumption, pneumonia, and smallpox claimed many victims. With the great demand for ex-slave men as military laborers and soldiers, contraband camps were largely populated by women, children, and the elderly. The cycle of life continued for these families, despite the many challenges they faced. Residents of contraband camps recreated aspects of their slave communities, cultivating small plots of land by daylight and gathering in the evenings to sing, dance, pray, sew, and gossip. Midwives served contraband camps in Helena, Arkansas, and on Edisto Island off the South Carolina coast. Some women started orphanages in the camps, as in Clarksville, Tennessee, and on President's Island in the Mississippi River. In Beaufort, South Carolina, Harriet Tubman appears to have run a soup kitchen for the poor.

One of the most disappointing aspects of freedom for former slaves likely was the treatment that some received from Union soldiers and officers. In June 1863, contrabands in Maryland suffered when members of the Second Maryland Infantry Regiment raided their tents, stealing from the former slaves and beating them. Many black women suffered from sexual assaults by white Union soldiers and officers. On the Sea Islands, women were shot for refusing sexual advances, and mothers were beaten for trying to shield their daughters. Similarly, laundresses at Fort Jackson, Louisiana, tried unsuccessfully to resist a group of officers who targeted the women for sexual harassment over several nights.

Despite these hardships, the desire for schooling among the former slaves thrived during the war. Although teachers from the North played an important role, indigenous efforts abounded as well. In Tennessee, African Americans began the first wartime schools in the fall of 1862. In many

Educating children and adults was closely associated with emancipation in the American South. The Freedmen's Bureau established this school in Beaufort, South Carolina, shown here around 1865. (*Corbis*)

Union-occupied areas, Northern teachers helped former slaves make the transition to freedom. In addition to the instruction and care that the teachers provided, they also gave ex-slaves other kinds of support. Teachers in occupied areas encouraged former slaves to marry and tried to help them reunite with their families. Although military officials often viewed slave women and their families as a nuisance at best, female teachers showed particular solicitude for women and their families. These teachers condemned the sexual abuse of ex-slave women and girls by Union officers and soldiers. Women teachers also lamented the Union Army's impressment of slave men, echoing the protests of ex-slave women.

The presence of women teachers in Union-occupied areas signaled to many newly emancipated slaves that freedom would be different from slavery. Former slaves appreciated the assistance they received from Northern teachers. However, they also usually encountered some of the same attitudes of possessiveness and control that they had long endured from Southern whites. Northern teachers, for example, became easily exasperated with former slaves and felt superior to them in terms of class and race. In addition, most Northern teachers promoted family stability for the ex-slaves, and also believed that freedwomen as well as men should work for wages.

The rapidly increasing demise of slavery in and near Union-occupied areas during 1863 rankled Confederate supporters, as well as Unionist slaveholders. Slaves who had not left used the threat of escape to negotiate better working conditions. Some slaves refused to carry out certain types of work; others came and went as they pleased. Slaveholders struggled to keep their farms and businesses going.

The Firm Grip of Union Occupation

Nonslaveholders had an even more difficult time feeding their families than the wealthier slaveholders because they had fewer resources to draw on when their farms were besieged by Union troops. Foraging, both official and unofficial, devastated many rural families. Living off the land was an essential component, for example, of General Ulysses S. Grant's Vicksburg campaign from May to July of 1863. Residents of Union-occupied rural areas often did not have enough to eat during the closing years of the war.

In addition, there were never enough troops to enforce Union control on a daily basis beyond garrisoned towns and cities, thus a dangerous power vacuum developed throughout the countryside. Beset by guerillas, Union stragglers, and simple thugs, rural occupied areas descended into chaos in the later years of the war. Community relations broke down completely as county governments ceased operations and as rural churches and stores closed. Vicious cycles of violence ensued between Unionists and Confederate supporters in such areas as western Tennessee and northwestern Arkansas. The bitterness engendered by guerilla activity would last long after the war ended.

Civilians who lived in Union-garrisoned towns and cities also saw their lives become more difficult in 1863. Occupation forces cracked down on active resistance with arrests, house burnings, and executions. In many towns and cities, military authorities instituted stricter oath policies, with those who refused to take the oath of allegiance sent beyond Union lines.

The Union Army's unrelenting assault on the Confederacy in 1863 introduced the hard hand of war to more Southern civilians. The Vicksburg campaign included the burning of Jackson, Mississippi, in May 1863. The siege of Vicksburg lasted from late in May to early July, trapping many civilians within the city. Many sought to protect themselves from the shelling by hiding in cellars and hillside caves. Little drinking water or food remained by the time the Confederates finally surrendered on July 4. Union forces distributed bacon and hardtack to starving civilians. At the same time, the troops celebrated their Independence Day victory with music and gunshots, to the chagrin of Vicksburg residents, who would not celebrate the Fourth again until the 1940s.

Many civilians lived in areas that changed hands several times during the war. Eliza Anderson Fain, who lived near Rogersville in northeastern Tennessee, recorded in her diary the comings and goings of Union troops from September 1863 until the end of the war. Fain, a Confederate supporter who had a husband and sons in the Rebel forces, nonetheless shared food with soldiers from both armies. A devout Presbyterian, she also passed out religious tracts to men on both sides. One evening in October 1863, a Union major from the 65th Indiana Regiment dined at the Fains's home. He said grace before the meal, and Eliza later recorded in her diary: "Oh to think Christian is arrayed against Christian in this struggle almost breaks my heart" (Stowell 2000, 161). As the war wore on, the Fains and many other families had less and less to eat for themselves. Foraging by the armies and wartime shortages depleted the Fains' resources so much that by May 1864 Eliza had to ask a neighbor to share some meat with her family. Later that year, she suffered another loss when the minister of her church became a refugee. From August 1864 to March 1865, she had no services to attend.

For Confederate supporters like Fain, 1864 brought disappointment and misery. Like residents of Vicksburg the year before, civilians in Atlanta endured the incessant shelling of a Union siege. People dug pits in their backyards and used metal sheets and railroad ties to erect roofs over the holes. Despite these precautions, 20 civilians were killed during the siege. When it ended with the city's surrender in September, General William T. Sherman's troops evacuated the civilians who had not yet left the city. Sherman's forces then destroyed the railroads and war industries, and many houses burned down as a result.

As more and more Confederate territory came under Union control, and as the number of refugees entering Union-held areas mounted, the federal government strained to assist civilians. The Nashville contraband camp, for example, was overwhelmed late in 1864 as Confederate general John Bell Hood's troops invaded Middle Tennessee.

Guerilla warfare continued to wreak havoc in rural areas of the occupied South in 1864. In particular, residents of Missouri, Kentucky, Virginia, and Tennessee suffered terribly from this irregular warfare. Confederate

Mary Greenhow Lee (1819–1907)

Avidly devoted to the Confederate cause, Mary Greenhow Lee of Winchester, Virginia, vocally opposed Union occupation of the town between 1862 and 1865. Forty-one years old when the war broke out, Lee was the widow of Hugh Holmes Lee, a lawyer who had died in 1856.

A native of Richmond, Virginia, Mary Greenhow Lee had adopted Winchester as her home upon her marriage. Located in Virginia's fertile Lower Shenandoah Valley, Winchester became one of the most fought-over towns in all of the Confederacy. By war's end, Winchester had officially changed hands 13 times.

Lee captured Winchester's tumultuous wartime existence in a journal that she began on March 11, 1862, the day Confederate troops first evacuated the town. At that time, Lee headed a household that included two sisters-in-law, two nieces, and five adult slaves. Both of the slave men in her household would later escape to Union lines. The Lee family and the town's other stalwart residents, who included many Union supporters, lived through six battles in or near the town, as well as countless raids.

Just as Winchester represents an extreme example of invasion and occupation, Lee exemplifies the zenith of fervent secessionism.

guerillas raided Union outposts. John Singleton Mosby, who commanded the Forty-third Virginia Partisan Ranger Battalion, was one of the most successful guerilla leaders. In Union-held north-central Virginia from 1863 to 1865, his unit attacked railroads, bridges, supply wagons, and telegraph lines. In Kentucky, John Hunt Morgan conducted many similar raids behind Union lines.

Civilians often found themselves caught in the middle. Guerillas burned the contraband camp in Pulaski, Tennessee, in 1864. In East Tennessee, Unionist bushwhackers threatened the Fain family farm in the closing year of the war. Early in April 1865, they stole food, a horse, and silver from the Fains' already depleted resources. Lizette Woodworth Reese, who lived north of Baltimore for most of the war, later wrote about the fear she experienced when caught between both sides. Reese's home was located near a Union encampment that was often visited by Confederate raiders. "Between the blue forces and the gray we were ground between two millstones of terror," she recalled (Bardaglio 2002, 321).

Despite mounting military defeats and pressing everyday needs, Confederate supporters continued to speak out against aspects of Yankee rule. Civilians who believed that they were being mistreated by occupation authorities protested, sometimes successfully. In Natchez, Mississippi, in 1864, civilians registered numerous complaints against General Mason Brayman, commander of the Union post. When Brayman ordered that all congregations pray for President Abraham Lincoln, the Roman Catholic bishop of Natchez, William Henry Elder, refused. Brayman exiled Elder to Vidalia, Louisiana, but Secretary of War Edwin Stanton overruled Brayman and rescinded his order, so that Elder could return to Natchez.

She rejoiced in being known as a "Secesh" by Union forces. Determined to maintain her independence under Union occupation, she dehumanized the Yankees as vulgar individuals not worthy of her consideration, much less her company. Although many Union officers sought lodging at her house during the war, she succeeded in putting them all off, save one, who stayed for only a few nights in 1863.

Like some other female Confederate supporters, Lee confronted occupying troops, identifying herself to them as their enemy. She intentionally defied even minor rules, including night curfews, lights-out commands, and orders to clean the sidewalk in front of her house. Even as she rejected Union rule, Lee worked for the Confederacy, running an underground mail service, making and collecting goods for Confederate forces, and doing hospital work. She depicted herself as a soldier for the cause.

For their constant annoyance to Union officers and soldiers, Lee and her family were banished from Winchester by General Philip H. Sheridan in February 1865. In October of that year Lee settled in Baltimore, Maryland, where she ran a boarding house and became involved in Confederate memorial activities. Mary Greenhow Lee died in Baltimore in 1907.

Other citizens of Natchez went to nearby Union authorities and complained of arbitrary arrests and confiscation of property from individuals who had taken the oath of allegiance. Transferred to Vidalia and later publicly censured, Brayman was replaced by General John W. Davidson, who eventually established a formal body to respond to complaints by Natchez citizens.

By December 1864, civilian charges of mistreatment and exploitation by Union occupiers led President Lincoln to appoint special commissioners for the occupied areas. These men had the task of investigating the activities of both civil and military officials.

Meanwhile, military officials, missionaries, and teachers promoted the legalization of slave marriages in occupied areas. In 1864 and 1865, many former slaves in Union-controlled territory got married legally, some in mass wedding ceremonies. New unions were formed, and existing ones made legal. Vicksburg, Davis Bend, and Natchez, Mississippi, for example, together registered more than 1,400 nuptials during these years.

According to one chaplain of a black regiment, ex-slaves did not just see the war as an opportunity for freedom but also as "the road to Responsibility; Competency; and an honorable Citizenship" (Berlin, Reidy, and Rowland 1982, 712). This citizenship included legal marriages. The chaplain approved of the popularity of weddings among the former slaves he ministered to in Little Rock.

Teachers played an important role in politicizing former slaves and introducing them to the rituals of citizenship. Early in 1865, teacher Anna Gardner in New Bern, North Carolina, introduced her ex-slave students to a ritual of Union citizenship when she had them present a flag to a black artillery unit. Holiday celebrations, such as those on the Sea Islands to commemorate Thanksgiving in 1862 and New Year's in 1863, included speeches and songs promoting the Union cause. An Emancipation Day celebration in Beaufort, South Carolina, on January 1, 1865, featured a former slave woman dressed as the Goddess of Liberty. She sang "In That New Jerusalem" and waved a banner. During Reconstruction and beyond, emancipation celebrations would become an integral part of black community and political life.

By 1865, some residents of occupied areas were looking toward the future and life in the postwar South. In January 1865, for example, the "colored citizens" of Nashville petitioned the Union Convention of Tennessee. The 62 individuals who signed the petition wanted blacks to be given the right to vote and to testify in court. The petitioners based their request in part on the sacrifices that black soldiers had made in their service to the Union cause. The Nashville civilians asked, "When has the colored citizen, in this rebellion been tried and found wanting?" (Berlin, Reidy, and Rowland 1982, 815).

In 1865, residents of the last bastions of the Confederacy experienced invasion and occupation. General Sherman's Carolinas campaign in February and March 1865 brought significant suffering to civilians, particularly in South Carolina. Sherman and his army, which numbered 60,000, wanted to destroy Confederate resources but also to inflict punishment on South Carolina for its rabid secessionism. At the Middleton Place plantation near Charleston, for example, slaves joined Union soldiers in destroying the plantation. Officers burned the house and many of the outbuildings. Slaves desecrated the family mausoleum. Although slaves and Union forces worked together in this instance, many blacks in the Carolinas were appalled by the destructiveness of Sherman's troops and disaffected when the soldiers mistreated them.

As Confederate troops evacuated strongholds like Richmond and Charleston, they set fire to the cities. Citizens desperately tired to subdue the flames. "It was a terrible scene," Susie King Taylor wrote of Charleston in her memoir of the war (Taylor 1904/1968, 42). For civilians in invaded and occupied areas, the South's devastated landscape served as a constant reminder of the war's heavy toll.

As Sherman's troops made their way through South and North Carolina, they encountered firm resistance from Confederate supporters, especially women. Throughout the South, civilians who had supported the Confederacy drew on a range of coping mechanisms to deal with defeat, from continued resistance to denial to religious resignation. In Norfolk, Virginia, for example, Confederate supporter Chloe Tyler Whittle flirted with despair but drew on her Christian faith to face the future. She dedicated herself to avoid taking the oath of allegiance to the United States at all costs.

Although invasion ceased with the Confederate surrender in 1865, occupation of areas of the South by Union troops would continue for 12 years. Reconstruction was not a new experiment but a continuation of the challenge of wartime occupation. Civilians would continue to work out the transition from slavery to freedom, the response to Northern rule, and

This photograph by George N. Barnard captures some of the damage done to Charleston, South Carolina, during Union general William T. Sherman's 1865 march. (*National Archives*)

the recreation of community life. Years after the Civil War, Susie King Taylor wrote, "I can and shall never forget that terrible war until my eyes close in death" (Taylor 1904/1968, 50). Countless civilians who witnessed the horrors of the conflict shared her sentiment.

References and Further Reading

Ash, Stephen. 1995. *When the Yankees Came: Conflict and Chaos in the Occupied South, 1861–1865*. Chapel Hill: University of North Carolina Press.

Bardaglio, Peter W. 2002. "On the Border: White Children and the Politics of War in Maryland." In *The War Was You and Me: Civilians in the American Civil War*, edited by Joan E. Cashin, 313–331. Princeton, NJ: Princeton University Press.

Berlin, Ira, Joseph P. Reidy, and Leslie S. Rowland, eds. 1982. *Freedom: A Documentary History of Emancipation, 1861–1867. Series II: The Black Military Experience*. New York: Cambridge University Press.

Furman, Jan, ed. 1998. *Slavery in the Clover Bottoms: John McCline's Narrative of His Life during Slavery and the Civil War*. Knoxville: University of Tennessee Press.

Gardenhire, Kibbie Tinsley Williams. 1939. "Memoir." Tennessee State Library and Archives, Nashville.

Grimsley, Mark. 1995. *The Hard Hand of War: Union Military Policy toward Southern Civilians, 1861–1865*. New York: Cambridge University Press.

Phipps, Sheila. 2004. *Genteel Rebel: The Life of Mary Greenhow Lee*. Baton Rouge: Louisiana State University Press.

Rable, George C. 2002b. ''Hearth, Home, and Family in the Fredericksburg Campaign.'' In *The War Was You and Me: Civilians in the American Civil War*, edited by Joan E. Cashin, 85–111. Princeton, NJ: Princeton University Press.

Rose, Willie Lee. 1964. *Rehearsal for Reconstruction: The Port Royal Experiment*. Indianapolis: Bobbs-Merrill.

Schwalm, Leslie. 1997. *A Hard Fight for We: Women's Transition from Slavery to Freedom in South Carolina*. Urbana: University of Illinois Press.

Spence, John C. 1993. *A Diary of the Civil War*. Nashville: Williams Printing Co. for the Rutherford County Historical Society.

Stevenson, Brenda, ed. 1988. *The Journals of Charlotte Forten Grimké*. New York: Oxford University Press.

Stowell, Daniel W. 2000. '''A Family of Women and Children': The Fains of East Tennessee during Wartime.'' In *Southern Families at War: Loyalty and Conflict in the Civil War South*, edited by Catherine Clinton, 155–173. New York: Oxford University Press.

Taylor, Susie King. 1904/1968. *Reminiscences of My Life in Camp*. New York: Arno Press and *New York Times*.

War on Two Fronts: Women during the Civil War

Lisa Tendrich Frank

In July 1861, Virginian Belle Boyd shot and killed a U.S. officer in her home. The young woman claimed self-defense, asserting that the drunken officer had threatened her and her mother. As a white woman, Boyd's actions were quickly excused and she faced no legal consequences for her actions. Taking a cue from her treatment after this event, Boyd began more fully employing her femininity to her advantage. On her own initiative, Boyd, an ardent supporter of the Confederacy, began openly associating and flirting with Union soldiers, many of whom had been stationed around her house as guards to prevent future incidents. Unbeknownst to them, however, the young woman had no romantic intentions toward them. Instead, she was using her feminine charms to gather information on military movements and passing it along to Southern troops. Her initial efforts as an unofficial spy did not last long. Unskilled in the work of espionage, Boyd hardly concealed her work as an unofficial spy and she was quickly discovered. Once again, Boyd discovered that her womanhood provided her protection. Even though there was solid evidence to confirm her treasonous role—Union officials discovered one of Boyd's uncoded messages, written in her own handwriting—the authorities did little to punish the budding spy. Boyd escaped with only a warning.

Boyd continued her efforts to aid the Confederacy by taking advantage of assumptions about white women and their ability to escape punishment. From Front Royal, Virginia, where she was sent to stay with an aunt and uncle, Boyd not only nursed wounded soldiers, but she also began to take weapons and supplies from Union troops for Confederates. Furthermore, she became an official Confederate courier, carrying messages between Generals P. G. T. Beauregard and Thomas "Stonewall" Jackson using federal passes she obtained from Union officers. In this capacity, Boyd became "the rebel spy," providing valuable information to Confederate officers during the Battle of Front Royal in May 1862 (Boyd 1865, 74).

After receiving a message from another courier and then garnishing information from local Union soldiers, Boyd ran through the battlefield to meet
the approaching Confederate Army. For her efforts, Jackson later awarded
her an honorary commission as a captain and an aide-de-camp. Northerners and Southerners publicly recognized Boyd's role in the Confederate
success, and her new status made it difficult for her to continue her espionage efforts. As a result, she was captured and imprisoned twice. The Federal Department of War imprisoned her in the Old Capitol Prison for a
month in July 1862 and in the Carroll Prison for a longer stay in the
summer of 1863. However, these prison stays did nothing to dampen
Boyd's commitment to the Confederacy. In May 1864, she headed to
Europe with secret Confederate government dispatches, but was arrested
again within a few days. She was exiled to Canada this time and from
there she traveled to England where, in 1865, she published her memoirs
of her wartime exploits.

Not all women took such extraordinary roles in the American Civil
War. Yet the nation's women all shaped and were shaped by the sectional
conflict and the realities of war. All women, regardless of their locale, age,

Confederate spy Maria
Isabella "Belle" Boyd
used her feminine
charms to obtain
information about
Union troop move-
ments and pass it to
Confederate officials
during the Civil War.
(*Library of Congress*)

race, or class, dealt with the direct and indirect results of the Civil War. As men marched off to the battlefields, it was the women left behind who had to keep society running—by raising children, feeding families, running farms and businesses, making uniforms, and provisioning armies. In both the North and South, the needs of war and a loss of manpower mandated that women take on expanded responsibilities. Some took control of family businesses and others took jobs in a growing industrial sector. Slave women also dealt with the shifting realities of wartime, as the conflict provided opportunities for emancipation while wartime tensions made their lives even more precarious. Other women—white and black—became active participants in the military, as nurses, cooks, laundresses, spies, and even soldiers. Even women who were lukewarm in regard to the war discovered that the war became everyone's business. Women across the nation discovered that they needed to deal with food shortages, fiscal inflation, the absence and deaths of family members, and the arrival of troops. Some women became refugees; others housed refugees. The war required the mobilization of the entire population, and in many cases, men, women, and children took up the rallying call. Although most scholarly attention focuses on men's political and military roles during the Civil War, women played a vital part.

The Coming of the War

Although war is frequently understood as being in the domain of men, the social history of the American Civil War demonstrates that the war could not have been waged without the nation's women. From the very outset of the conflict, women became integral to both the Union's and Confederate's ability and willingness to fight the war. Many women helped fill the ranks by encouraging men to enlist, but women were also among the most vocal opponents of mobilization efforts and the war itself, especially as their effects on the home front and family life became known. In this way, women made themselves central participants in the brewing conflict.

The active participation of women began before the first shots were fired on the battlefields. Just as the secession crisis consumed the thoughts of husbands and fathers, the nation's women also recognized it as a momentous and important event. Women everywhere commented upon secession in their diaries, some even starting a journal for the first time to commemorate what they knew were historic events. As one Tennessee woman explained in 1861, "The War is the all absorbing topic of conversation and of letters" (Jabour 2007, 246). With the high stakes involved in secession and then the war, it should not be surprising that many women were, like Virginian Kate Corbin, "all . . . intimately concerned in the threatened [and] inevitable war that it is not to be wondered at after all" (Jabour 2007, 248). Northern white women, too, were similarly preoccupied with the political realm. Author Louisa May Alcott, for example, observed "of course the town is in a high state of topsey turveyness, for every one is boiling over with excitement" (Sizer 2000, 75). Although women were expected to refrain from publicly engaging in politics, many women did more than simply follow politics and talk about it among themselves. Around the Confederacy, women attended the secession conventions, cheered raucously in support of their political positions, presented flowers and wreaths to admired speakers, and made banners to voice their public views. In Boston, as elsewhere in the North, "windows were flung up; and women leaned out into the rain waving flags and handkerchiefs" to salute the first volunteers for the Union Army (Attie 1998, 19). As another woman from Massachusetts explained, "I neither know, nor care for politics in any form, and yet I am drawn into the vortex" (Attie 1998, 23). Although they were occasionally scorned for their brazen public behavior, the nation's women recognized the importance of secession and the political events swirling around them.

African American communities similarly recognized the importance of the secession crisis. In the North, their involvement in the political realm often occurred as an extension of their abolitionist activities. Although slave women were expected to be especially ignorant about public affairs—on account of their race, gender, lack of education, and status as chattel property—they too followed the secession crisis closely. In the low-country of South Carolina, for example, slave owners observed that their slaves "all think this a crisis in their lives that must be taken advantage of" (Schwalm 1997, 77).

Enlistment

At the outset of the conflict, women on both sides helped rally the troops as well as outfit the units. As the Union and Confederate governments both called for recruits, Northern and Southern communities scrambled to organize regiments that they could send off to defend their respective nations. On occasion, women made their voices heard in public. A crowd of women, for example, watched Abolitionist Frances Dana Barker Gage make an impassioned and "beautiful appeal to the mothers, urging them not to keep back their sons from the war . . . but to send them forth willingly and gladly as she had done hers, to fight for liberty" (Silber 2002, 50). Other women made similar appeals in the private realm, personally urging husbands, sons, sweethearts, and brothers to enlist.

Women played an integral part in raising these local regiments. They cajoled family members and sweethearts to join the ranks, often proclaiming that they would not tolerate a shirker in their society. Some women postponed engagements until their fiancés had enlisted in the local unit, refused to talk to nonenlisted men, and publicly scorned those not willing to wear a military uniform. Stories abound of women who shamed men into service by sending nonenlistees a piece of women's clothing, thereby solidifying the connection between military service and masculinity. Many women made it known that they were more than willing to judge those who served against those who did not. Some single women made it clear that they would not allow men to court them if they were unwilling to serve their nation. Some wives made similar threats. A British observer proclaimed that wives "won't let a man capable of carrying and handling a rifle stay round home. If he can walk he must be off" (Gallagher 1997a, 78). Women of both regions were willing to shame men into enlisting. Maria Patec of Kansas observed that "Men who love their homes, country, and firesides are willing to fight for them" (Silber 2005, 25). Women took seriously their roles as unofficial recruitment officers.

Concurrent with women's efforts to raise regiments and aid their nations, many women felt severely the conflict between country and family. Many women prioritized the public good over their personal needs. Eliza Oatis, for example, recognized that "It's hard to do without him and yet . . . his country has higher claims upon him now than I have" (Silber 2005, 26). Others came to different conclusions about sacrifice. "What do I care for patriotism?" a wife from South Carolina asked. "My husband is my country. What is country to me if he be killed?" (Faust 1996, 13.) An Ohio woman's comments reveal similar concerns. "I am more a wife than a patriot [and] although I do care for my country, I care for you [my husband] much more" (Silber 2005, 14). Although these women saw the patriotic necessity of sending men to the battlefield, they were reluctant to sacrifice their personal interests in favor of national interests. They hoped they would not have to make the choice between their husband and their nation.

In addition, women of both regions played a significant part in the elaborate ceremonies held before local soldiers headed off to join the armies. In addition to cheering for the recruits and wishing them well in their war endeavors, women also made the flags that the men carried off to battle. The flags subsequently served as a reminder to the soldiers of the families and homes that they fought for on the battlefield. Some flags had political messages on them, while others instead focused on local images. As another constant reminder of the women who had made the flag, some flags even incorporated material from women's dresses. At the flag presentations, prominent women made elaborate speeches encouraging the new soldiers to remember what they were fighting for—the freedom and survival of their homes and their loved ones. In these speeches, women also drew a link between soldiers' protection of the flag as a metaphorical protection of the women who had made it so lovingly. The soldiers took a piece of home with them as they marched into battle. In Tampa, Florida, for example, the community's women presented a flag with silk trimmings as a "memento of regard from those whom your self devotion is so highly esteemed" (Revels 2004, 15). When African American troops were raised in the North, their women organized similar flag presentations.

Outfitting Armies

Once the community's men had formed companies, women helped outfit them for battle by raising funds, sewing uniforms, and gathering supplies for the troops. On an individual and community level, women made blankets, clothes, bandages, and other wartime necessities for the enlisted men. Women on both sides were knitting so often that countless women referred to the "everlasting sock" or "everlasting mitten" that was on their knitting needles (Massey 1966, 35). As one woman in Pennsylvania explained, their obligation was "to supply regularly the Hospital at this place, with all the comforts necessary for the sick soldiers" (Silber 2005, 19). Just as they routinely did before the war, Southern white women often took credit for the work that was performed by their African American slaves. Julius Porcher, for example, "made the uniforms for the entire company of eighty men—she and her coloured seamstresses. The wool from their own sheep was spun into yarn. . . . This was then woven by her women on hand looms, cut out by her own hands, and made by her and her seamstresses" (Weiner 1998, 157).

The sewing societies and other aid societies formed in both the North and the South at the outset of the conflict to make flags and supplies for new regiments continued their work throughout the war and were joined by countless others. Women's aid efforts ranged in size and scope. Across the Confederacy, aid societies were locally run and independent of each other. Some were composed of two or three related women or friends who sewed together in the evenings for the soldiers. Others were community-based groups that met in church basements. For many women, these aid societies provided them with their first opportunities to work outside of the home—even if it was in the homes of their neighbors. In North Carolina, Catherine Anne Devereaux Edmondston observed that "Thousands of ladies who have never worked before are hard at work on coarse sewing all over our whole country" (1979, 60). Although many women enthusiastically incorporated textile work into their busy lives, many found it exhausting. Near the end of the war, for example, Sarah Wadley shamefully admitted that she just recently "commenced to card and spin, and I never tried anything so difficult to me, or so tiring" (Faust 1996, 47). Whatever its form, women's voluntary efforts on behalf of their soldiers proved vital to the armies on both sides.

As the war lengthened, wartime shortages became more severe and basic supplies became scarcer. Despite these problems, the scale of private donations to the war effort remained remarkably high. For example, in January 1865, as William T. Sherman's Union troops were rapidly approaching Columbia, South Carolina, a fund-raising bazaar raised between $150,000 and $350,000 for Confederate soldiers. The bazaar, which was organized and run by elite white women, offered everything from fortune telling to a wide assortment of donated food—including roasted turkey, salmon, lobster, duck, venison, and a variety of desserts. The bazaar also offered a wide range of other donated products for sale, including jewelry, cutlery, dolls, fancy clothes, tobacco, and livestock. "You would never imagine there was a war in our land, could you have seen, the delicacies of every description" (Frank 2001, 163). After much success, the sumptuous bazaar closed early to avoid the danger of enemy troops.

The U.S. Sanitary Commission

In June 1861, the U.S. Sanitary Commission (USSC) formed in the North to coordinate the efforts of local women and aid societies to supply the Union Army. With approximately 7,000 aid societies supporting the Union, the USSC's task was profound. As an umbrella organization, the USSC coordinated millions of dollars of food, medicine, and clothing for Union soldiers, and it provided a structure for the thousands of individual women who volunteered to serve as nurses, knit socks, make uniforms, raise money, or donate supplies. The USSC created formal branches in 10 cities—with the largest headquartered in Chicago—and also created 25 soldiers' homes to provide for the needs for soldiers who were heading to and from the front. At the soldiers' homes, an estimated average of 2,300 mostly sick and injured soldiers daily received food, medical care, a bed, and help with pension forms and other paperwork. Elizabeth Blackwell, one of the founders of the USSC and the first woman to earn a professional medical degree in the United States, recognized the chaos that existed before the creation of the USSC. "There has been a perfect mania amongst the women to 'act Florence Nightingale'" (Giesberg 2000, 22). The USSC successfully channeled women's desires to be wartime nurses into areas where they were needed.

In addition to distributing supplies and placing nurses where they were needed, the USSC also conducted Sanitary Fairs to raise money to support the soldiers and the efforts of smaller branches. In late 1863, a fair in Chicago raised more than $100,000 and subsequent fairs elsewhere raised even more money. The New York Metropolitan Fair was the most successful of its kind, raising $1,183,505. These fund-raisers required a tremendous amount of organization as well as skills that were hardly common before the war. More than 3,000 volunteers helped with the spring 1864 Philadelphia Fair. The sight of women selling goods, let alone organizing the entire affair, certainly shocked many Northerners. As William Sherman explained to his wife, "I don't approve of ladies selling things at a table. So far as superintending the management of such things, I don't object, but it merely looks unbecoming for a lady to stand behind a table to sell things" (Lewis 1932, 520). Despite these concerns, the USSC eventually conducted about 30 fairs and raised millions of dollars for the Union war effort.

Hospitals

Although it was primarily a male occupation before the war, necessity demanded that thousands of women become nurses. The frequency of amputations, gruesome wounds, and naked male patients made nursing—especially wartime nursing—a potentially unfeminine prospect. North Carolinian Lucy Capehart, for example, explained

> I never in my life could go to one [hospital], [and] never expect to unless I am compelled. Not that I am not willing to do everything I can for the Soldiers, but simply because I don't like so *much mess*, [and] so *many different odours*—it makes me sick to smell soldiers anyway. (Frank 2001, 148fn)

Mary Ashton Rice Livermore (1820–1905)

Mary Ashton Rice was born to wealthy white parents in Boston in 1820 and received the education afforded to women of her class. In the early 1840s she spent three years as a tutor to children in Virginia. Her life on a slave plantation during this period opened her eyes to the horrors of slavery and formed in her a hatred of the institution. In 1845, Mary married Universalist minister Daniel Livermore, who shared her belief in abolitionism and temperance. An accomplished author, she published several socially conscious stories that covered topics such as temperance and religion. In 1857, the family moved to Chicago, where Mary Livermore became active in the community and its voluntary organizations. She covered the 1860 Republican National Convention's nomination of Abraham Lincoln for the *Northwestern Christian Advocate*, the only woman

Mary Livermore worked as director of the Northwestern branch of the United States Sanitary Commission during the Civil War, helping to run several Sanitary Fairs. (*Library of Congress*)

Others overcame their reticence and came to different conclusions. Thousands of female nurses performed a wide range of tasks in formal and makeshift hospitals. They comforted and fed patients, helped change bandages, obtained supplies, cooked food, shook out ticks, did laundry, cleaned the wards, lifted patients, and helped soldiers write letters home. At least 21,000 female nurses served in the Union Army and others served as nurses in unofficial capacities. The number of female Confederate nurses is more elusive, but soldiers and doctors all noted their omnipresence. Even with volunteers in short supply, African American nurses were frequently relegated to menial tasks as "wardboys." At Tunnel Hill Hospital in Atlanta, for example, "negro women who aid in cleaning the wards are also required to wash" (Mohr 2005, 278). Despite their varied roles, the work that women provided in military hospitals, at all levels, proved invaluable.

Fighting the War

Some women were directly involved in the fighting. Because both the Union and Confederacy restricted women from joining their armies, women who wanted to enlist had to conceal their sex. Hundreds of women bound their breasts, cut their hair, and dressed like men to serve their nation. Fortunately for them, both the Union and Confederacy only correspondent in attendance. The Civil War, however, brought the greatest opportunities to her.

During the Civil War, Mary Livermore became a vital part of the U.S. Sanitary Commission. After rising through the ranks of voluntary associations in Chicago, she became an Associate Manager of the Northwestern Branch of the Sanitary Commission. She worked closely with Jane Hoge. As managers, Livermore and Hoge oversaw the sorting of donated goods as well as the packing and sealing of boxes headed to soldiers on the battlefields. In addition, Livermore recruited nurses to serve at army posts, visited numerous battlefields and local aid societies, gave public speeches on behalf of the commission, planned two Sanitary Fairs in Chicago, and tirelessly raised money for and awareness of the Sanitary Commission. Livermore became

a public face of the Sanitary Commission who helped recruit donations, aid, and volunteers for the Union cause.

Livermore's wartime work with the Sanitary Commission ultimately led her to an active role in the postwar suffrage movement and a public role in American life. She had a busy speaking career that took her around the United States giving lectures on women's rights. In addition, in 1889 she published her popular memoir, *My Story of the War*, which detailed her experiences on the home front, in military hospitals, and with Union officials.

Mary Livermore died in Boston in 1905.

required remarkably superficial medical exams for enlistees, so their sex was rarely discovered. Consequently, there is no way of determining the full extent of female soldiers' participation in the Civil War, because no one knows how many female soldiers were ever revealed as such. The service of women that came to light did so as a result of several factors. In some instances, doctors or fellow soldiers discovered disguised women when they were killed or wounded, when they became pregnant and delivered a baby, or when they were captured. Other female combatants revealed their identities after the end of the war.

Scholars have been able to document the participation of female soldiers in every major Civil War battle. For example, at least 10 fought at Antietam and five fought at Gettysburg. These women joined the military with similar justifications as their male counterparts: to collect bounties and wages, to demonstrate their patriotism, and even to escape the general ennui that many claimed characterized the home. Once in the army, the performance of women did not contrast sharply with that of male soldiers. Female soldiers often rose in the ranks, a reality confirmed by the dismissal of several sergeants from duty. Although they broke the law by concealing their identities, neither the Confederacy nor the Union court-martialed women for their deceptions. Sarah Emma Edmonds, who fought for the Union as Franklin Thompson, received a pension for her service in the

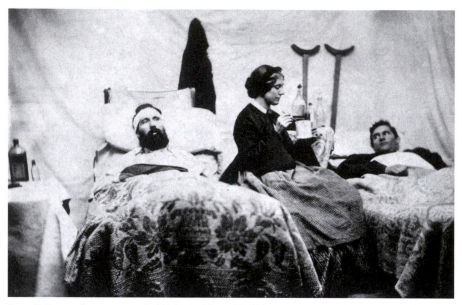

Anne Bell cares for two wounded Union soldiers. (*Corbis*)

1880s. The petitions of her former infantrymen helped convince Congress that she had earned a soldiers' pension despite her desertion—one made necessary by her feared discovery. After running from the ranks to avoid discovery, Edmonds became a nurse for the Union Army.

Female Spies

Throughout the war, female spies aided both the Union and Confederate war efforts. White women frequently relied on their feminine charms to disarm enemy soldiers and officials and convince them that they had no political motives. Allan Pinkerton, who created the U.S. Secret Service, explained that when the war began "it was not deemed possible that any danger could result from the utterances of non-combatant females . . . That this policy was a mistaken one was soon proved" (Leonard 1999, 21). Abolitionist Elizabeth Van Lew, for example, spent most of the war in her Richmond, Virginia, home. Unbeknownst to her Confederate neighbors, she headed an extensive spy network in the Confederate capital. She hosted Confederate officers and nursed wounded soldiers in her home, and she used these opportunities to gather information and ameliorate suspicious neighbors who were aware of her antislavery attitudes and resistance to donating supplies to the Confederate Army. Van Lew helped several dozen Union soldiers escape from Richmond's Libby Prison and passed information to the Union on the military positions of the Confederates. She sent encrypted messages in the spines of books, in the shoes of her servants, and even in a hollow egg in a basket of eggs.

Congress expressed its appreciation for Van Lew's service in 1867 with a reward of $5,000.

Slave women, too, provided the Union with additional information—"black dispatches" that they gathered while performing domestic chores for white Southerners, who rarely noticed the presence of their black slaves or assumed them unable to understand political and military discussions. For example, while working as a house servant for Jefferson Davis in the Confederate White House, Mary Elizabeth Bowser listened carefully to the Confederate president's discussions of military affairs and later passed them on to the Union. In addition, Mary Louveste, who was employed at the Gosport Navy Yard in Norfolk, Virginia, passed information about the state of the Confederate Navy on to U.S. secretary of the Navy Gideon Welles. Others, like former slave Harriet Tubman, served as formal spies during the war. Although Tubman earned a reputation for leading slaves to freedom through the Underground Railroad, she also used her contacts in the South and in the slave communities to gather information and pass it on to Major General David Hunter. For three years, "General Moses," as Tubman was called served as a Union scout in South Carolina and Florida. The importance of espionage by black spies was not lost on Robert E. Lee who concluded, "The chief source of information to the enemy is through our Negroes" (Fellman 2000, 201).

Home-Front Work

When the men of both regions marched off to battle, they left women of all ages and classes to keep everything running smoothly. Women on the home front faced new challenges as they were left in charge as the primary decision makers in households and businesses, and on farms and plantations. These adjustments were not always easy ones, but home-front women had no choice. Some women became the heads of family businesses and others took jobs in the industrial sector to support their families. In some cases, wartime women publicly took on roles and jobs that they had previously done in the domestic sphere. In other instances, women were new to the tasks at hand. Many women jumped at the opportunity to expand their responsibilities; others found it burdensome.

In the wealthy plantation areas of the South, elite slave mistresses often took on the tasks of the plantation master, including the role of overseer of not just household slaves but also of field hands. Although before the war women had run the households, these jobs did little to prepare them for full-time plantation management. Some fulfilled their new positions with little trouble, while others struggled to maintain the control necessary for efficient plantation management. For some, managing the household in the most trying of times was burdensome, especially when many African American slaves were increasingly expressing their independence. Mississippian G. W. Gayle, for example, worried that if any more white men left for the army, "anarchy will prevail and the slaves become one nation, if they can" (Edwards 2000, 78).

Furthermore, white women on plantations as well as those on smaller farms also had to take on the tasks of farm work that previously had been done by men or slaves. Many, unaccustomed to the hard labor of fieldwork, struggled with these tasks and complained about them to friends or in diaries.

In addition, this lack of a male workforce, black and white, placed even more emphasis on the labor of African American slave women. As the Confederate Army impressed slave men, the women who remained in the slave communities were given the additional responsibility of doing the labor previously done by men. As some female house slaves were moved into the fields to work, others gained additional tasks inside the house. For example, one former slave recalled that during the Civil War, "I worked in the big house, washed, ironed, cleaned up, and was nurse in the house when the war was going on" (Weiner 1998, 165). Slave women also had to deal with the isolation and trepidation that came with loved ones living at a distance. Although the Confederate Army did not impress slave women, many slave owners hired out their female slaves to compensate for the white family's financial needs. Slave Ellen Campbell, for example, recalled that "My young missus wus fixin' to git married, but she couldn't on account de war, so she brought me to town and rented me out to a lady runnin' a boarding house" (Hunter 1997, 10). Hired-out slaves performed a myriad of tasks. Some were hired out to nurse, chop wood, work in fields, iron, carry water, cook, and do laundry. One former slave recalled that when she was hired out as a 6-year-old, her job description was "in general just do everything" (Hunter 1997, 12).

Household Decisions

With the men in the military, women of both regions and all classes had to make all household decisions on their own. They had to ensure that they had the resources necessary to feed and clothe themselves and their children. This often meant coping with less. One Southern white woman recognized that "a year ago we would have considered it impossible to get on for a day without the things that we have been doing without for months" (Edwards 2000, 74). Women also had to keep up with the daily chores necessary to running their households. Some initially wrote to their husbands asking for advice, but slow communication and women's growing confidence in their abilities eventually led women to make these decisions entirely on their own. Many women moved in with relatives or opened their doors to neighbors on their own initiative and enjoyed the companionship afforded by sharing quarters.

Industrial Work

In addition, women filled positions previously held by men in factories, government posts, and other jobs. In return, women received desperately needed wages, although their wages were not as high as those given to men doing the same work. With few male breadwinners left on the home front and with prices rapidly increasing, many women had to find ways to bring in money to support their households. In the North, hundreds of "Government Girls" met the labor shortage created by the widespread enlistment of clerks in the Union Army. These women worked in the Treasury, Patent Office, War Department, Quartermaster's General Office, and elsewhere. Similarly, several hundred women—from middle- and upper-class Southern families—worked for the Confederate Treasury in Columbia, South Carolina, and Richmond, Virginia. Although there was resistance to hiring women to work as clerks, the absence of qualified men led to women signing treasury notes and performing other clerking tasks. In addition to government work, women filled in wherever their labor was needed—at textile mills, shoe-making factories, iron works, and telegraph offices. At the war's end, many of these workers were forced to relinquish their positions, even though they had more than proved their proficiency.

Industrial work was remarkably dangerous during the Civil War—especially in the munitions plants. Although cartridge making was naturally hazardous, the clothes worn by female workers exacerbated the risks. Women's long dresses not only caught fire easily, but also helped spread fire as they caught upon each other when female workers crowded together to flee danger. Explosions in several munitions factories in the Confederacy and Union—including those in Richmond, Virginia; Washington, D.C.; Jackson, Mississippi; Allegheny, Pennsylvania; and Waterbury, Connecticut—turned deadly. For example, in September 1862, the explosion at the Allegheny Arsenal killed 78 workers, most of whom were young women. Sparks from wagon wheels ignited the loose gunpowder on the stone road within the compound and then ignited the arsenal's main supply of gunpowder. The ensuing explosion could be heard for miles. Employees rushed to the doors to escape, but got trapped by the inward opening doors. Some were blown apart while others caught fire. The bodies of 54 of the dead employees were unidentifiable. Although the explosion was undoubtedly caused by avoidable dangerous conditions, the commanders of the factory received no punishment.

Home-Front Shortages

Making life even more difficult for those on the home front, the Civil War initiated shortages and high inflation. Prices skyrocketed and supplies dwindled in both the Union and the Confederacy. The impressment of supplies by both governments contributed to the lack of food and clothing for many. In addition, especially in the Confederacy, which faced a blockade of its ports from the beginning of the war as well as destructive foraging by enemy troops, women had to find ways to cope with the lack of food, textiles, and other things that they had considered necessities during peacetime. As a result, women had to be resourceful throughout the conflict and find substitutes for daily items, including coffee, sugar, tea, paper, ink, needles, thread, cloth, buttons, shoes, medicines, and candles.

African American slaves, who were hardly accustomed to a world of plenty, especially struggled with the shortage of supplies. Masters across the South cut back on provisioning their slaves with shoes, coats, shirts, and other basic supplies, often providing even less for women than for men. When clothing was necessary, slaves made it out of blankets and carpets. Slave women were expected to spin cotton for the needs of their master, but homespun cotton clothing became an even scarcer luxury for slaves. Thomas Porcher Ravenel, for example, provided new pants for his slave men, but concluded that women "can do without" (Schwalm 1997, 77). Food supplies also became more limited, especially items like salt that were diverted to the war. As a result, complaints of sickness and hunger became increasingly common in the slave quarters.

Protests and Riots

When unsatisfied with the conditions on the home front, women of both regions willingly took to the streets to make their opinions known. In the South, feminine protests often took the form of urban food riots. Women who had willingly sacrificed their husbands, brothers, and fathers to the Confederate war effort expected their government to help them survive if they could not manage it on their own. Consequently, when faced with unbearable shortages and drastic inflation, women took to the streets to demand the assistance they thought they deserved. Bread riots took place in cities in Georgia, Louisiana, Virginia, Tennessee, Alabama, and North Carolina. The largest riot took place in the Confederate capital of Richmond, Virginia, on April 2, 1863. One woman explained her decision to participate by stating:

> We celebrate our right to live. We are starving. As soon as enough of us
> get together we are going to the bakery and each of us will take a loaf of
> bread. That is little enough for the government to give us after it has taken
> all our men. (Rable 1989, 109)

Close to 500 women raided stores, taking coffee, candles, shoes, flour, bacon, and beef. Some were armed, but did not use their weapons. Approximately four dozen women were arrested for their participation in this disturbance, which was ultimately dispersed by the city's public guard.

Northern women, not faced with the same desperate and widespread shortages as their Southern sisters, did not need to turn to bread riots. Instead, their frustrations often played out in protests over conscription. Their anger at the prospect of losing their male loved ones to the armies manifested itself in physical violence. As individuals, some women threw things at enrollment officers; other women joined together to chase away these officers. In more drastic instances, women took to the streets in mob violence to protest conscription. Although draft riots occurred in several cities, the two biggest, and most violent, riots were in New York City and Boston. The draft riot in New York City—which served to vent many of the frustrations of the city's working-class Irish community—began with the destruction of a conscription office and rapidly expanded into assaults on manifestations of the Republican Party and the war. The most brutal behavior was directed at African Americans—with unthinkable assaults and murders routinely taking place across the city and in New Jersey. Although black men faced the most horrors, black women were assaulted when they tried to intervene on behalf of their sons and fathers. Only Union troops who had recently fought at Gettysburg were able to restore order.

Refugees

Many women on both sides of the Mason Dixon line became refugees because of the war. Although it is impossible to know the exact number of refugees, Southerner Eliza Frances Andrews hyperbolically concluded that "half the world is refugeeing" (Massey 1964, 47). At the outset of the war, some women followed their soldier husbands or sweethearts to the front lines, becoming camp followers that both aided and hindered the armies. Others left their homes to join female family members nearby, assuming that there was safety, and knowing that there was good company, in numbers. The tendency of women to group together with other female family

Camp of the 31st Pennsylvania Infantry near Washington, D.C., 1862. Many women became camp followers, working as laundresses or cooks and living in the military camps with their enlisted husbands. (*Library of Congress*)

Emma Florence LeConte (1847–1932)

Elite Southerner Emma LeConte, like many of her countrywomen, experienced the Civil War on the home front. LeConte, the daughter of a prominent scientist, kept a brief, but descriptive, journal of her time in Columbia, South Carolina. Her journal, which she began on December 31, 1864, illuminates home front life through August 6, 1865. In her journal, LeConte details shortages, volunteer efforts, attitudes about the Confederacy, and the Union invasion of the state's capital. Throughout the war, and despite the mounting Southern losses, LeConte remained an ardent Confederate who maintained her belief in slavery and rejoiced at U.S. president Abraham Lincoln's assassination and mourned Confederate president Jefferson Davis's capture.

During the Civil War, LeConte and her family lived near the campus of South Carolina College (now the University of South Carolina), where her father had been a science professor until the outbreak of war. As her father helped the Confederacy by producing medicines and working at the niter works, Emma, her mother, and her sisters spent much of their time sewing clothes and blankets for Confederate soldiers as they themselves dealt with wartime shortages. Like other women of their class, they also continued their social life during the war, visiting

members whose kinsmen had departed for the battlefield resulted in numerous female enclaves, especially across the South. Additionally, assuming that they could find safety and food there, many Confederate women refugeed to Southern cities, whose populations ballooned during wartime. For example, the population of Richmond, Virginia, which was approximately 40,000 at the start of the war, doubled in size by 1861, and continued to grow throughout the war. The mass influx of people contributed to food shortages and poor sanitary conditions in the city. In 1863, one observer concluded that the city "was never intended to hold so many people" (Massey 1964, 75). Still other women, who had no relatives nearby or could not make it to the cities, sometimes took refuge in caves in the hilly areas. For example, hundreds of women sought safety in the caves surrounding Vicksburg, Mississippi.

African American women, too, often experienced the war as refugees. Some enslaved women accompanied owners who moved during the war. Still others ran from slavery. Although they did not run away as frequently as did their male counterparts, many African American women fled for safety when the opportunity presented itself, leaving their homes in the slave quarters for freedom behind Union lines. There they often volunteered as laundresses or nurses for the Union Army or simply followed the soldiers on their marches. Approximately 25,000 slaves followed Union general William T. Sherman for at least part of his March through Georgia and the Carolinas. The dangers of running from slavery and the fears of retribution from white slaveholders kept many African Americans in the South.

Not all refugees had a choice of whether they should risk staying in the homes or take flight. Union military policies intentionally created friends and family when the opportunities presented themselves.

Emma and her family experienced a Union invasion firsthand when Union general William Tecumseh Sherman and his soldiers attacked and ultimately captured Columbia in February 1865. Although relatively confident that enemy soldiers were headed their way, Emma and many of her countrywomen went about their efforts on behalf of the Confederacy throughout January and early February 1865. In particular, they planned and attended a bazaar to raise funds for Southern soldiers. Sherman's approach forced the bazaar to close a few days early, but did not necessarily dampen the spirits of the participants. In her journal, Emma described not only the Columbia bazaar, but also the preparations for the Union invasion, the evacuation of some of the city's residents and all of its soldiers, the arrival of Union troops, and the destruction that the enemy visited upon the city.

Although unhappy with the ultimate failure of the Confederate bid for independence, Emma did not waver in her commitment to Southern ideals. She attended local dances with returning Confederate soldiers and married a Confederate veteran, Farish Carter Furman. Emma LeConte Furman died in 1932.

thousands of refugees in Atlanta, Georgia, and a few other towns. After his capture of the Atlanta in September 1864, for example, Sherman ordered the evacuation of all of the city's civilians. On September 8, Sherman issued Special Field Order Number 67, requiring the removal of the hostile civilian population. Of the more than 1,600 evacuees, most were women and children. The policy's effect on women roused the ire of people throughout the Confederacy, who thought that the policy was immoral.

The War Comes Home

When enemy soldiers approached the towns and farms, women directly confronted the war. In these instances, the home front and war front became conflated. Many women did not wait to see what would happen when the enemy arrived. This was especially true in the South, where much of the fighting occurred. Wearing as many of their clothes as possible, women in the path of Union armies left for safety with family members or fled to cities. Similar fears faced African Americans in areas invaded by Confederate soldiers. For example, many free blacks in Gettysburg, Pennsylvania, feared being enslaved by invading Confederate troops. Their fears were not unfounded. In nearby Chambersburg, one woman observed that the soldiers

> were hunting up the contrabands [and] driving them off by droves! O! how it grated on our hearts to have to sit quietly & look at such brutal deeds—I saw no men among the contrabands—all women [and] children. Some of the colored people who were raised here were taken along. (Creighton 2002, 213)

Women who stayed in their homes as enemy soldiers approached rarely passively waited for the impending invasion. Southern women, especially those in the Upper South, repeatedly faced the prospect of meeting Union troops. Civilians in port towns similarly feared invasion and occupation. Many women prepared by hiding their prized possessions—jewelry, family heirlooms, silver, letters from loved ones, sewing supplies, and journals—wherever they thought they would be safe, including under floorboards, in fields, under and in mattresses, on their bodies, and even in baby cribs. Some women hid guns under their dresses, in case enemy soldiers threatened their personal safety or virtue. Others made makeshift pockets under their skirts to hold personal treasures. For example, in Virginia's Shenandoah Valley, Susan Blackford hung so many items, including her silver, under her skirt that "as I walked and when I sat down the clanking destroyed all hope of concealment" (Frank 2005, 129). Women also attempted to hide food from the invaders.

In occupied areas of the Confederacy, women had to figure out how to live among Union troops. This reality of occupation had social and political ramifications. In Vicksburg, Mississippi, as elsewhere in the occupied South, women were compelled to take loyalty oaths or live without the resources and business of the occupying Union troops. Elsewhere, Confederate women pestered the occupying troops, refused to submit to their demands, crossed streets to avoid coming in contact with the enemy, and otherwise snubbed the invaders. In New Orleans, Louisiana, General Benjamin Butler dealt with the disrespect of Southern women with his infamous "Woman Order." In it, he ordered disrespectful women would be "regarded and held liable to be treated as a woman of the town plying her avocation" (McPherson 1988, 551–552). His referral to Southern ladies as prostitutes enraged Confederates everywhere and earned him the nickname "Beast."

African American women had a very different understanding of invading Union soldiers than did their white counterparts, presuming that the arrival of Union troops would lead to freedom and greeting them as liberators. Many slaves and free blacks frequently formed bread companies to carry food to the Union Army when they were passing nearby, and thousands of slaves left their plantations to seek safety behind Union lines. The arrival of Union soldiers, however, did not always lead to widespread emancipation, and some soldiers instead visited physical and sexual abuse on female slaves. Rapes of black women occurred during many Union incursions into the plantation South. Nevertheless, as the Union Army conquered and occupied much of the Confederacy, African American women took the opportunity to gain their own freedom and to track down loved ones.

Objections to War

Although most white women supported the war at its outset and urged their husbands to enlist, the realities and difficulties of wartime eventually led many women to rescind their support. Women's objections to the course of the war or the cause that their men supported often proved equally powerful. Some white women, unable to handle the business at home on their own, urged their husbands to desert. Whether or not their husbands complied with these requests is difficult to discern, but women's disillusionment with war goals and sacrifices changed their views of the Confederacy and the Union. Other women created underground groups of protest within their communities, such as the secret Unionist circle in Atlanta frequented by Cyrena Stone. In more drastic instances, women took to the streets to make their voices heard. In cities across the South, for example, hundreds of women participated in food riots in 1863, drawing attention to their needs in a time of shortage. That same year, many Northern women participated in draft riots throughout Northern cities.

African American women did not passively await freedom, as if it were an expected and inevitable gift. On the contrary, throughout the conflict enslaved women maneuvered to transform the war into a campaign for their own emancipation. They took advantage of the disruptions of war and the arrival of Union troops to transform their immediate conditions. They claimed safety behind Union lines, left their masters to begin the difficult process of reuniting with family members, and found various ways to expand their freedoms even while they remained slaves.

Free black women also worked tirelessly on behalf of their slave sisters—often confronting and sometimes acquiescing to the racism that permeated the nation. They, like their white counterparts, performed a myriad of tasks. They helped to raise and outfit Union regiments, served as nurses and laundresses, and formed aid societies to help African American soldiers and widows. Susie King Taylor, for example, served as a nurse and laundress for the Union's First South Carolina Regiment.

Conclusion

In 1866, Frank Moore asserted that "the story of the war will never be fully or fairly written if the achievements of women in it are untold" (Moore 1866, v). The study of women's roles during the Civil War adds dimension to early military-based explorations of the conflict. Women across the spectrum of race, class, region, and nationality helped shape the outcome of the war and in turn were shaped by the events around them. Some did the exotic, dressing up as men to serve in armies or using their feminine charms to participate in rampant espionage. Others did the more mundane, but equally essential, tasks of recruiters, political cheerleaders, nurses, fund raisers, seamstresses, cooks, laundresses, factory workers, and household managers. By performing these tasks, women fulfilled a need for labor and goods that would have otherwise drawn men from their positions on the battlefront. Often at the same time, women proved their mettle in the face of adversity as they confronted enemy troops, dealt with shortages and inflation, and became refugees. These varied experiences forced women to adapt to harsh conditions, but also allowed them the opportunity to gain confidence in their abilities and their fortitude. Women could not avoid the

Civil War, even from the presumed safety of the home front. In short, the Civil War was hardly confined to the world of men—it was women's work.

References and Further Reading

Attie, Jeanie. 1998. *Patriotic Toil: Northern Women and the American Civil War*. Ithaca, NY: Cornell University Press.

Boyd, Belle. 1865. *Belle Boyd, In Camp and Prison*. New York: Blelock.

Creighton, Margaret S. 2002. "Living on the Fault Line: African American Civilians and the Gettysburg Campaign." In *The War Was You and Me: Civilians in the American Civil War*, edited by Joan E. Cashin, 209–236. Princeton, NJ: Princeton University Press.

Dyer, Thomas G. 1999. *Secret Yankees: The Union Circle in Confederate Atlanta*. Baltimore, MD: Johns Hopkins University Press.

Edmondston, Catherine Anne Devereaux. 1979. *Journal of a Secesh Lady: The Diary of Catherine Ann Devereaux Edmondston, 1860–1866*, edited by Beth G. Crabtree and James Welch Patton. Raleigh: North Carolina Division of Archives and History, Department of Cultural Resources.

Edwards, Laura F. 2000. *Scarlett Doesn't Live Here Anymore: Southern Women in the Civil War Era*. Urbana: University of Illinois Press.

Faust, Drew Gilpin. 1996. *Mothers of Invention: Women of the Slaveholding South in the Civil War*. Chapel Hill: University of North Carolina Press.

Fellman, Michael. 2000. *The Making of Robert E. Lee*. New York: Random House.

Frank, Lisa Tendrich. 2001. "To 'Cure Her of Her Pride and Boasting': The Gendered Implications of Sherman's March." PhD diss., University of Florida.

Frank, Lisa Tendrich. 2005. "War Comes Home: Confederate Women and Union Soldiers." In *Virginia's Civil War*, edited by Peter Wallenstein and Bertram Wyatt-Brown, 123–136. Charlottesville: University of Virginia Press.

Gallagher, Gary W. 1997a. *The Confederate War: How Popular Will, Nationalism, and Military Strategy Could Not Stave Off Defeat*. Cambridge, MA: Harvard University Press.

Gutman, Herbert G. 1976. *The Black Family in Slavery and Freedom, 1750–1925*. New York: Pantheon Books.

Giesberg, Judith Ann. 2000. *Civil War Sisterhood: The U.S. Sanitary Commission and Women's Politics in Transition*. Boston: Northeastern University Press.

Hunter, Tera W. 1997. *To 'Joy My Freedom: Southern Black Women's Lives and Labors After the Civil War*. Cambridge, MA: Harvard University Press.

Jabour, Anya. 2007. *Southern Sisters: Young Women in the Old South*. Chapel Hill: University of North Carolina Press.

Leonard, Elizabeth D. 1999. *All the Daring of the Soldier: Women of the Civil War Armies*. New York: W. W. Norton & Company.

Lewis, Lloyd. 1932. *Sherman: Fighting Prophet*. New York: Harcourt, Bracc and Company.

Livermore, Mary A. 1887. *My Story of the War: A Woman's Narrative of Four Years' Personal Experience*. Hartford, CT: A. D. Worthington and Company.

Massey, Mary Elizabeth. 1964/2001. *Refugee Life in the Confederacy*. Baton Rouge: Louisiana State University Press.

Massey, Mary Elizabeth. 1966/1994. *Women in the Civil War* (Reprint of *Bonnet Brigades*). Lincoln: University of Nebraska Press.

McPherson, James. 1988. *Battle Cry of Freedom*. New York: Oxford University Press.

Mohr, Clarence. 2005. ''The Atlanta Campaign and the African American Experience in Civil War Georgia.'' In *Inside the Confederate Nation*, edited by Lesley J. Gordon and John C. Inscoe, 272–294. Baton Rouge: Louisiana State University Press.

Moore, Frank. 1866. *Women of the War: Their Heroism and Self-sacrifice, True Stories of Brave Women in the Civil War*. Hartford, CT: S. S. Scranton.

Rable, George C. 1989. *Civil Wars: Women and the Crisis of Southern Nationalism*. Urbana: University of Illinois Press.

Revels, Tracy J. 2004. *Grander in Her Daughters: Florida's Women during the Civil War*. Columbia: University of South Carolina Press.

Schwalm, Leslie A. 1997. *A Hard Fight for We: Women's Transition from Slavery to Freedom in South Carolina*. Urbana: University of Illinois Press.

Silber, Nina. 2002. ''A Compound of Wonderful Potency: Women Teachers of the North in the Civil War South.'' In *The War Was You and Me: Civilians in the American Civil War*, edited by Joan E. Cashin, 35–59. Princeton, NJ: Princeton University Press.

Silber, Nina. 2005. *Daughters of the Union: Northern Women Fight the Civil War*. Cambridge, MA: Harvard University Press.

Sizer, Lyde Cullen. 2000. *The Political Work of Northern Women Writers and the Civil War, 1850–1872*. Chapel Hill: University of North Carolina Press.

Weiner, Marli F. 1998. *Mistresses and Slaves: Plantation Women in South Carolina, 1830–1880*. Urbana: University of Illinois Press.

Whites, LeeAnn. 1995. *The Civil War as a Crisis in Gender, Augusta, Georgia, 1860–1890*. Athens: University of Georgia Press.

Children and the Civil War | 4

Karen A. Kehoe

Fifteen-year-old Tillie Pierce recorded her memories of life in Gettys-burg, Pennsylvania, during the memorable July of 1863. She reported rumors that swept the town for weeks and then wrote: "We were having our regular literary exercises on Friday afternoon, at our Seminary, when the cry reached our ears. Rushing to the door, and standing on the front portico we beheld in the direction of the Theological Seminary, a dark, dense mass, moving toward town" (Alleman 1889, 21). After great anticipation, the war had finally come to her Pennsylvania home. Like most Northern children, before that summer she experienced the war as she wished, seeking out contact through her play, schooling, the copying of adult behaviors, or her willing entrance into the adult world of the soldiers. Like some other children, particularly Southerners and African Americans, in that summer Pierce found the war had come to her doorstep whether or not she wished it. No matter how they experienced it, the war changed American children and American childhood forever.

Play during the War

The location of their homes and the economic status of their parents determined the kinds of toys and games available to young people of the time. Generally speaking, 19th-century youngsters had as many things as their families could provide. In that century, children began to be considered as precious and special parts of their families. An increase in the number of white-collar workers in the country created a larger middle class than in earlier generations, and these middle-class families had more expendable income. The children of middle-class parents did not have to work to ensure the survival of the family. Instead, parents showered attention on their children, making sure they attended school and enriching their lives

Matilda Tillie Pierce Alleman (1848–1914)

Tillie Pierce was 13 years old when the Civil War broke out and almost 15 when the fighting came to her home in Gettysburg, Pennsylvania, where she was attending classes at the Gettysburg Seminary. During the summer of 1863, local girls shared the local rumors about Rebels headed for their town. With growing fear, Pierce observed people leaving with bundles of belongings and watched as the old men and boys who remained in town practiced their military drill.

Fear gave wings to her feet and Pierce ran home as fast as she could the day the soldiers arrived in Gettysburg. Anger replaced some of her fear as Confederates began to steal supplies her family needed, including the family horse. When the Union soldiers arrived, Pierce and her friends did their best to help the blue-clad soldiers, singing national songs for them and preparing little bouquets of flowers to cheer the tired men.

Her mother thought she would be safer in the countryside, so Pierce left town with a neighbor on the day the battle began. Their route took them past Union gun emplacements and gathering Union forces and, at last, brought them to the Weikert farm right

with books, toys, and interesting experiences. For the first time, childhood was seen as a unique phase in development, not just a period when children were small adults.

Rural children and children of the poor had different experiences of play during the period than did children of white-collar workers. The homes of rural and poor children had fewer books about a more limited range of topics than those of the middle and upper classes. A Quaker boy encountering marbles for the first time in his life, referred to them as "marvels," an indication of the rarity of toys in some American homes (Marten 2004, 10). Despite the lack of formal toys, children played and had fun before the war. Their games were simply made up from the worlds of their imaginations. They pretended to be teachers, lawyers, storekeepers, parents, ministers, and politicians, mimicking the actions and words of the adults that populated their lives. They manufactured dolls from materials at hand and roamed the world around them. However, they also filled their days with chores and work.

The war changed these patterns of play. For some children, especially those in the South, new toys, playthings, and play became rare indeed. Northern children had new games and toys from which to choose. Some toys featured particular Northern military leaders and their armies; some dolls came dressed in military uniforms. These toys and games familiarized the youngsters with the events of the day and reinforced national attitudes.

Even Abraham Lincoln's children had dolls dressed in the flashy uniforms of Zouaves, who wore clothes inspired by those of European soldiers serving in Africa. The Zouave style of dress was extremely popular with children. It featured bright scarlet or striped trousers and unusual headgear like fezzes or turbans. Children could buy paper soldiers and toy cannons to mow those soldiers down. Toy guns, drums, and miniature uniforms fed at the edge of the battle. Pierce spent much of her day drawing water for soldiers wounded in the fight. She was terrified by the numbers of dead and dying men that she found in the barn, but smiled bravely and tried to comfort them.

The following day she was asked to take a group of officers to the roof so they could observe the battle. Their presence attracted the attention of the enemy, and Pierce and the other women and children ran across the battlefield to another home. From that position, it appeared that the whole of Gettysburg was ablaze and for the first time she was frightened

for her family. She felt a keen sense of relief when her brother and his comrades in the Pennsylvania Reserves arrived.

On the last day of the fight, Pierce again moved locations during the bombardment. She spent most of the day among a crowd of people seeking shelter, but returned to the Weikert house as the battle ended. It was many days before Pierce learned that her entire family had survived the battle. Schoolgirl games and gossip filled her days as she cared for the wounded before rejoining her family.

the imaginations of those whose tastes tended toward the warlike. In other war games, boys and girls in the North and the South made and manned forts. For a while, the White House featured a mock cannon on the roof, where Willie and Tad Lincoln kept watch for Rebel intruders.

Nineteenth-century children liked to accumulate things. Their collections of "novelties" or "oddities" were usually small items that they found, purchased, or were given. Birds' nests, colored stones, arrowheads, leaves, odd buttons, stamps, anything that caught their attention or came from special people, joined their other treasures. During the war, children added bits of memorabilia from visits to army camps or places of special interest and encounters with famous people. Most adults who lived through the war as children remembered having collections that included material sent to them by friends or relatives in the military. When children lived close enough to where soldiers passed, they searched for bits of cloth from uniforms, spent bullets, pieces of exploded shells, or other pieces of discarded material. Many hours were spent studying and rearranging the items or preparing them to be displayed for friends or family.

Wartime Literature

Children's literature developed into a separate category of writing before the war. Prior to the war, the authors and editors used the material to teach children moral lessons. Hard work, charity, tolerance, kindness, and obedience were typical kinds of lessons illustrated in the stories. Wartime literature focused on the idea of sacrifice. The youthful characters willingly surrendered their food for soldiers or the poor, their jackets to the cold, and their free time to do work for a tired mother. Both Northern and

Southern children learned that the small sacrifices on their part would help their causes and would prepare them for the larger sacrifices their lives might require. The stories taught children that they had to contribute to others to benefit from their sacrifices and that the benefit they would earn was life in a secure community.

Children's magazines, another source of wartime entertainment and reading, also sought to instill values in their young readers. These journals featured all kinds of literature—long stories broken into monthly install-ments, the words to songs and poems, including some by the young read-ers, as well as games provided to educate and entertain. William Taylor Adams, writing as Oliver Optic, edited one of the most popular children's magazines. Optic played to the war interests of his young readers, provid-ing articles that carefully described army life and organization so that his junior soldiers understood the proper terms to use in their play. He rein-forced the sectional loyalties of the adults by giving his readers games and information specific to Northern children. Optic also helped to popularize a new sort of literature for children—the adventure story. These tales cast a young person, usually a boy, in the role of hero. As a result of some set of circumstances, the young man left his hometown and participated directly in the action of the war. The young people were usually opposed by evil adults and always prevailed in their endeavors. Optic provided two trilogies in the genre, his army and navy stories, featuring the brothers Tom and Jack Somers. Unlike earlier literature, these books did not emphasize the contributions the children could make for the benefit of others. Instead, the main characters worked for their own benefit and sur-vival. The new format seemed much more exciting than the old kind of writing. The young characters faced dangers that the readers could experi-ence in their imaginations, recasting themselves in the patriotic roles.

Children also published their own newspapers during the years of con-flict. Some were single pages, randomly produced sheets, but others were regularly published papers that reflected the interests of their authors. Like the magazines the boys read, the newspapers were full of articles of all descriptions, but a nationalistic theme ran through all of them.

Girls received a much different message through literature written for them. The youthful heroines fulfilled very traditional roles. They joined their mothers in helping raise money for the soldiers or the poor. They helped smaller children to succeed at some task. Few girl characters wan-dered into the thick of a battle or struggled to overcome evil adults. Girls attended the hospital rounds their mothers made, helping to care for the men who were less seriously wounded. They would read to or sing for the men, provide water, fan the soldiers, or simply sit by their cots. Dolls, rep-resenting wounded or sick soldiers, were nursed back to health and those who had deserted were executed and buried.

Although the wartime literature tended to reinforce the gender roles of earlier days, it connected the lives of both girls and boys to the strength of the nation. Young male characters were supposed to be pious, coura-geous, loyal, and ambitious, traits they used for the good of their nation, communities, and families. Girls were supposed to practice domestic arts, like cooking, cleaning, and nursing, and they were supposed use their abilities for the benefit of others. Adults, who wrote most of the literature, included children in the stories of the war and the events that surrounded the conflict not only because children wanted to see themselves as active participants in those events but also because the scope of the struggle required the participation of every segment of society.

Education

The war also changed school experiences. For many children whose fathers answered the call of the bugle, North or South, school was no longer possible. During battles, schools were suspended. In many Southern towns, schools closed, more or less permanently, when teachers joined the armies. Many children left school when they had to assume the duties of those who enlisted. Some took on most of the farm chores, while others went to work to support their mothers or sisters.

In areas where schools stayed in session, curricula changed during the war. Partisans on both sides influenced the materials studied. Methods of instruction emphasized memorization and recitation. Both Northern and Southern children learned to repeat pieces of speeches teachers carefully chose. The material reflected the patriotic messages of each side. Southerners rushed to produce textbooks that eradicated any possible negative presentation of the institution of slavery and that glorified their new nation. In both the North and the South, textbooks, particularly spellers, familiarized the children with new terms and their meanings. These included military terms like brigadier, garrison, guerilla, and commissary. The lessons helped the children enrich their playing at war and subtly indoctrinated the older boys into the language and culture they would need if they joined the armies. In addition, children from the schools were "drafted" to participate in special community ceremonies. In the North, inauguration day was observed by parades and children marched among the adults, and the schools of New Orleans reopened during the war with great fanfare and special programs put on by the youngsters.

Changes in school materials did not escape the attention of the military. The Union Army policed Southern schools, watching for any sign of rebellion among the students. They inspected the children's things for hidden Confederate flags and paged through books, tearing out any pages that had material that seemed to support the Southern cause. The result, inevitably, was that children in occupied areas often became stronger supporters of the Confederacy than they had been before the inspections.

Northern schools repeated the message of sacrifice in children's stories and linked education to the work of the U.S. Sanitary Commission, a group devoted to helping Northern soldiers. Children were recruited to join those working for the Sanitary Commission just as soldiers were recruited to join the ranks of the armies. In addition, children were encouraged to join other patriotic organizations. Alfred Sewell began an organization known as the Army of the American Eagle. Youngsters could join the group for a dime, and in return, they received a copy of a photo-graph of "Old Abe, the Battle Eagle," a real eagle that served as the mascot of the Eighth Wisconsin Infantry. Children who signed up enough of their friends could earn extra materials and become officers in the youth army. Schoolmates made good recruits, and Sewell's plan raised much money for the relief of the soldiers.

Children Supporting the War Effort

During the years of the war, the Sanitary Commission developed a number of ways to raise the large sums of money it needed to support its work. The most successful strategy devised was holding large, regional fairs. The elaborate events included children's departments designed to get children to visit and to allow them to help in the Union war effort. Youngsters took part in recreations of folk tales, concerts, and recitations. Schools displayed examples of the children's work. Girls sent examples of their handcrafts and boys loaned their collections of "oddities" to help bring in pennies for the cause. Some of the children even offered their own dear pets to be sold to raise money for the soldiers. Fortunately for everyone, in most cases a philanthropic relative, neighbor, or charitable stranger would purchase the animal and return it to the grieving but determined child. The fairs also provided all sorts of treats to eat. At a great fair held in Chicago, a bevy of young girls lined up to pay for the privilege of kissing General Ulysses S. Grant. The act of kissing a stranger was much too promiscuous for the era, but the girls were forgiven because the kisses were rained down on the great hero and the cause was a good one.

Although 19th-century girls did not kiss boys, they did think about the next phase of their lives and watched older girls for signals about what was proper behavior. The little ones admired the latest trend in wartime jewelry sported by young women who made a practice of wearing copies of the corps badges of their sweethearts, fathers, or brothers. The badges were sim-ple shapes, such as diamonds, clovers, and crescents cut from brightly col-ored wool felt. They indicated a connection to a man in the army and a patriotic style that seemed very adult. Adolescent girls found the usual tran-sitions in their lives complicated by the war. The political climate even affected their choices of potential mates. Like the adults in their lives, the girls patriotically took a Union pledge, promising their loyalty and sacrifice for the nation. The girls extended the idea, taking public pledges not to look at or kiss men that had never been in the army. They flatly rejected the pos-sibility of marrying a "shirker" and scorned the advances of "home guards," men in units organized to help out in case the enemy moved into the area.

Both boys and girls were familiar with the varieties of people around the armies and, when possible, the children visited the drill fields of the armies. When the men retired from the field, the children took their places. They did their best to duplicate the intricate movements of the men, using sticks, broomsticks, or whatever they could find to replace the firearms. For the boys, the "drilling" became a large part of the activities of the day.

They formed their own units and carefully chose names that reflected the seriousness of their intents. The country was peppered with "Garibaldi's Guards" and other fierce-sounding units. Sometimes girls were admitted to the ranks, especially if they were tall, and in the North even African Americans were admitted to the ranks, although never as officers.

Both boys and girls formed groups that sewed "housewives," little sewing kits supplied with thread, needles, and spare buttons that would be sent to the soldiers. They all worked collecting pennies that were sent off to a relief society of one sort or another, and many men who had been small boys at the time of the war could remember spending precious hours scraping lint that was packaged and used by hospital workers to pack off wounds.

Girls accompanied their mothers to meetings of local soldiers' aid societies. Some, like the young women who lived on Milwaukee's fashionable east side, formed their own girls' aid societies. They planned and completed quilts and other items that soldiers who were convalescing could use, and they participated in most of the activities planned by the adults. By teaching the children to serve in aid groups, the adults assured themselves that the next generation would be ready to assume its responsibility of caring for the less fortunate. Although girls could not control armies, real or play, or strike blows for their nations, the tasks each undertook were understood to be the duties of "a patriotic and loyal girl" (Alleman 1889, 9).

The patriotic duties that young people became involved in indicated that even children understood political questions to surprising degrees. For some, the interest began when their parents took them to political events. For most, the interest began after they overheard parents in intense conversations about their own political concerns. The children did not simply repeat the words of the adults. They read about and debated the issues on a sophisticated level.

In the 19th century, children were regular participants in political events. Processions of adults who supported one candidate or another were of interest to many, because they were frequently accompanied by lantern illuminations, bright symbols of the candidates, and bands. Groups of children heckled candidates that did not represent the views of their parents. Fathers took their children to see parades, speeches, and conventions. Aware that they were living in important times, the adults wanted to guide the youngsters in their understanding of what was happening. Children discussed the events and learned the positions of the candidates on the conduct of the war. Schoolyards became partisan battlegrounds as the children discussed their favorites. They created their own versions of the events, taking turns adopting the roles of the main political figures of the day, although few could remember playing the role of Abraham Lincoln. Children willingly participated in the adult response to events of the day. When the draft riots of New York turned to racial violence, young boys acted as scouts, marking the houses of African Americans by throwing rocks through windows. Although such actions had the hallmarks of boys testing their marksmanship skills without being stopped by an adult, they also had a deadly intent.

Entertainment

Public entertainment of all sorts attracted children, especially in the North where circuses and museums continued to be popular. Of much interest were panoramas, extremely detailed illustrations. For a small fee, patrons could watch as the painting moved across a space, unwinding off one huge spool and onto the other accompanied by appropriate music. The works depicted the life stories of famous individuals such as the founding fathers, generals, or Abraham Lincoln. Panoramas often illustrated the stories from the Bible or the action of major battles. In the prewar years, the exhibitions tried to reinforce the lessons and values of the middle class. During the war, such things provided information, but their main purpose was to entertain and to distract the observers from the stresses of life in a nation at war. One panorama featured a fictional character that appeared in several of the panels and the children had fun looking for the figure and determining his meaning in the illustration.

Children who lived near the camps where the armies trained had a ready source of entertainment. They accompanied adults, or snuck off on their own, to watch the soldiers drill and to attend dress parades. The crisp uniforms, the martial music, and the gaily fluttering flags made the early days of the war exciting. Following the ceremonies, the children and the adults mingled among the tents and inspected the soldiers' gear. The prominence of the military in national life presented new possibilities for entertainment. For children near major waterways, naval vessels could be visited when they were in port. In an attempt to mimic the noise guns made, little boys wanted firecrackers to celebrate events large or small.

Boys whose older relatives planned to enlist had clear role models. One 10-year-old boy watched in awe as his two uncles tried to learn the manual arms. The men bought an old musket and a copy of a book of tactics and "worked seriously in a business like manner" so they would be ready for service (Elmore 1910, 54–59). The boy kept a constant vigil, not so much from admiration but on the off chance that he might be able to play with the weapon once in a while.

Visits to camps and ships and the presence of men preparing for war led to a new spirit of militarization among the children, who begged for their own miniature uniforms, toy guns, and small drums. Popular periodicals for adults took note of the change just as those for children did. An illustration in one, labeled "The Fourth of July," showed two small children dressed in military uniforms beating bright drums while their mother cowered in the background with her hands clapped over her ears and a look of pain on her face.

The war brought many new items into the world of children. Valentines were fairly new to the people of the 19th century. During the war, Valentine's Day cards with images of soldiers were available. They reflected the longing of both the soldiers and the members of their families for a restoration of the family circle. Other cards made fun of the home guards. These units recruited men too old for the rigors of long campaigns, boys

Like many young boys across America, P. H. Martin dressed up in a uniform to play war (1862). (*Library of Congress*)

too young for the regular army, and men home on long furloughs because of illness or injury. Among the members were men who were suspected of using their membership in the home guard as an excuse for avoiding regular service—thus the term "shirkers."

Schoolyards soon reflected the observations the children made about the uses of the military men. The simple play of children became politicized and militarized. Name-calling reflected the sides in the war. Like gang members in modern day America, children often wore symbols that indicated their connections. Those that represented the Northern forces pinned or sewed the brass buttons of the Union Army onto their clothing, while Southern sympathizers fastened the halves of walnut hulls to theirs. The symbols attracted much attention and caused many schoolyard fights. Gangs also adopted such signals, and whether the groups were just friends who wandered around together getting into mischief or groups with more sinister intents, their activities took on a more warlike manner than they had in the prewar years.

Music

Recruiting activities naturally attracted the attention of the youngsters. If available, a military brass band would be sent into town in full dress uniform. The musicians kept a large number of patriotic songs in their parts books for just such occasions. The bandsmen accompanied local people in the singing of popular songs, including "Dixie's Land" and "The Bonny Blue Flag" in the South and "Battle Cry of Freedom," "The Star Spangled Banner," and, later, "The Battle Hymn of the Republic" in the North, to rally support and volunteers for the armies. Volunteers would step forward and sign enrollment sheets. When finished, the soldiers, accompanied by the throb of the drum cadence, marched away. Any sound of drums invariably drew scores of children into the streets, where they paced along with the passing soldiers.

Drums did not only mark exciting, patriotic ceremonies. Many towns also heard the solemn thump of muffled drums that marked the funerals of local men. Although many soldiers were buried near the spot they were killed, some families searched for the bodies of their loved ones and returned them to their homes for burial. For some children, these solemn ceremonies provided their first realistic understanding of the costs of war. For others, who had no direct relatives or friends in the conflict, the loss was abstract until April 1865, when President Abraham Lincoln was assassinated by John Wilkes Booth. All but the smallest children of the Civil War generation could remember throughout their lifetimes the circumstances of the very moment the news reached them. Yet, for children, the aftermath of the assassination was just as memorable. Parents took them to see the body of the president or his casket as it was carried in solemn processions, pulled in ornate hearses, or passed by on a slowly moving train. Some 10,000 Chicago children, decked out in black mourning sashes, participated in the parade down Chicago's Michigan Avenue as the president's body returned to Illinois. Bands, with uniforms trimmed with black ribbons, played newly composed death marches, and the drums were swathed in black to muffle their usual crisp taps. The grandeur of these moments added to the usual excitement of military ceremonies the children had so long enjoyed.

Adults became concerned about some of the changes the war caused in the behavior of children. While the play of girls seemed to reinforce positive behavior, the actions of boys seemed less positive. The connection to battle play not only caused difficulties by encouraging rowdiness that brought conflict with shopkeepers and townsfolk, but it also seemed to cause confusion for boys who had trouble telling the difference between their military play and preparation for real combat. Boys began trying to enlist long before they were legally qualified to do so. To stem the wave of young boys trying to join the army, home guard units began accepting boy members as young as 14 years of age. Their presence in the ranks served as examples of how easy it was to enlist in the 19th century. Although soldiers were supposed to be at least 18, many served who were younger because they lied about their ages and the system that could verify the

The Union Army employed boys to keep gun crews supplied with gunpowder and shot. This "powder monkey" is pictured on the USS *New Hampshire*, off Charleston, South Carolina (1864–1865). (*Library of Congress*)

ages had not been created. Officials of the Sanitary Commission recorded at least 127 men who were just 13 years old when they entered the army. Alva Cleveland enlisted in the Twenty-fourth Wisconsin Infantry and brought his 12-year-old son, George, with him. George served as a drummer for the regiment, like many other young soldiers. As drummers, these boys did not have to carry the heavy equipment of a regular soldier, but they worked long hours and often were located in some of the most dangerous parts of the battlefields providing battlefield communication. Along with fifers and buglers, drummers helped regulate the military day by playing a different musical "call," a short phrase that was repeated over and over, for various activities. One woke the troops, one sounded sick call, one announced the arrival of mail, one indicated the unit should charge, and another indicated that they should retreat. Field musicians could control every single movement of the army, so although many drummers were young boys, they had a huge responsibility placed on their small shoulders.

George Cleveland was only one of a large number of drummer boys who were admired and envied by the boys at home and whose positions became symbols of the war. An entire set of popular music, stories, and poetry were written to enshrine their memories. The song "The Drummer Boy of Shiloh" is typical of its kind. According to the words, a wounded drummer was lifted up by his comrades so that he could fold his hands in prayer before his death. He prayed for the men he served with and at the last called out to his mother, pleading that he be allowed to join her in Heaven. His fellow soldiers gathered near to hear him pray and left the scene determined to be better men. The drummer boy served as an example of the adventure, courage, piety, honor, and loyalty looked for in heroes of children's literature, but these heroes also reflected the reality of children in the ranks of Civil War soldiers. The most famous of the drummers was Johnny Clem from Ohio who enlisted in a Michigan Regiment at the age of nine. Seventeen of the youthful "ponies," as the underage soldiers were known, received the Medal of Honor for their service and more than 250,000, perhaps as many as 400,000, underage boys served in the armies.

Life on the Home Front

Men and boys who enlisted in the war broke the close-knit circle formed by 19th-century families. Children longed for the presence of their fathers and brothers and the men longed for the families at home. In their letters, the men asked for any news from home, especially news of the development of their small children. They tried to share in the lives of the youngsters and pleaded with their wives to tell them everything they were missing. No detail was too small—first teeth, first steps, first words— the fathers wanted to know it all. The news was not always positive and some of the letters reflect the attempts of desperate fathers to learn the fate of sick or injured children. Some of the pages reflect the grief of fathers at war who learned of the death of their beloved children.

Fathers also used their letters to provide the kinds of advice that they would give children if they were at home. They told them to behave and to listen to the adults left around them. They suggested reading programs, and warned the young people to care for their health. Most added that their sons should be sure to help their mothers. Many of the letters provided positive reinforcement, showing the great affection that the men had for the youngsters. These instructions were an attempt by the men to remain active in the lives of their children. The men also wanted to let their children know what the army experience was like. They chatted about camp conditions, sometimes describing their living arrangements or daily routines in great detail. Many avoided discussing the dangers around them, but others seemed to want the children to understand the peril they lived with and they tried to describe the sound of bullets or the effects of shells on the men in the camp. In some cases, it seemed that the men were trying to assure themselves that they had survived, although such descriptions undoubtedly scared some children.

Children in the South experienced the war much more directly than did those in the North. A much greater percentage of the white Southern male population participated in the fighting, and the majority of battles were fought in the South. Consequently, Southern children were plagued by shortages of food and clothing and had few toys. In addition, many had to contend with poor and dangerous living conditions. Southern children also faced the fear of invasion and occupation by enemy troops.

For families that sent men to the armies, whether for the North or the South, the impact was devastating and could not be avoided. The departure was filled with excitement. The men marched through the town with bands playing while the townspeople cheered and waved. Children thought the uniforms, horses, flags, and bands were wonderful. The sight of the national flag on such occasions caused feelings of nationalism that the young people had not felt before. As on all military occasions, the small boys and girls tried to march along with the men, falling back as fatigue overtook them. It was only when the crowds dispersed, or the men passed, or the bands ceased playing that the children had to face the grief and fear that also accompanied such departures. For middle-class women not used to managing household affairs, the burden was unimaginable, and the breakdown was immediate. Those children old enough to understand were left trying to shore up their remaining parent, a task made more difficult if the man of the house was killed in the conflict. Young boys quickly took on additional responsibilities, trying to do as much of their father's work as possible. The messages delivered from pulpits and in schoolbooks, taught them that doing so was part of their patriotic duty. As historian James Marten noted, assuming these tasks "became their greatest contribution to saving the Union." But the patriotism came with a price—cutting short the childhoods of many of the war generation (Marten 2004, 63).

The war made many children, North and South, "partial orphans" when their fathers died or were incapacitated by their wounds. Women had to learn to care for their children while trying to earn money to support their families. For many, the job was overwhelming and they tried to find individuals or institutions to provide for the youngsters. All over the country, people worked to fill in for the parents. Northerners reacted by building homes that served as symbols of the link between the sacrifice of the men and the responsibility the community had as a result of that sacrifice. In the South, the children were treated with great reverence because of their connection to what Southerners saw as a sort of perfect past. Most of the aid for the orphans came from local governments, churches, and organizations that already were helping the soldiers. In an effort to make the care more regular and more permanent, the people of Wisconsin petitioned their state government to create a home for the children. During the war, the widow of Governor Louis P. Harvey convinced the federal government to establish a hospital at Madison to care for sick soldiers. Harvey Hospital, as it was called, was no longer needed by the last year of the war. Rather than wasting the facility, Cordelia Harvey worked to convert the buildings for the use of the orphans of Wisconsin's soldiers. The task was important because, by 1865, half of the children in the asylums of the state's largest city, Milwaukee, were orphans.

The war was an alien but unmistakable presence in the lives of children close to the action. For some, the possibility of conflict was a strange new adventure, but for others, it was a frightening reality that threatened those they loved and their homes. When looking back at the war years,

Susie Baker King Taylor (1848–1912)

Susie King was born into slavery in Georgia in 1848. Because teaching slaves was illegal, she, her sister, and her brother went to school in secret, hiding their books and never entering or leaving the school as a group. Some of her education came from a white girl who chose to ignore the law. King used her education to help other slaves, writing them passes so they could move about the community.

In April 1862, King left the city she lived in with her grandmother to be with her mother in the countryside, where the adults thought she would be safer. On her journey, she experienced the bombardment of Fort Pulaski. When the shells fell on the fort the ground shook for miles around. Her uncle decided to move his family and King to a safer location, an island off the coast of Georgia protected by the Union's navy gunboats. After a few days all of the people there went to St. Simon's Island where the 13-year-old girl was put in charge of a school for the children of former slaves.

Life on St. Simon's was hectic and frightening. Families separated by slavery and war

they often identified the first moment they saw soldiers as the end of their childhood innocence. In the first moments of the conflict, they helped with the hasty, secret burial of family treasures and were rapidly moved away from perceived danger. The assumed security of home was missing from the lives of children in towns contested by the two sides. Those youngsters became refugees, living from hand to mouth and never quite secure in their temporary or their permanent homes. At Vicksburg, Richmond, and Petersburg, towns that were under siege, the children had to be ready to race to areas of shelter whenever bombardments began. If at all possible, the women and children packed up and moved to the homes of relatives living in the country, adding another level of stress to their lives. Those who stayed behind in their own homes had to hide during the day to avoid becoming victims of robbers or worse. At night, candlelight needed to be hidden so that some soldier did not interpret the light as a signal, resulting in an attack on the home.

African American children became refugees in much larger numbers than other children. As the fighting moved close to plantations where they were enslaved, whole groups ran away to enter the Union lines. In places where the Rebels threatened to overrun communities with large numbers of contrabands or large numbers of freedmen, African Americans took to the roads to avoid being swept into slavery. Carrying everything they could with them, the children suffered from the same privations and pressures as their parents. In some ways, slavery seemed to prepare them for the challenges. Parents emphasized their lessons about sacrifice with stern, often physical punishments. Rather than teaching the youngsters to sacrifice for the common good, they taught them to sacrifice so they would be searched for each other. Rebels slipped onto the poorly protected island and tried to capture any black people that walked alone. As King thought about books and lessons, she also contemplated her future. The Yankee officers constantly searched for able-bodied men that could fill the ranks of the black regiment they were forming and King left her uncertainty behind by enlisting to serve as laundress for that unit.

Many of King's relatives, including uncles, cousins, and eventually a husband, served in the unit. Unafraid of infectious diseases like smallpox, she soon became a nurse as well as a laundress. At night, when the men had no other duties, she taught the eager soldiers to read and write. She became a well-loved and well-respected member of the regiment. When her hospital was located too near the spots where shells fell, her officers would remove her from the danger zone. Although she worked tirelessly for the remaining years of the war, Susie King Taylor was not paid for her services. Following her childhood as a slave, she labored for the right to live life as a free woman.

strong enough to survive slavery. As these refugees found safety, they began to search for the education that had been denied to them for so long. They believed that education would be another tool that would help them survive whatever came after the war. Northern children helped provide books and supplies for African American schools.

Modern Americans reading about the Civil War are frequently surprised at the number of civilians in the army camps. In addition to local citizens who visited as part of their entertainment, slaves who ran away from their homes, contrabands and freedmen, other workers, and family members came to the front to try to locate their loved ones. Mothers sometimes brought their children along. The soldiers loved the visits of the little children and showered them with attention. The men saluted the youngsters as if they were officers, told them stories, and generally treated them like royalty. Nurses in one hospital were surprised when a visiting woman gave birth there. Although the newborn caused the ladies additional work providing food for the child and locating clothing for it, they gladly endured the labor because the men so loved to hold the baby. The nurses believed that having the child in the area helped give the men the will to survive.

Youngsters were among the many people who flocked to the battlefields of the Civil War shortly after any fight. The sites remained pilgrimage goals for years. Although girls were likely to report on the grass that was growing over the location of the carnage, or to comment on the wild flowers that had reappeared, boys delighted in the wreckage of men and animals that resulted from the fighting. They went to the fields as soon as they could, sometimes before the battle ended, eagerly searching for items to add to their collections.

African American children often took refuge with their parents as contrabands behind Union lines (1863). (*Library of Congress*)

Girls seemed to have useful skills to offer at the edges of the battles. When Tillie Pierce and her friends observed the Union Army beginning to pass through the streets of Gettysburg before the battle there, they stood on the corner and sang national songs to entertain and motivate the men as they passed. Following the battle, soldiers that heard them commented about how much the moment meant. Although the girls prepared bouquets of flowers to give to the men, in their excitement over their roles as greeters, they forgot the flowers completely. As the battle grew, the girls busied themselves handing out water to all who passed, including General George Gordon Meade, who Pierce failed to recognize. Other girls spent the days helping their mothers bake bread for the men. When all else failed, girls would simply sit with wounded soldiers, comforting the men by their presence. The games of girlhood prepared them well for their part in the "grand and awful spectacle" that was taking place all around them (Alleman 1889, 52).

Gender did not protect the girls from the realities all around them. As parents determined that one place was safer than another, the girls hurried to reach the new spot. While on the move, they were exposed to the same sights that the boys would run to see—exploding shells, dead animals and men, cannons, and smoke—all the thrilling images of imagination and novel. If the new spot was indeed out of direct fire, it tended to fill up with wounded soldiers seeking shelter and aid. Wherever possible, surgeons set up hospitals and the girls saw amputation and the aftermath of the surgeries—blood, gore, and unattached arms and legs—as they moved about the farms they were on. Pierce helped some officers find their way onto a rooftop to better observe the battle, and they allowed the girl to look for herself, a reward the boys she knew would have loved to share.

Conclusion

The children that emerged from the Civil War were different than those of the prewar years. These changes occurred whether the child had direct contact with the war or was hardly touched by it. Some of the changes were simply passing fads—like wearing Union buttons or walnut shell halves and playing war. New games took the place of the wartime versions, and doll fashions altered over time. Other changes were more permanent. Children's literature, especially dime novels that were devoured as quickly as they were produced, emphasized the individual choices that children made during the years of conflict. In these stories, young men were forced or chose to leave the homes of their families and the protecting influences of schools and churches to embrace the adventure of the battlefronts. The boys were always bright and managed to outsmart their opponents. They remained loyal to their beliefs and the values inculcated in their homes and were unfailingly courageous. Although the heroes exhibited worthy traits, the new characteristics undercut the sense of community of earlier generations and encouraged a sense of individual interests of the future, rather than community action of the past.

The boys that populated the United States after the war were different from the boys before the war, and that difference made its way into the literature of the postwar period. The new stories suggested that the independence learned during the war years might not all be positive. They were "bad boy" tales featuring youths who operated independently of their parents. They had a clear set of admirable characteristics—courage, loyalty, humor—and they used those qualities to outsmart adults, but these boys were different. They did not outsmart evil adults, but they instead outsmarted all adults. They lacked the respect for authority that wartime characters had. Most of their adventures seem more like practical jokes than serious wrongdoing, but they demonstrate the real effects the war had on children. The stress and uncertainty of the war years tore down the security of the prewar years. In its place, the children of the Civil War created new realties and new roles for themselves. Like the veterans, they had to learn to live in a world changed by war.

References and Further Reading

Alleman, Tillie Pierce. 1889. *At Gettysburg or What a Girl Saw and Heard of the Battle*. New York: W. Lake Borland.

Bardaglio, Peter. 1992. "The Children of Jubilee: African American Childhood in Wartime." In *Divided Houses: Gender and the Civil War*, edited by Catherine Clinton and Nina Silber. New York: Oxford University Press.

Elmore, Elting, in Old Schoolmates Association. 1910. ''Reunion of Former Attendants of Milwaukee University and the Milwaukee High School.'' *Children in Urban America Project*, Hotel Pfister, September 8, 1910, Marquette University, Milwaukee, Wisconsin.

Hays, William Shakespeare. 1863. *The Drummer Boy of Shiloh*. Augusta, GA: Blackmar & Bro.

Marten, James A. 1998. *The Children's Civil War*. Chapel Hill: The University of North Carolina Press.

Marten, James A. 2004. *Children for the Union: The War Spirit on the Northern Home Front*. Chicago: Ivan R. Dee.

Patriotism, Preparation, and Reputation: Immigrants in Battle and on the Home Front in the American Civil War

5

Fiona Deans Halloran

In the 20 years before the Civil War, a massive wave of immigration swelled the American population. More than 3 million Europeans left their native lands to live in the United States. Although immigrants came from many countries, two areas contributed the largest numbers. These were Ireland and the various states of what is now Germany. Most immigrants entered through the port of New York, and most settled either in Northern cities or in port cities and towns in the upper Midwest. Chicago and St. Louis, in particular, experienced significant growth. By 1860, half of Chicago's residents were foreign born, slightly less than St. Louis's 60 percent.

A New Wave of Immigration

There had been Irish immigration into the American colonies from the beginning of their settlement. Significant populations of Irish immigrants settled the mountains of western North Carolina and the upcountry of South Carolina. They also populated New York City and New York State and a variety of other areas. Irish immigration to America was steady and significant between 1800 and 1840, but in the 1840s Irish immigration surged because of a terrible famine in Ireland.

In the Ireland of the 1840s, many families survived on tiny family farms. These farms produced various items, but survival depended primarily on the potato. When, in 1846, the potato crop failed because of a fungus, the Irish had few resources to sustain them. Mismanagement by the British government made the crisis worse. For several years, potato crops failed and the population of Ireland starved. In response, thousands of Irish families chose to immigrate to North America. For various reasons, the majority came to the United States.

German immigration to the American colonies began in the early 18th century. By the 19th century, a small but thriving German-American community populated both cities—especially Philadelphia—and rural areas. Towns like Germantown, Pennsylvania, were held up as examples of admirable immigrant communities: thrifty, diligent, and law-abiding. German immigration in the early 19th century was relatively minor but steady. Like the Irish, however, German immigrants began to pour into the United States as a result of a regional trauma. Whereas the Irish fled poverty and famine, the wave of German immigration in the late 1840s and early 1850s was the result of political conflict.

The year 1848 was a pivotal one in European politics. Liberals across Europe agitated for greater popular political participation, restrictions on royal privilege, and a greater role for intellectuals and the middle class. The resulting conflicts over representation are known as the Revolutions of 1848, and they convulsed cities and countries across Europe. In their wake, many intellectuals and activists abandoned their homelands in favor of the promise of greater political freedom in the United States. The Revolutions provoked, as well, a widespread sense of economic insecurity. As a result, an enormous number of German-speaking immigrants arrived on American soil seeking economic opportunity and a respite from political and religious conflict.

German immigration rose massively in the years following the Revolutions of 1848. By the end of the 1850s, more than 1.5 million German-speaking migrants had joined the nation. The year of greatest immigration was 1854, when more than 200,000 German-speaking immigrants arrived on American shores. For many, New York was the initial destination. From there, they spread out both to cities and rural communities. In New York City alone, the German population swelled so massively that by the time the Civil War began, New York was the second-largest German-speaking city in the world, after Berlin. In the Midwest, Cincinnati swelled with German immigrants, supporting four German-language newspapers, numerous German-speaking churches, and demands for German language instruction in public schools. By the Civil War, German-speaking immigrants and their families accounted for nearly 30 percent of the total population of foreign-born residents in the United States.

Other migrant groups also flocked to American shores. These included more than 200,000 French immigrants, and smaller groups of Swedes, Norwegians, Italians, Scots, and Spaniards. Jews came to the United States from a variety of lands, although they did so in relatively small numbers. Like their German-speaking counterparts, these immigrants founded cultural organizations, newspapers, clubs and benevolent organizations, and schools. In short, they built immigrant communities based both on shared heritage and a forward-looking vision.

One exception should be noted. Beginning with the gold rush in the late 1840s, thousands of Chinese immigrants settled along the west coast, primarily in California. Between 1850 and 1864, in particular, thousands of Chinese fled the country as a result of the Taiping Rebellion. Although the Chinese population grew steadily during the decades between 1850 and 1882, when Congress passed the Chinese Exclusion Act, Chinese immigrants rarely were free to establish the same strong ethnic communities as their European counterparts. Chinese newspapers, businesses, clubs, and neighborhoods did appear, but they faced constant scrutiny from native-born and European immigrant locals—especially the Irish. Violence against Chinese residents was common both in cities like San Francisco and in the mountain areas where men sought gold. American culture and politics were usually closed to Chinese immigrants, sometimes by statutes banning Chinese from obtaining citizenship or voting.

By the time the Civil War broke out, immigrant populations had grown to such an extent that no government, no party, and no leader could ignore them. German-language daily newspapers debated the merits of Republican and Democratic politics, examined slavery as a labor system and a political choice, and asserted a political role for German immigrants in the nation. Irish politicians, likewise, participated in the many debates that prefaced the conflict. Immigrant communities smaller than either the Irish or the Germans read, wrote, and argued about the sectional conflict both within their enclaves and with their native-born neighbors.

For many of the families who had immigrated in the decades before the war, the conflict sharpened both their commitment to American citizenship and their opinions about America's goals and limitations. In other words, they approached the conflict much as other Americans did, with anger, concern, fear, and patriotism.

Immigrants and Politics

Many American politicians considered immigrant communities a serious problem, both in terms of policy and politics. For those concerned with American culture and national identity, immigration posed a set of serious challenges to the assumptions of the native born. Could immigrants assimilate into American culture? What ought their political rights be? What was the effect of their culture on American society, and was it positive? And, sometimes most pressing, what could the role of Catholic immigrants be in a nation so wedded to its Protestant history?

Politically, a different set of questions emerged. As the Civil War approached, America's parties began to clash in more and more bitter contests. Reform movements in favor of temperance, women's rights, and abolition exerted ever-greater pressure on existing parties and sometimes succeeded in splintering parties into factions. Thus, as party leaders and candidates examined election strategies, they were increasingly aware of the potential of the immigrant vote. If immigrant voters could be mobilized in favor of one party or another, they might sway entire elections, especially in the North. Yet cultivation of the immigrant vote required compromise on some points. Irish and German communities, for example, were unlikely to respond favorably to temperance advocacy. And although the many Irish immigrants were indifferent to slavery, Germans were, on the whole, in favor of abolition on principle.

Thomas Nast (1840–1902)

The most famous and influential American political cartoonist of his time, Thomas Nast left Bavaria for the United States in 1846, when he was six years old. The Nast family emigrated because of the political conflicts that eventually would cause the Revolutions of 1848. Thus, Nast shared with many other German-speaking immigrants the experience of fleeing political strife.

Many of Nast's earliest opinions emerged from his family's immigrant experience. Like many older Forty-Eighters, political refugees of the 1848 European revolutions, Nast believed in representative democracy, written constitutions, and popular political participation. He idolized European liberal leaders like Garibaldi and Kossuth. Growing up in a community of immigrants—Irish, German, English, Jewish, Scandinavian, and Italian— Nast learned a complex form of American politics composed of both the native-born and the recently arrived citizen.

German-American Thomas Nast was the most famous political cartoonist during the American Civil War. (*National Archives*)

These two sets of questions led to a complex array of responses. The Democrats, Whigs, and Republicans all tried to combine various positions and issues to attract votes while retaining core constituencies. Winding through the politics of slavery, sectionalism, rising industrial economics, and social policy was the ever-growing immigrant population. Thus, as the Civil War approached, immigrants found themselves at the center of many political debates.

Immigrant Units

When the war began, immigrants fought on both sides for many reasons. For some, service as a soldier offered a path to citizenship. Just as military service reflected the responsibilities of citizenship for the native born, it could confer membership in society by demonstrating commitment to shared values. Military salaries provided a second reason to enlist. Not only did soldiers earn a monthly salary, but also bounty payments meant that immigrants who arrived with little or no financial assets could immediately support themselves.

Practical considerations were not the only motivation to enlist. In numerous cases, immigrants fought for political or social principles. Many

At 15, Nast obtained a job drawing for *Frank Leslie's Illustrated News*. By 1861, Nast was an illustrator for the premier illustrated paper of his day, *Harper's Weekly*. While at *Frank Leslie's* Nast helped to illustrate coverage of two local controversies—against spoiled milk and police corruption—but it was at *Harper's* that his political work really began. There, his drawings reflected public ideas, emotions, and discussions about the Civil War.

Early on, Nast provided readers of *Harper's* with detailed battle scenes. Later, as the political tensions of the war became increasingly strained, Nast began to produce drawings that were both illustrative and politically pointed. Through his work, *Harper's* commented approvingly on the Emancipation Proclamation and the leadership of Abraham Lincoln. Nast also provided powerful evocations of the personal costs of war. Most famously, Nast supported Lincoln's 1864 reelection campaign with a cartoon demonstrating the cost of "Compromise with the South."

Nast's career is especially interesting with regard to immigrants and the Civil War because Nast was sometimes openly anti-immigrant. He lampooned Irish residents of New York and occasionally mocked his fellow German immigrants, as well. After the draft riots, Nast transformed the stereotypical image of the Irish thug into a symbol of the dangers of immigration to the war effort, Reconstruction, and the national political system.

By the end of the war, Nast was a rising star. In the next 20 years he would become America's most famous political cartoonist, and would comment often on the status of immigrants—especially Catholics—in America. Nast left *Harper's Weekly* in the late 1880s and died in 1902.

German immigrants, for example, opposed slavery and believed it to be incompatible with democratic government. For them, a war to end slavery was philosophically appealing. Others believed that the Union could not be severed by secession. They fought to preserve the Union and to repress what they perceived as a rebellion.

For Irish immigrants, recruiters pitched the war in anti-English terms. Because the Confederacy sought English support, Union boosters argued, Irish men could fight the English by fighting the South. Even more powerful was the promise of military training. Many Irish people came to the United States as famine refugees. For these immigrants, English rule meant starvation and penury. Some hoped that after a period of renewal in America, Irish nationalism could rise up against the English and take Ireland back under Irish rule. Military service offered training for that eventual conflict, and some soldiers believed that the Civil War was an opportunity to battle-harden Irishmen.

Although most immigrants fought as ordinary soldiers, there were immigrants among the highest ranks of military leadership. In some cases, these men led units composed almost entirely of immigrant recruits, units which proudly identified themselves as German, Scandinavian, French,

THE GREAT REPUBLICAN REFORM PARTY,
Calling on their Candidate.

This 1856 political cartoon lampoons the newly formed Republican Party for embracing immigrants, women, African Americans, and Catholics as "radicals and reformers." (*Library of Congress*)

Italian, or Irish. On the battlefront, the story of immigrants and the Civil War is one built around the creation and experience of immigrant units.

Many immigrants took great pride in fighting for the Union or Confederacy. In fact, immigrant units proudly proclaimed their heritage through official and unofficial names, flags, and banners. It is important to recognize that most immigrants who served in the Civil War did so in mixed units. Almost one-fifth of the men in the Union armies were immigrants or sons of immigrants and, of those, most did not join the units generally recognized as "ethnic."

Units associated with specific immigrant groups were important, however, and they were distinguished by three characteristics. First, other Americans viewed them as immigrant units. Second, they perceived themselves, and represented themselves, as immigrant units. This identification was especially important for those that adopted specialized flags or uniforms, like the Louisiana Tigers or the Irish Brigade. Finally, immigrant units included men who were overwhelmingly drawn from one immigrant group or one kind of immigrant group (Scandinavians, for example). In many cases, immigrant units came to symbolize the incorporation of the immigrant group into American society and politics. In some cases, though, the immigrant units represented both heroism and negative stereotypes.

Even small immigrant communities sent units to war. The Norwegian community of Wisconsin heard, in 1861, that local Germans were raising a regiment of volunteers. Not to be outdone, the Norwegians raised their own unit, the Fifteenth Wisconsin, also known as the Scandinavian Regiment and the Norwegian Regiment. This unit included men from a variety of Norwegian settlements, including those in Iowa and Illinois. A group of Chicago volunteers formed St. Olaf's Rifles, a celebrated part of the regiment. Also from Chicago came the regimental flag. On one side flew the stars and stripes, while on the other raged the Norwegian lion. The flag was the work of the Norwegian Society of Chicago.

The Fifteenth Wisconsin fought in 26 engagements, under the leadership of its celebrated colonel, Hans Christian Heg. Heg died at Chickamauga in September 1863, alongside more than half of the regiment. Heg's Civil War service, and that of the regiment he led, has remained a part of the historical memory of the Civil War among members of the Norwegian-American community.

Swedes, too, contributed men and enthusiasm to the Union war effort. Most opposed slavery, although they had little experience with black Americans and held many of the same prejudices as their native-born neighbors. Overwhelmingly, they supported the preservation of the Union, and they volunteered to fight in that cause. Swedes joined existing units, including the Fifteenth Wisconsin, and fought with distinction. Some of the volunteers brought Swedish military experience to their Civil War service. Colonel Oscar Malmborg, for example, trained the Fifty-fifth Illinois, fought at Corinth, and attracted admiring attention from General Ulysses S. Grant (as well as criticism for his bad temper). John Ericsson designed the ironclad *Monitor* and convinced Abraham Lincoln that it could be an asset to the Union Navy. When the *Monitor* was finally afloat, its assistant engineer and one of its crewmen were also Swedish. John Adolph Dahlgren, also a Navy man, invented the "Dahlgren gun," led the initial naval blockade of the war, and participated in the 1865 siege of Charleston, South Carolina.

In other cases, Swedish officers fought for the Union. A. C. Warberg did so, and wrote back to Sweden that he was confident that "officers from no nation have done their fatherland so much honor in the ranks of the American army as have ours" (Warberg in Barton 1975, 96). American Swedes pointed with pride to the contributions both of immigrant Swedes and those still in the service of Sweden. Like many other immigrant groups, Swedes looked, in later years, to Civil War veterans for community leadership. Colonel Hans Mattson, for example, became secretary of state for Minnesota from 1870 until 1872.

Like Norwegian and Swedish immigrants, Italians entered the United States through the port of New York City. Unlike the others, though, many Italians remained in the city to live. Politically active and socially cohesive, Italians in New York observed and participated in the party politics of the late 1850s and were powerfully motivated to fight in 1861. Francesco Casale, who founded the first English-Italian newspaper in America, recruited a group of volunteers called the Italian Legion. Later, he helped to create the Thirty-ninth New York Regiment, also known as the Italian Garibaldi Guard. Many of the men who fought with the Thirty-ninth were veterans of the wars of Italian unification and fought for Garibaldi in Italy. As a link to that

Immigrants such as Captain Schwartz, a sharpshooter in the 29th New York, proved essential to the Union's wartime success. (*Library of Congress*)

experience, the unit wore red shirts, echoing Garibaldi's army. They also linked the Garibaldi message of political liberalization, equality under the law, and personal freedom to the Union cause. The 39th Regiment is interesting from another perspective, as well. It contained not only Italian units, but five other immigrant companies. These included companies of French, Hungarian, German, Swiss, and Spanish immigrants. It is easy to imagine the challenges of language alone for commanders of this regiment.

Other Italians also raised volunteer units. Francesco Spinola recruited and commanded four regiments for New York. Count Luigi Palma di Cesnola used his experiences in the Crimean War to train numerous young Italian men who went on to fight for the Union. Cesnola commanded Union forces himself, as well. In June 1863, he was wounded and pinned under his horse after an engagement with Confederate J. E. B. Stuart in Virginia. Taken prisoner, Cesnola became an advocate for better treatment of prisoners of war.

Although their numbers were small, French immigrants were similarly eager to fight for the Union. In New York, they formed the Lafayette Guards, a company led by Colonel Regis de Trobriand. The Guards fought at Fredericksburg, Chancellorsville, and Gettysburg. Trobriand was an unusual person. Descended from a distinguished French family, and married to an American banking heiress, Trobriand lived in a variety of locales. He settled in New York City in 1841, writing for its French-language newspaper and writing a novel. He then moved to Venice. In 1847 he returned to New York City, resuming his work as a writer and man-about-town. Thus, he was unlike many immigrants in that he had not emigrated directly and then started to establish roots in America. It was war service, from which he emerged a major general and an American citizen, which seemed to cement his commitment to the United States. After the war, Trobriand produced a history of the Army of the Potomac in French and commanded garrisons in North Dakota, Montana, Utah, Wyoming, and New Orleans. Trobriand died on Long Island, New York, in 1897.

As a measure of the possibility for confusion in an army composed of regulars, volunteers, and local and state units, there was another Lafayette Guard. This unit, a group of 80 men designated Company E of the Second Ohio Infantry, was composed mostly of German immigrants. It left Ohio on the governor's orders to protect Washington, D.C., in 1861. Later, the Fifty-fifth New York Volunteers recruited heavily among French immigrants.

Although no Chinese units were formed, individual Chinese immigrants fought in both Union and Confederate units. The total number of Chinese soldiers is difficult to establish, in part because some fought under names that did not reflect their ethnicity. An example is Corporal Joseph Pierce of the Fourteenth Connecticut Volunteer Infantry. Sold to sea by his parents, Pierce caught the attention of Amos Peck, a descendant of one of the founders of Hartford. Raised by the Peck family, he joined a local unit at the beginning of the war. With his regiments, Pierce fought from Antietam to Appomattox. In addition, at least one Chinese soldier fought with the Avegno Zouaves, a unit of the Confederacy's 13th Louisiana Infantry. The total number of Chinese immigrant soldiers is believed to be about 50.

The two largest immigrant groups, the Germans and Irish, contributed enormous numbers of men to the war effort. As many as 200,000 German immigrants and German Americans fought for the Union, and Irish soldiers filled regiments across the nation. The Eleventh Corps of the Army of the Potomac, the most famous of the German units, and the Irish Brigade both attracted intense public scrutiny as immigrant units. But many other smaller groups of men fought as well. In several cases, leaders forged in battle would go on to become active examples of the participation of immigrants in American politics.

German-speaking Americans raised numerous units, and German immigrants provided fighting men from the rank of private all the way up the command chain. Although about half of the Eleventh Corps' men were native-born Americans, so many were either German-speaking immigrants, naturalized citizens of German origin, or Americans born to German immigrant parents that the unit was forever associated with German immigrants in the public eye.

Although Germany was not a unified country in the 1860s, German-speaking immigrants to America were usually lumped together as "Dutch" or "German" by their native-born neighbors. Likewise, the distinction between a new immigrant, a naturalized citizen, and the child of immigrants was only sometimes meaningful. American disinterest in differentiating between Bavarian and Prussian immigrants—or among the various citizenship statuses—reflected a common tendency to retreat into stereotypes. The Eleventh Corps suffered from this tendency, most notably in the aftermath of the Battle of Chancellorsville.

At Chancellorsville, the disastrous miscalculation of General Joseph Hooker was compounded in the press by the supposed cowardice of the German troops. On May 2, around 5:30 P.M., the Eleventh Corps found itself under fire from three directions. As the line crumbled, a disorderly retreat sent men tumbling back into the lines of their compatriots. Some of Carl Schurz's men held their line briefly, but it, too, broke at about 6:15 P.M. In the end, the Eleventh Corps fought for more than an hour and a half without reinforcement, and suffered massive losses. When the Battle of Chancellorsville was over, there was plenty of blame to go around. The German units, though, bore an enormous share. They were mocked in the press and abused in letters and among army leaders. Schurz spent much of the rest of his life trying to rehabilitate the reputation of his men and of German fighters in the Union Army.

Schurz's career was a testament to the leadership potential realized by German fighters. Four German Americans would become major generals in the Union Army. In addition to Schurz were Franz Sigel, Peter Joseph Oster-haus, and Adolph Steinwehr. Germans appeared among brigadier generals, as well. These men included Alexander Schimmelfennig, Louis Blenker, Frederick Salomon, August Willich, and Joseph Weydemeyer. German generals represented much of the history of German immigration into the United States. Sigel, for example, was a refugee of the Revolutions of 1848, in which he led radicals in Baden. Likewise, Salomon and his brother—who was governor of Wisconsin—escaped the Revolutions from Halberstadt.

As with everything else to do with immigrants and the war, these men did not necessarily agree about politics. Just as they had debated the merits of Republican versus Democrat before the war, Germans in America continued to participate in American politics throughout the war. This participation included conflict over military leadership. Louis Blenker, for example, supported General George McClellan so passionately that he led a torchlight procession of 2,000 men through Washington, D.C. His military career ended not long after.

The German-Jewish minority also supplied fighting men for the Union. Although many German immigrant areas, particularly in New York City, were divided between Catholic and Protestant religious groups, a portion of immigrants from German- and Polish-speaking areas were Jewish. Louis Gratz, for example, emigrated from Prussian-controlled Inowrazlaw, or Jung-Breslau, now called Inowraclaw and a part of Poland. Gratz came to the United States with $10 and no English language skills. Unable to find work, he spent $7.50 on sewing notions, stockings, and shoelaces, and became a peddler. Life as a peddler was almost unimaginably hard. To make more money and out of desperation at his condition, Gratz studied at night to learn English. Eventually, he forged a partnership with another immigrant from Inowrazlaw. When the war broke out, Gratz found it impossible to continue in business.

Like many other men, Gratz was swept up in the fervor of the early months of the war. He volunteered for service in the Union Army. Although Gratz spoke good English, he could not read or write well enough to win a promotion. After his first four-month enlistment expired, Gratz obtained a meeting with Secretary of War Simon Cameron. Examining Gratz, Cameron found him capable enough for a position as first lieutenant in the cavalry and promoted him. Gratz ended the war as a regimental commander. In a letter to family, Gratz expressed pride in his accomplishments, satisfaction that he was "treated with utmost consideration by Jews and Christians," and a determination that if he survived the war he would "return to Germany to live with you" (Marcus 1996, 220–224).

The most famous immigrant unit in the Civil War was the Irish Brigade. Organized in 1861 by Thomas Francis Meagher, the Brigade would see some of the most brutal fighting of the war. Included in the Brigade were the Sixty-ninth, Sixty-third, and Eighty-eighth New York Regiments, and later the Twenty-eighth Massachusetts Regiments, and the 116th Pennsylvania Regiment. The men who served in the Brigade were overwhelmingly Irish-born or the children of Irish immigrants. Like the Norwegians of the Fifteenth Wisconsin, the members of the Irish Brigade proudly displayed Irish imagery on their regimental flag. Green, with a golden harp or a golden shamrock in the middle, the flag came to symbolize the pride of the brigade in its immigrant heritage and the valor it displayed in combat.

In 1862, the men of the Irish Brigade fought all over the eastern theater, including at Second Manassas, Antietam, and Fredericksburg. Losses were enormous, and the bravery of the Brigade became famous. At Fredericksburg, on December 13, an attack on the stone wall at Marye's Heights was nearly successful because of the willingness of the Brigade to charge without regard to massive casualties. Of 1,300 men in the Brigade then, 50 died in the assault, 421 were wounded, and 74 were either captured or unaccounted for.

Five men led the Brigade during the war. Three were killed in action. In the Sixty-ninth New York, 16 of 19 officers died. In the course of the war, the brigade included 7,000 men, but at war's end only 1,000 remained. Casualties sapped unit strength and required constant recruiting to replace fallen men.

The immense losses helped to undermine Irish support for the war, as did the perception that the Irish Brigade was always fighting at the front line. Like so much else in the history of the Irish in America, the Brigade was both a blessing and a curse. It helped to demonstrate the fierce patriotism and impressive physical courage of the Irish. As casualty lists grew longer, however, the Brigade's courage began to seem more like exploitation. Eventually, tension over the role of Irish men in the Union armies, and over the relationship of the war to slavery, would spark some of the worst riots in American history. Still, Irish-American pride in the exploits and sacrifices of the Irish Brigade was substantial and remains so.

Combat Experience

Immigrants experienced the war in a variety of ways. Motives for enlistment varied from Irish nationalism to American patriotism to simple economic need. Combat experience could be both triumphant and tragic,

Thomas Francis Meagher (1823–1867)

Activist, orator, lawyer, Democrat, Irish nationalist, and defender of the Union, Thomas Francis Meagher helped to mobilize the Irish community in America on behalf of the Union. Born August 23, 1823, in Waterford, Ireland, Meagher was the scion of a prominent merchant family. Meagher rejected a career in business, however, in favor of political activism. Between 1843 and 1848, he immersed himself in Irish politics, embracing the nondenominational, culturally oriented patriotism of the Young Ireland movement. As the Revolutions of 1848 convulsed European states, Meagher began to speak of an Irish revolution against British rule. Nicknamed "Meagher of the Sword," his public embrace of violence attracted the attention of the British government. Conviction for treason resulted in exile to Tasmania.

Meagher escaped from Tasmania in 1852. Making his way to New York City, he became a part of the growing Irish-American community, speaking widely and to popular acclaim about Irish nationalism. He became a member of the New York City bar, edited the *Irish News*, and joined enthusiastically in Democratic politics. Like many other Irish immigrants, Meagher was passionately devoted to Irish nationalist causes, while also immersed in American political debates.

Politics proved troublesome in 1861, however, when the nation plunged into civil war.

while camp life was often frustrating for everyone. Immigrant units, however, helped to establish a precedent for the place of immigrants in American life. By proclaiming simultaneously immigrant identity and a commitment to the Union, soldiers could assert their ability both to assimilate and to retain their heritage. Before the war, immigration had been the source of a great deal of political tension. After the war, communities could point to the service of their sons as proof that they had both a right to stay and a role to play in American culture.

Immigrants as Confederate Soldiers

Immigrants fought for the Confederacy, but usually in smaller numbers and in less homogenous units than did those in the Union armies. This difference was partly due to demographics. Fewer Americans lived in the South (as a proportion of the total population of the nation), and of those, only a small portion were foreign born. The South lacked the industrial development to lure immigrants seeking easily obtained work, and it lacked the major port activity that brought in immigrants to cities like New York and Boston.

However, one port city, New Orleans, supplied numerous foreign-born fighters for the Confederacy. In Robert E. Lee's Army of Northern Virginia, the Louisiana Brigade was known as the Louisiana Tigers. Famous for their drinking and fighting, these men were also famously courageous. Immigrants from more than 20 countries joined their ranks, but the Irish accounted for the greatest proportion of foreign-born soldiers in the

Meagher was a Democrat and opposed federal intervention in the slavery question, but he believed in the preservation of the Union. Eventually, the Confederate assault on Fort Sumter pushed him into the camp of the Union for good. He began to mobilize his considerable oratorical and organizational talents for the Union war effort.

First, he organized his countrymen in the Sixty-Ninth New York Volunteer Militia Regiment. With this unit, he would fight at First Manassas in July 1861. In the fall of that year, Meagher helped to create the Irish Brigade. He became its commanding officer in February 1862. With the brigade, Meagher fought in the eastern theater throughout 1862.

Frustrated by the massive losses sustained by his unit, Meagher resigned in early 1863, supportive of the war but angry at its management. In 1864, he returned to service as a brigadier general, and in 1865 he worked under William T. Sherman in Savannah, Georgia. Meagher died in 1867, while serving as acting territorial governor of Montana.

Meagher was a symbolic figure both for Irish immigrants and for native-born Americans. He represented the powerful nationalist feelings within the Irish community, and its resentment of the sacrifices of Irish soldiers in the Union Army, while at the same time demonstrating the commitment of the Irish to American politics and to the Union.

Louisiana Brigade. The Sixth Louisiana was almost entirely Irish, in fact. Recruited from New Orleans's scruffy docks, Louisiana Tigers were sometimes called "Wharf Rats," and their behavior reinforced the sense that their courage was matched only by their inability to obey orders. Thus, immigrants in the Confederate forces faced the same double experience as those in Union forces; their value as fighters was undeniable, but their status as immigrants attracted disapproving attention to behaviors common among many soldiers.

Farther north, St. Louis boasted both a large population of immigrant Irish and substantial Confederate sympathies. Those two qualities combined in the First Missouri Brigade, a unit of about 8,000 men that had substantial enrollments from the Irish and German populations of St. Louis and its rural hinterlands. The First Missouri fought long and hard, and it was considered one of the best units the Confederacy could field. Of the 8,000 men who comprised it, only a few hundred survived to surrender in 1865. The Missouri Brigade is of special interest in part because it was so well led and so courageous, and in part because it is an example of a unit in which native-born and immigrant men commingled without apparent tension. At the very least, the brigade represents a unit in which social difference did not interfere with unit cohesion and battlefield effectiveness.

St. Louis was not the only Southern city to supply German soldiers. Germans lived in a variety of locations throughout the South, notably in Richmond, Virginia, New Orleans, and Texas. Many shared the antislavery sentiments of Northern immigrants, but they also felt a strong tie to the land they had chosen. Just as in the North, prominent German confederates provided a model for immigrants loyal to the Confederacy. Charles

Minnigerode preached to Jefferson Davis at St. Paul's church in Richmond. In the Confederate cabinet, Charles Memminger served as secretary of the treasury. Captain Henry Wirz, superintendent of Andersonville Prison and another of the Forty-Eighters, provided an example to his fellow immigrants, if an ugly one.

Similar examples attest to the Irish who fought for the Confederacy. The most prominent of these men was Major General Patrick Cleburne, who arrived in the United States in 1849 and died at the Battle of Franklin. Many ordinary soldiers fought for a variety of Confederate units, including one that christened itself the Confederate Irish Brigade.

A small number of Norwegian immigrants also fought for the Confederacy. These men were drawn mainly from settlers to Texas, and numbered only in the hundreds before the war. Some evidence suggests that these Norwegians fought out of duty rather than with the compelling patriotic commitment of the Norwegians who fought for the Union. Complicating their service was antislavery sentiment, which was prevalent among Norwegians in Texas as elsewhere.

After the war, the South attracted even fewer immigrants than it had before the war. The region was not just defeated but devastated. As a result, service in Confederate units could not play the same role in asserting a national place for immigrants. Still, as the myth of the Lost Cause took hold, many immigrant communities in the South pointed with pride to the experiences of their soldiers. In that sense, the Northern and Southern immigrant soldiers were just alike.

Nativism

The heroism of Irish, German, and other immigrant soldiers drew admiring comment from many Americans. Immigrant contributions on the battlefield assuaged tensions about the role of immigrant peoples in American national identity, but those tensions remained. There had always been Americans who opposed immigration and who felt that immigrants did not belong on American soil.

In the 1840s and 1850s, the streets of New York City saw many violent confrontations between criminal gangs. Some of these gangs replicated the ties of Ireland, attracting men from a particular county or village. Other gangs gathered men who hated the Irish. These men, who called themselves Native Americans and who are often called Nativists by historians, believed that immigration in general, and Irish immigration specifically, posed a threat to American society.

Nativism was both a social and a political force. It not only underlay gang activity in the streets of American cities, but it also formed the foundational political philosophy for political parties such as the Know-Nothings. Thus, as existing political parties competed for office, broke apart, and reformed in new configurations, Nativism and the status of immigrants moved to the center of political debates. The argument over slave

The 1863 draft riots in New York City revealed tensions over conscription and racial politics in the North. Illustration from *The New York Illustrated News*, July 25, 1863. (*Library of Congress*)

labor versus free labor, for example, also required Americans to consider the role of the industrial worker, who was often an immigrant.

The Civil War both ameliorated and exacerbated existing tensions. Immigrant units performed well on the battlefield and attracted positive attention, but not all immigrants wanted to fight. In some areas, immigrant opposition to the draft became, in fact, a central part of the argument over the role of immigrants in American society. The eruption of violent riots in New York City in the summer of 1863 cemented the sense, among some Americans, that Irish immigrants were a dangerous element within the body politic.

The riots began with the Conscription Act of 1863. As the war progressed, it became more and more difficult to attract volunteer soldiers. Finally, the federal government assessed each state a quota. Should that state fail to provide the requisite number of soldiers, it would have to institute a draft. In New York, volunteers were hard to come by, and even large bounties failed to secure the necessary numbers. Finally, the governor instituted a draft.

Objections to the draft came not only from the immigrant community, but also from many other poor New Yorkers. The famous statement that the war was ''a rich man's war but a poor man's fight'' reflected the conviction that although wealthy Northerners planned and executed the conflict, it was the poor who fought and died. The ability of wealthy men to buy a substitute only added to the outrage. Race played a role, as well.

Many Irish New Yorkers accepted racist stereotypes about black Americans. For years, conflict in the Irish neighborhoods of New York—especially Five Points—had victimized black New Yorkers.

The proximity of the Emancipation Proclamation and the Conscription Act, therefore, offered observers a racial explanation for the draft. To free the slaves, many thought, Irish men would be sacrificed. Opposition to the draft, then, was both class based and racialized. It rejected the idea that only the poor should fight, but it also rejected a war for emancipation.

New Yorkers were not the only Americans to oppose the Emancipation Proclamation, nor were Irish immigrants the only immigrants to oppose it. Democratic politicians convinced many working-class white Americans that freed slaves would take industrial jobs in the North. Some immigrant volunteer units, including a German unit from Wisconsin, disbanded rather than fight for emancipation. There was widespread tension over the proclamation and its relationship to the war. In New York, however, that tension joined with existing discontent, the losses sustained by Irish units, and the anxiety over the draft. The combination would prove deadly.

As the date set for a New York City draft approached, tensions in the city ran high. The incredible death toll from the Battle of Gettysburg only reinforced the sense that the war was destroying the nation's young. When, on July 12, 1863, the names of the men who had been drafted the day before appeared in the newspaper, riots broke out almost immediately. Within a day, as many as 50,000 rioters had taken to the streets. Four days of violence ensued, leaving homes and businesses burned, more than 100 citizens dead, and the city government in disarray. Prominent abolitionists were targeted, and some feared not only for property but also for their lives. Black New Yorkers were a special target, and many died at the hands of the mob. In addition, rioters burned the Colored Orphan Asylum, a symbol of benevolent activism on behalf of free black Americans.

Draft riots erupted in cities other than New York. Working-class Americans of a variety of ethnicities objected to both the draft and the Emancipation Proclamation. But the New York City draft riots stuck in the American imagination. The threat of poor, Catholic, unskilled, and whiskey-soaked Irish immigrants, so long enumerated by Nativists, seemed to have come true. The heroic contributions of the Irish Brigade and other units like it were forced to compete against this mental image in the American mind from 1863 forward.

The vision of Irish men as violent thugs persisted long after the war. Chinese labor on the transcontinental railroad attracted Irish opposition from laborers who felt that the Chinese depressed wages. When Irish immigrant laborers attacked Chinese workers, the popular press compared that violence with the Irish attack on the Colored Orphan Asylum. As the century progressed, politicians exploited anti-Irish and anti-Catholic prejudice by referring to the draft riots as proof that even in the nation's greatest crisis, the Irish had been more liability than asset.

For Jews, anti-immigrant feeling combined with widespread American anti-Semitism. In 1862, facing a chaotic trade in black-market Southern cotton, General Ulysses S. Grant issued General Order Number 11, which expelled Jews from Kentucky, Tennessee, and Mississippi. In another order, Grant wrote that "Cotton-Speculators, Jews, and other Vagrants," must leave the Department of Tennessee because they were engaged in "trading on the miseries of their Country" (Marcus 1996, 198). Protests from Jewish leaders in affected areas, particularly Paducah, Kentucky, elicited a revocation from President Lincoln. Although Grant's motives and personal feelings are the subject of some debate, the connection he drew between speculators and Jews was widespread among military and civilian leaders. Jewish residents of occupied areas, Jewish traders, and Jewish soldiers confronted anti-Jewish sentiment frequently. Because some Jews were native born, and others were immigrants, it is difficult to separate a specifically immigrant experience from that faced by a Jewish-American citizen.

For immigrants as a whole, however, the home front was a place much in step with the rest of the nation. The wives and families of immigrants confronted the same food shortages in the South and the same casualty lists in the North. Patriotic sentiment, too, motivated soldiers and their families, as letters home attest.

Conclusion

Millions of immigrants arrived in the United States in the years before the Civil War. They populated cities, founded newspapers and cultural organizations, and began to participate in American politics. Americans, however, were unsure about immigration. In politics and society, the status of the immigrant was a subject for debate and the focus of a variety of prejudices. Nativist politicians railed against the presumed decline of American culture and the dangers inherent in a Roman Catholic minority within the nation. As the nation approached a conflict over sectionalism and slavery, it also found itself grappling with complex questions about the role of foreign-born residents in American culture, economy, and government.

When the Civil War began, immigrant-dominated units became celebrated—and sometimes excoriated—parts of the armies of both the Union and the Confederacy. Immigrants fought for both sides, but the vast majority fought for the Union. This reflected both demographic differences between the sections and philosophical convictions on the part of immigrants. In addition, just as the citizen-soldier was a symbol of adulthood and political independence for native-born young men, the soldier as citizen offered an alluring opportunity for many immigrant men.

In the aftermath of the war, combat leaders rose from the ranks of immigrant units into national political positions. Ordinary men, too, claimed membership in the body politic and American society based on Civil War combat experience. Especially in the North, service in the war legitimated the presence of many immigrants and asserted a place for them in the nation. Like their neighbors, immigrants exploited the massive growth of the postwar period, moving west, starting businesses, and participating in the expanding consumer and industrial culture of the Gilded Age.

References and Further Reading

Barton, H. Arnold. 1975. *Letters from the Promised Land: Swedes in America, 1840–1914*. Minneapolis: University of Minnesota Press.

Bernstein, Iver. 1991. *The New York City Draft Riots: Their Significance for American Society and Politics in the Age of the Civil War*. New York: Oxford University Press.

Creighton, Margaret S. 2005. *The Colors of Courage: Gettysburg's Forgotten History, Immigrants, Women, and African Americans in the Civil War's Defining Battle*. New York: Basic Books.

Gannon, James P. 1995. *Irish Rebels, Confederate Tigers: A History of the 6th Louisiana Volunteers, 1861–1865*. New York: Cambridge University Press.

Levine, Bruce. 1992. *The Spirit of 1848: German Immigrants, Labor Conflict, and the Coming of the Civil War*. Urbana: University of Illinois Press.

Marcus, Jacob Rader, ed. 1996. *The Jew in the American World*. Detroit: Wayne State University Press.

Symonds, Craig L. 1998. *Stonewall of the West: Patrick Cleburne and the Civil War*. Kansas City: University Press of Kansas.

From Enslaved to Liberators: African Americans and the Civil War

6

Julie Holcomb

In 1857, the Supreme Court ruled that, as a black man, Dred Scott was not a citizen of the United States. Both a cause and an effect of sectional conflict, the *Dred Scott* decision surprised few Americans at the time, although it angered abolitionists who had consistently challenged the idea that African Americans—free or enslaved—were not citizens of the United States. In 1860, as the United States hovered on the brink of civil war, 4 million African Americans living in the South were legally defined as articles of property. As property, African American families could be separated at will by white masters, who wielded absolute power over their slaves. Laws excluded slaves from education, property ownership, and even the freedom to leave their master's property. Conditions for the 250,000 free blacks living in the South were hardly better. Free Southern blacks had few civic rights, lacked the right to vote, and were generally as illiterate as the slaves. The 225,000 blacks who lived in the North enjoyed greater freedom and more economic opportunities than their Southern brethren, and, in a few states, even had the right to vote; however, their lives were closely circumscribed by racism and segregation and they were clearly defined as second-class citizens.

Fighting for Freedom

With the passage of the Thirteenth Amendment and Union victory, the American Civil War represented a watershed in African American freedom; in four years, millions of African Americans moved from bondage to freedom through their own actions and those of the men on the battlefields. Many African Americans realized that they needed to participate personally in the fight to free the slaves. Former slave and abolitionist Frederick Douglass, like many African Americans at the time, recognized

Frederick Douglass (ca. 1818–1895)

Born into slavery as Frederick Augustus Washington Bailey in Maryland, Frederick Douglass was separated at a young age from his mother, Harriet Bailey. Douglass remained with his grandmother on a nearby plantation until, at age eight, he was sent by his owner to Baltimore to work for Hugh Auld. In Baltimore, Auld's wife taught Douglass to read and write despite legal statutes prohibiting slave literacy. At the age of 16, Douglass was returned to the plantation in Maryland to work as a field hand. He was later sent back to Baltimore to work as a ship caulker. In 1838, using borrowed papers, Douglass was able to present himself as a free African American sailor and escape.

Once in the North, he adopted the last name of "Douglass" and married Anna Murray, a free African American woman he had met while he was enslaved in Baltimore. After meeting William Lloyd Garrison in 1841, Douglass became an agent for the Massachusetts Anti-Slavery Society. He traveled throughout the North speaking on behalf of the antislavery movement and describing his enslavement. After publishing his autobiography, *Narrative of the Life of Frederick Douglass* in 1845, Douglass left for Great Britain for a two-

both the promise and the importance of black participation in the Union war effort:

> Let the black man get upon his person the brass letters 'U.S.'; let him get an
> eagle on his button, and a musket on his shoulder and bullets in his
> pocket, and there is no power on earth which can deny that he has earned
> the right to citizenship in the United States. (Douglass as quoted in
> Litwack 1980, 72)

Others agreed. "God will help no one that refuses to help himself," a Philadelphia man wrote the *Anglo-African*, a metropolitan weekly. He continued, "the prejudiced white man North or South never will respect us until they are forced to by deeds of our own." (Alfred M. Green as quoted in McPherson 1982, 32). Free blacks had "great obligations," African American relief organizer Elizabeth Keckley declared.

> It has been asserted that we, as a people, do not sympathize with this
> oppressed portion of our race. Let us, my friends, by our benefactions, by
> words and by acts of kindness, disprove these assertions . . . great obligations
> rest upon us to do all we can to assist, both morally and physically, those
> whose lot has hitherto been cast in the dark, rough paths of life. (Keckley as
> quoted in Forbes 1998, 69).

As Douglass, Green, and Keckley recognized, patriotism, liberty, racial equality, and African American participation were inseparable. Whether on the home front or the battlefield, African American actions shaped the black experience of the Civil War and hastened the arrival of black emancipation.

At the outbreak of war in 1861, African American men and women offered their assistance to the war effort. However, Northern and Southern year speaking tour. His tour not only helped promote his book and the American antislavery movement, but also protected him from recapture and a return to Southern slavery.

In 1847, Douglass returned to the United States. Friends in England and the United States helped purchase his freedom and provide the financial backing for his abolitionist newspaper, the *North Star*. Throughout the antebellum period Douglass remained an outspoken and well-known advocate of abolitionism, women's rights, and temperance.

Despite Union policy to the contrary, Douglass saw the Civil War as a crusade for the freedom of millions of African Americans. He clashed with Abraham Lincoln when in the early months of the war the president refused to adopt emancipation as a military strategy and to enlist black soldiers. After the Emancipation Proclamation was issued on January 1, 1863, Douglass recruited two African American regiments in Massachusetts, enlisting among others his two oldest sons.

After the war, Douglass continued to fight for African American rights. He held numerous political appointments, including a stint as consul general to Haiti. He died in 1895 in Washington, D.C.

whites generally rejected all African American offers of assistance in the first two years of the war. Because secession, not slavery, was the pretext for the war, President Abraham Lincoln rejected any consideration of abolition or black military assistance through government means. Throughout his 1860 presidential campaign, Lincoln made numerous assurances that if elected he would not pose a threat to slavery where it existed. Even after Southern states seceded in the wake of his election, Lincoln continued to reassure all Americans that his only objective was preservation of the Union: "If I could save the Union without freeing any slave I would do it, and if I could save it by freeing all the slaves I would do it; and if I could save it by freeing some and leaving others alone I would also do that," Lincoln declared (Lincoln as quoted in Jenkins 2002, 3). Lincoln's emphasis on preservation of the Union was part of a calculated effort to court the Border States of Delaware, Maryland, Missouri, and Kentucky. He believed that the abolition of slavery or the arming of black soldiers might cause those states to secede and lend their support to the Confederate cause. Furthermore, the abolition of slavery or the arming of black soldiers potentially could arouse Northern prejudices and stiffen Confederate resistance. Throughout 1861 and into the early months of 1862, Lincoln maintained his conservative stance toward abolition and the use of black soldiers.

The Issue of Slavery and the War Effort

Still, the disruption of the Civil War, which forced men and women, black and white, free and enslaved, to labor in new settings and in new ways, ensured that black emancipation would be central to the war effort regardless of Lincoln's assurances to the contrary. By the time the war officially began with the surrender of Union forces to the Confederates at Fort

African American families take refuge as "contrabands" behind Union lines in 1863. Image by David B. Woodbury. (*Library of Congress*)

Sumter, South Carolina, in April 1861, the ideas of war and secession had already severely disrupted plantation life throughout the South. In late 1860 and early 1861, South Carolina slave owners removed slave men from plantations to build coastal defenses on Morris Island and Sullivan's Island in Charleston Harbor. Large numbers of slave men were also moved to the South Carolina coast to increase Southern production of salt, which was vital to the war effort. Men were not the only slaves subject to forced removal, however, as coastal planters moved any of those slaves who were not needed on the coastline to protected interior areas to prevent slaves from escaping or being impressed by the Confederacy. The shifting of the slave population separated families and disrupted patterns of agriculture, domestic networks, and social relations.

Moreover, as the war progressed, Union occupation affected slave families for good and bad. The presence of Union troops and the exigencies of the Civil War provided an unprecedented opportunity for slaves to escape. Although the bulk of escaped slaves in the antebellum years were men, during wartime, large numbers of women, children, and older slaves escaped to safety behind Northern lines. Their escapes further disrupted life throughout the South. Furthermore, Union blockades and war demands led to shortages for free and slave families, as well as for white Southerners. The declining availability of cloth and its increasing cost meant that slaves often went without suitable clothing and often without shoes. As a result, the rate of sickness and death among slave families increased during the war. In addition, the absence of male slaves and the wartime shortages in textiles meant that slave mistresses often appropriated the fruits of women's domestic production such as spinning and weaving. Planters cut food rations to their slaves as wartime shortages took a toll on the home front. Because slaves lacked supplies like shot, powder, and fish hooks, they frequently were unable to supplement their meager rations with self-caught game and fish. Slave men and women who remained on the plantation often resisted declining conditions and increased planter demands by slowing down production and engaging in other forms of passive resistance.

Slave resistance bolstered by the Union war effort helped undermine slavery in the early months of the war despite the lack of a federal proclamation on black emancipation. Indeed, because Lincoln refused to link black emancipation to the war effort, slaves in Union-occupied areas of the South faced an uncertain status. That ambiguity was exacerbated by the actions of Union commanders. In May 1861, Benjamin Butler refused to return three slaves to their owner, a Confederate colonel who had demanded their return under the provisions of the fugitive slave law. Butler said the law did not apply because Virginia had seceded and the three slaves had been working on Southern fortifications at the time of their escape. While Butler refused to return the fugitives, he carefully avoided the question of emancipation simply declaring the three "contraband of war" and putting them to work in his own camp.

Uncertain Status

The freed slaves still faced an ambiguous legal status, however. Although not legally emancipated, the contrabands received a wage for their work and enjoyed a relative amount of freedom. In a letter to her sister in June 1861, white Northerner Laura Hildreth described the situation as slaves flocked to Butler's camp:

> Negroes come in every day from outside, and one day as many as forty
> came into the backyard; of all ages from babies up to old men and women.
> It was a ludicrous and at the same time a sad sight to see the poor creatures,
> homeless, not knowing when or where they were to get their next meal.
> (Quoted in Silber 2005, 223)

For Northern whites, black freedom, however vague, carried a host of social problems that the federal government had yet to deal with. In August 1861, Congress voted on the First Confiscation Act in an attempt to deal with the contraband question. The act allowed only for the confiscation of property, including slaves, used directly in the Confederate war effort; it did not grant freedom or answer the question of freedom for slaves confiscated under the act's authority. The act declared that any master who permitted his slave to labor in Confederate service forfeited his ownership of that slave. Despite the careful wording, all but three of the Democratic and Border State congressmen voted against the bill. Thus, although the act successfully passed Congress, the vote made it clear that emancipation was a Republican issue. However, despite the lack of an emancipation edict, slaves flocked to Union lines in hopes of gaining their freedom. By the end of July 1861, nearly 1,000 slaves had fled to Butler's camp.

Major General John C. Frémont, commander of the Western department at St. Louis, Missouri, issued his own edict of freedom for the slaves during the same month that Congress voted on the Confiscation Act. Frémont had been the Republican presidential nominee in 1856 and a prominent member of the party's antislavery wing in 1861. On August 30, Frémont placed the state of Missouri under martial law and declared all property of Missourians fighting against the United States confiscated and liable to use by the Union. He also pronounced the slaves of Confederate Missourians free. Frémont's actions exceeded both the bounds of martial law and the First Confiscation Act. Moreover, his actions contributed to the severe dislocation suffered by slaves throughout the South, particularly as the federal government attempted to avoid any stance on black emancipation. Lincoln privately asked Frémont to modify his proclamation. When Frémont refused, Lincoln announced that he had altered Frémont's proclamation to comply with the conditions of the First Confiscation Act passed six weeks earlier. Just weeks after Lincoln's reversal, Frémont was removed from command of the Western Department and replaced by Major General David Hunter.

Despite these reversals, however, slaves continued to view Union soldiers as liberators and frequently used the presence of Union occupation forces as the impetus for and means to escape. In some cases, the government stepped in to make freedom a reality for these African Americans. For example, in November 1861, a Union fleet captured Port Royal Island and the rest of the South Carolina Sea Islands south of Charleston. Nearly all of the white inhabitants fled, leaving behind cotton-rich plantations and more than 8,000 slaves. Thus began the North's first experiment in reconstructing the South and its slave economy. The Treasury Department sent agents to the Sea Islands to supervise contraband labor in the harvest of cotton for Northern mills. Abolitionists and other reformers—black and white—organized freedmen's aid societies to educate these African Americans. At the same time, Major General David Hunter ran afoul of Lincoln's conciliatory policy toward black emancipation. On March 31, Hunter was given command of the Department of the South, which covered the Sea Islands off the coast of Georgia. Six weeks later, Hunter declared all slaves in Georgia, Florida, and South Carolina free. Moreover, he requested his commanders to arm the freed slaves for military service. Hunter also organized the First South Carolina Volunteers, the first Union regiment organized among escaped slaves. Lincoln quickly disbanded the regiment over concern about public opinion, however, and also revoked Hunter's order freeing the slaves.

In addition to Northern support, escaped slaves like Susie King helped their fellow runaways. King, who secretly had learned to read and write while enslaved, fled with her uncle to Union lines at Fort Pulaski, Georgia, in April 1862. She spent the remainder of the war teaching other freed slaves and working as a laundress in the Union camps on the Sea Islands. Thousands of other slave men, women, and children throughout the low-country fled to the Sea Islands and to Union lines. However, Union lines did not guarantee safety or better living conditions. As white contraband teacher Elizabeth Botume observed, "The refugees were vastly worse off than the plantation people. They literally had nothing to wear" (Botume as quoted in Schwalm 1997, 98). Former slaves lived in makeshift quarters, had few resources, and received inequitable pay. Moreover, slave women were frequently subject to rape or the threat of rape as Esther Hawk, a missionary and teacher with the Freedmen's Aid Society noted: "[N]o colored woman or girl was safe from the brutal lusts of the [white] soldiers—and by soldiers I mean both officers and men." Furthermore, "Mothers were brutally treated for trying to protect their daughters, and there are now several women in our little hospital who have been shot by soldiers for resisting their vile demands" (Hawk as quoted by Schwalm 1997, 102).

The Tide Turns

By mid-1862, the tide against emancipation had started to turn. In the summer of 1862, Congress passed the Second Confiscation Act, which prohibited under penalty of court martial the return of fugitive slaves even to masters who claimed loyalty to the Union. Congress also abolished slavery in Washington, D.C. Events of 1861 and 1862 hastened this change. In the early months of the war, Northerners, most notably Lincoln, had believed victory would come quickly to powerful Northern forces. However, by mid-1862, Northerners were frustrated by the military stalemate. Significant Union defeats at First Bull Run in 1861 and the Seven Days' Battle and Second Bull Run in 1862 sapped Northern morale. Lincoln and others realized that emancipation and recruitment of fugitive slaves could weaken the Confederate military while simultaneously strengthening Union forces. Lincoln also realized the inconsistency of fighting a government based on slavery without striking a blow at slavery. Slavery was indeed the core of Southern economic and social life; even though slaves were not engaged in combat, their service in support roles continued to aid the Southern cause. As emancipation increasingly became linked with military necessity, emancipation was also becoming detached from any moral imperative. However, Lincoln did not want to take action against slavery in the midst of Northern defeat. As the summer of 1862 wound down, Lincoln drafted his Emancipation Proclamation. Union success at Antietam on September 17, 1862, gave Lincoln the victory he needed and on September 22 he issued his preliminary Emancipation Proclamation. The final proclamation took effect on January 1.

Blacks and some whites greeted the Emancipation Proclamation with enthusiasm. Henry M. Turner, a freeborn African American and pastor of the Israel Bethel Church in Washington, D.C., described the reaction: "As many as could get around me lifted me to a great platform." When he found himself unable to read the document because of breathlessness, he handed it to someone who, he reported, "read it with great force and clearness." The large crowd was overwhelmed with emotion and

> while he was reading every kind of demonstration and gesticulation was going on. Men squealed, women fainted, dogs barked, white and colored people shook hands, songs were sung, and by this time cannons began to fire at the

navy-yard, and follow in the wake of the roar that had for some time been
going on behind the White House. (Quoted in McPherson 1992, 20)

Furthermore, Turner observed the numerous black and white men who
came to the White House and congratulated the president on the path-
breaking proclamation.

Lincoln's proclamation linked emancipation with the arming of blacks,
thus striking a significant blow to the economic and social base of the
South. However, in truth, Lincoln's proclamation failed to free a single
slave. Slaves in the Border States and in Union-controlled areas of the
Confederacy were exempted from the proclamation, and it had no immediate effect in parts of the South still under Confederate control. Yet, the
proclamation changed the tone of war. No longer was the North fighting
solely to preserve the Union; the North now fought to establish a new
United States free of slavery. That new Union would be formed in large
part through the actions of slaves and free blacks.

African Americans recognized the implications of the Emancipation
Proclamation and celebrated those who had brought about its existence.
For slaves, the Union Army had always been seen as an army of liberation.
As Susie King of Savannah, Georgia, recalled, "I wanted to see these wonderful 'Yankees' so much, as I heard my parents say the Yankee was going
to set all the slaves free" (McPherson 1992, 26–27). After Lincoln issued his
preliminary Emancipation Proclamation, the army of liberation included a
following of hundreds of runaway slaves and free blacks. The 1st South
Carolina Volunteers, the first black regiment formed under Lincoln's new
policy, was organized on November 7, 1862, under the command of white
abolitionist Thomas Wentworth Higginson. The success of the 1st South
Carolina prepared the way for other black regiments authorized in 1863. In
a letter to one of his commanders, Lincoln noted that "the colored population is the great *available* and yet *unavailed of* force for restoring the Union.
The bare sight of 50,000 armed and drilled black soldiers upon the banks of
the Mississippi would end the rebellion at once" (McPherson 1992, 60–61).

Still, many Northern whites feared the consequences of arming black
soldiers to fight for black freedom. In the summer of 1863, draft riots broke
out throughout the North, revealing class and racial lines. In New York
City, antiblack and antidraft rioters burned a draft office and destroyed a
black orphanage as well as the homes of well-known abolitionists and
Republicans. Rioters linked black emancipation to amalgamation, a charge
antiabolitionists had leveled against abolitionists since at least the 1830s.
The New York City riots, fueled in part by fears of miscegenation and loss of
jobs to free African Americans, targeted New York City blacks. One eyewitness known only as Mrs. Statts described the violence against one black
woman and her newborn baby. She described how the rioters "broke
through the front door with pick axes, and came rushing into the room
where this poor woman lay, and commenced to pull the clothes off from
her." Later she "saw the innocent babe, of three days old, come crashing
down into the yards; some of the rioters had dashed it out of the back window, killing it instantly." Before the attack began, Statts and her young son

had sought refuge in the basement of the unnamed woman's home. Discovering Statts and her son, "Two ruffians seized him, while a third, armed with a crow-bar, deliberately struck him a heavy blow over the head." Statts's son died two days later (Statts as quoted in King 2006, 173–174). Rioters also burned an orphanage and otherwise terrorized the African American residents of the city and those who supported them.

Black Support for the Union Cause

Northern blacks' support of the Union war effort was critical. Just as white women took action to support Union troops in 1861 and 1862 through volunteer efforts and aid societies, African American women similarly focused their voluntary efforts on helping other African Americans. Initially, they sent aid to former slaves in the South. After the Emancipation Proclamation was issued, black women took a more active role in soldier relief. Just as white women had done at the outset of the war, African American women formed soldiers' aid societies. For example, in Philadelphia, black women formed the Colored Women's Sanitary Committee and the Ladies Sanitary Association of St. Thomas African Episcopal Church. Elizabeth Keckley of Boston formed the Contraband Relief Association to provide care for recently freed slaves. These were among the many soldier and contraband relief groups formed in the wake of freedom. The women who organized and ran these relief societies saw their work as more than aid to specific soldiers and often defined soldiers' aid as a step in advancing the causes of emancipation and racial equality. For African American women, freedmen's aid and soldier relief were "joint projects in the same struggle" (Silber 2005, 166–167).

African American women's relief efforts on behalf of other African Americans differed markedly from those of white women. Because white Northern women worried about social control of a hitherto dependent group of people, they often placed conditions on their relief efforts to freed slaves. African American women, however, emphasized racial solidarity and generally did not place qualifications on their aid.

Black Northern support included military as well as home-front support. However, for the nearly 180,000 black men who fought in the Union Army, military service was a complex, ambiguous experience. Initially rejected and then finally actively recruited after Lincoln's proclamation in 1862, blacks volunteered in large numbers to hasten their own liberation and that of their people. Union rosters list 166 black regiments: 145 infantry, 7 cavalry, 12 heavy artillery, 1 light artillery, and 1 engineer. On May 22, 1863, the Union War Department established the Bureau of Colored Troops to oversee black recruitment and create examining boards to screen applicants for officer's commissions. The U.S. Colored Troops (USCT) mustered 7,122 officers and 178,895 enlisted men. More than 80 percent of the enlisted men came from the Confederate states and were former slaves. By the end of the war, 110 African American men had received commissions; however, more than 70 were so badly harassed by their

Sojourner Truth [Isabella Baumfree] (ca. 1797–1883)

Sojourner Truth was one of the most highly regarded and recognized African American women in the 19th century. In 1863, Harriet Beecher Stowe noted that she was impressed not only by Truth's tall, slender physical appearance but also by her clear sense of self-worth. An unstinting advocate of the rights of women and African Americans, Truth traveled widely in support of both movements.

Truth was born into slavery as Isabella Baumfree around 1797 in New York State. Enduring harsh physical punishments, Isabella was sold several times. She grew to adulthood on John Dumont's farm in New Paltz, New York. Dumont had promised to emancipate Isabella early rather than waiting for New York's emancipation law to take effect. When Dumont reneged on his promise, Isabella took her youngest child and walked to freedom in 1826, seeking refuge

Sojourner Truth was a former slave and preacher who fought for the abolition of slavery and for women's rights. (Library of Congress)

superiors that they resigned. Ninety percent of the USCT's commissioned white officers were combat veterans who received their commissions after passing a rigorous exam. USCT commissions were highly sought after and widely accepted because they offered opportunities for promotion. The experienced leadership of the USCT meant African American soldiers had a higher quality of leadership than the average white soldier. By war's end, African Americans made up 12 percent of the Union Army, had participated in 41 major battles and 449 smaller actions, and had earned 16 Medals of Honor.

Still, African American soldiers were subject to the persistent racism of the period. All black enlisted men, including noncommissioned officers, were paid $10 a month, $3 less than white privates. Additionally, black soldiers had another $3 per month deducted for their uniforms, while white soldiers were given their uniforms. Black soldiers protested the inequitable pay. Finally, on June 15, 1864, Congress voted for equal pay for USCT, but only for men who were free at the start of the war, thus further depressing morale and driving a deeper wedge between Northern and Southern blacks. This pay distinction remained in place until March 3, 1865.

African American soldiers had the greater share of fatigue duty. Indeed, many Union generals thought USCT units should be used as labor with the Van Wagenen family, who bought out her remaining time as a slave.

In 1828, Truth became the first black woman to sue a white man in a New York court. Truth's son Peter had been illegally sold to an Alabama plantation owner. She prevailed in court and secured her son's freedom. In 1835, Truth sought justice in the court system again when she sued for slander and won damages of $135.

In 1843, Truth adopted her well-known name and began her life as a traveling preacher. Soon after, she relocated to Northampton, Massachusetts, where she worked with other social and antislavery reformers, including Frederick Douglass. In 1850, with the aid of a white friend, she published her autobiography.

During the Civil War, Truth remained a prominent and active reformer. She recruited African American soldiers for the Union Army, nursed black soldiers in Washington, D.C., hospitals, and aided newly freed slaves. She also met with Abraham Lincoln as well as with Harriet Tubman, who had visited black solders in South Carolina. Truth was responsible for initiating the lawsuit that led to the desegregation of Washington, D.C., streetcars.

After the Civil War, Truth continued to aid freedpeople, helping them to relocate throughout the North. She called for the distribution of western lands to former slaves. She died in Battle Creek, Michigan, in 1883.

and garrison battalions. When African American soldiers went into combat, they often carried inferior weapons. Fatigue duty impaired morale, contributed to a higher disease rate, and wore out the soldiers as well as their meager supplies. Consequently, one in five African American servicemen died of disease compared with one in 12 whites. Ten black soldiers died of disease for every one who died in battle; for white soldiers the ratio was two to one.

In sharp contrast, African American sailors were an active part of the Union Navy from the beginning of the Civil War. Indeed, the navy provided African Americans the best opportunity to actively support the Union war effort. African American naval service dated back to the American Revolution, and many African Americans possessed maritime skills gained through service in the merchant marines in the first half of the 19th century. Unlike military service, naval service lacked any connotations of social uplift and generally sailors—white and black—were seen as the dregs of society. Black sailors fared better than their later military counterparts. The navy was fully integrated because segregation was difficult if not impossible to achieve on a ship. Black sailors received equal pay and an equal share of all prize money from captured Confederate merchant ships and blockade runners. An equal standard of equipment, decent

Nine uniformed black soldiers are seen aboard the gunboat *Mendota* (1864). (*National Archives*)

medical care, similar opportunities to earn distinction in combat, and an equitable naval criminal justice system also ensured that black sailors had a better wartime experience than black soldiers. Furthermore, the navy retained control of its recruiting responsibilities, thus eliminating the racism that pervaded state recruitments for the army. Black sailors were primarily urban, Northern free blacks or foreign blacks, while black soldiers were largely rural slaves.

The Emancipation Proclamation also provided African American women with the opportunity to take a more active role in Republican rallies and activities as politicians realized that their support was critical to the Union cause. Because black men had been excluded from voting and from military service, Republicans had little incentive to seek their support. With emancipation and recruitment, however, the political climate changed. Several Northern black women served as recruiters for African American Union regiments. Black women expressed support and renewed faith in Lincoln and the remainder of the nation's leaders. In late 1862, Frances Harper wrote to a friend that "We may thank God that in the hour when the nation's life was convulsed . . . the President reached out his hand through the darkness to break the chains on which the rust of centuries had gathered" (quoted in Silber 2005, 140–141). Black schoolteacher Edmonia Highgate spoke in support of Lincoln at a meeting of the National Convention of Colored Men in the fall of 1864. One newspaper reporter said her public comments demonstrated that she was a "strong Lincoln MAN" (quoted in Silber 2005, 140–141).

Free African American women faced harsh economic conditions. The better-paying jobs were often denied to black women. As black soldiers were recruited for the Union Army, the lack of employment opportunities and the absence of male wage earners placed Northern black women in an acute economic position. David Demus, a soldier in the famed 54th Massachusetts, pleaded with his wife to stop doing field work for a local farmer. In a letter to Secretary of War Edwin Stanton, Mrs. John Davis asked for a furlough for her husband, a member of the 102nd USCT: "I have no support except what I can earn by my own labor." This problem resulted from the fact that her husband had received no pay, and it ensured that she was "completely distitute." Rosanne Henson explained to Lincoln that "being a colored woman [I] do not get any state pay" (quoted in Silber 2005, 63–64). The federal government made some initial steps in relieving the economic plight of African American women after the massacre of black soldiers at Fort Pillow by amending pension laws so that wives of black soldiers could receive pensions. With greater economic opportunity came greater government oversight, however, as the federal government investigated "proper" and "improper" marriages among a people who had never been legally permitted to marry.

Blacks in the Army

Although black men were consistently barred from military service for the Union Army early in the war, they were included in the Confederate Army from the beginning. However, black Confederate military service was built on the conventions of Southern society, which put blacks to work performing the menial tasks of heavy labor. Harvey's Scouts, a group that rode with Confederate general Nathan Bedford Forrest, the Third Georgia Infantry, and the Louisiana Native Guards and who would later join the Union Army after Benjamin Butler's occupation of New Orleans in 1862, all served support functions for the Confederate Army. The use of coerced or "voluntary" black military service for manual labor freed white Confederate soldiers for frontline duty and kept firearms from African Americans. The Confederate Congress passed several bills, including the Negro Musicians Bill (1862) and the Regimental Cooks Bills (1862 and 1863), ensuring that free and enslaved blacks filled support roles and did not serve as soldiers. Slaves and conscripted blacks also built fortifications, expanded river defenses, repaired railroads, and assisted in the manufacture of armaments. In the early years of the war, there was no talk in the Confederacy of arming slaves for combat.

Although Major General Patrick Cleburne called for the enlistment of slaves as soldiers in January 1864, Confederate president Jefferson Davis would not consider Cleburne's plan. Later that year, Confederate Secretary of State Judah Benjamin also called for the enlistment of blacks, and by January 1865, Confederate commander Robert E. Lee similarly called for the use of black soldiers to fill the thinning ranks of the Confederate States Army. On March 13, 1865, the Confederate Congress authorized recruitment of black soldiers promising a loosely defined emancipation in exchange for service. Few blacks were recruited, however, and the surrender documents at Appomattox one month later showed no black soldiers among those who surrendered. Generally, black soldiers who served the

A few African American men worked in the Confederate Army, especially as "servants" to their enlisted owners or as cooks, general laborers, teamsters, and musicians. This photo shows a man identified as Marlboro, a servant to Major Raleigh Spinks's Camp of the 40th Georgia Infantry of the Army of Tennessee. (*AP/ Wide World Photos*)

Confederacy did so because they were conscripted, coerced by their masters or other whites, or sought economic gain or protection for their families and communities. There is no evidence that blacks fought to support the South or its so-called peculiar institution.

Free and enslaved black men and women in both the North and South interacted with the Union and Confederate causes and troops in some way or another during the war, and thus the "world came to the plantation" (Bardaglio 1992, 219). Slave children's workload increased as white men left for military service and black men were either impressed into service or ran away. The war meant more than an increased workload for African American children. The Civil War further destabilized African American families in a myriad of ways. Slave fathers' control over their children could and often was trumped by the master's absolute power over slave lives. During the Civil War, fathers and mothers ran away. When families reunited, fathers asserted their authority in ways that had been completely unknown under slavery. Families were destabilized and divided as slaves sought freedom behind Union lines. The military accepted male slaves into military service, particularly after 1862, but families were expected to remain behind on the plantation. Enslaved women and children who were left behind on the plantation were often brutalized by vengeful masters. Patsey Leach of Kentucky recalled how her master became particularly abusive after her husband left and later died on the battlefield: "When my husband was killed my master whipped me severely saying my husband had gone into the army to fight against white folks and he my master would let me know that I was foolish to let my husband go." Leach was so badly beaten that "blood oozed from the lacerations" on her back. Desperate to escape, Leach fled without four of her children (Leach as quoted in Taylor 2005, 194).

Thus, for African American men and women the decision to flee or to stay, to fight or to sit idly by was fraught with painful choices. Adding to the chaos of African American family life was increased government interest in slave marriages, which marked a dramatic change for black families. As the federal government passed legislation allowing the wives of black soldiers to receive pensions, the government expressed a heightened interest in "proper" and "improper" marriages and "moral" and "immoral" activities of the widows. Still black families generally welcomed the intrusion of the public worlds of politics and war into their domestic affairs because they saw in such a blending of the public and private a means of achieving liberation.

Abolition

The adoption of the Thirteenth Amendment in January 1865 forever settled the status of slavery in the United States and "placed reunification at the forefront of ex-slave families' quest for freedom" (Taylor 2005, 196). Although the Emancipation Proclamation did not free a single slave, its implementation reinforced the movement for the destruction of slavery. With the passage of the Thirteenth Amendment, the provisions of Lincoln's Emancipation Proclamation could not be overturned by a future presidential administration, Congress, or the courts. Furthermore, the amendment prepared the way for the expansion of civil rights that were later guaranteed for African Americans in the Fourteenth and Fifteenth Amendments.

After Lincoln issued the Emancipation Proclamation in January 1863, several versions of an antislavery constitutional amendment were considered. Missouri congressman John Henderson presented a draft proposal to Congress in January 1864. Charles Sumner also submitted a version of an abolition amendment. Congressman James Ashley of Ohio emerged as the leading spokesperson for a constitutional amendment abolishing slavery. Ashley argued that Congress had unrestricted amending power that allowed for the abolition of slavery. The final version of the amendment was prepared by the Senate Judiciary Committee under the direction of Lyman Trumbull of Illinois. Using language similar to that of the

Northwest Ordinance of 1787, the committee's version called simply for the prohibition of slavery. The committee believed the amendment accomplished the desires of abolitionists while avoiding the anger and potential loss of support from War Democrats. The Thirteenth Amendment was passed in the Senate in April 1864, but was voted down in the House of Representatives as Democrats rallied supporters under the banner of states' rights.

Popular support for abolition grew as war casualties mounted. The elections in the fall of 1864 would provide the final impetus for passage of the amendment. Lincoln claimed his overwhelming victory in his reelection bid as a mandate on the abolition amendment. While Lincoln could have simply waited until March when the new, Republican-majority Congress was seated, he chose instead to push for passage of the amendment by the lame-duck Congress. Lincoln believed passage by a bipartisan majority would stand as a sign of wartime unity, and he used his prestige and his influence to persuade Democrats to change their votes. On January 31, 1865, the Thirteenth Amendment finally passed the House with unanimous Republican support and many Democrats either reversing their position or absenting themselves from the vote. By December 1865, the requisite three-fourths of all states—Union and former Confederate states—had ratified the Thirteenth Amendment.

With ratification of the Thirteenth Amendment and Union victory in 1865, African Americans witnessed and participated in their transcendence from slavery to freedom. In February 1865, after Confederate evacuation of Charleston, South Carolina, the Twenty-First USCT and detachments of the Fifty-Fourth and Fifty-Fifth Massachusetts regiments were the first Union troops to enter the city. As Colonel Charles B. Fox of the Fifty-Fifth Massachusetts put it:

> Words would fail to describe the scene which those who witnessed it will never forget—the welcome given to a regiment of colored troops by their people redeemed from slavery . . . Cheers, blessings, prayers, and songs were heard on every side. Men and women crowded to shake hands with men and officers. (Fox as quoted in McPherson 1992, 90)

The enslaved had become the liberators.

References and Further Reading

Bardaglio, Peter. 1992. "The Children of the Jubilee: African American Childhood in Wartime." In *Divided Houses: Gender and the Civil War*, edited by Catherine Clinton and Nina Silber, 213–229. New York: Oxford University Press.

Berlin, Ira, Joseph P. Reidy, and Leslie S. Rowland, eds. 1998. *Freedom's Soldiers: The Black Military Experience in the Civil War*. Cambridge: Cambridge University Press.

Blight, David W. 1991. *Frederick Douglass' Civil War: Keeping Faith in Jubilee.* Baton Rouge: Louisiana State University Press.

Cimprich, John. 2005. *Fort Pillow, a Civil War Massacre, and Public Memory.* Baton Rouge: Louisiana State University Press.

Cornish, Dudley Taylor. 1987. *The Sable Arm: Black Troops in the Union Army, 1861–1865.* Lawrence: University Press of Kansas.

Cullen, Jim. 1992. "'I's a Man Now': Gender and African American Men." In *Divided Houses: Gender and the Civil War,* edited by Catherine Clinton and Nina Silber, 76–91. New York: Oxford University Press.

Edwards, Laura F. 1997. *Gendered Strife and Confusion: The Political Culture of Reconstruction.* Urbana: University of Illinois Press.

Forbes, Ella. 1998. *African American Women During the Civil War.* New York: Garland Publishing, Inc.

Frankel, Noralee. 1999. *Freedom's Women: Black Women and Families in Civil War Era Mississippi.* Bloomington: Indiana University Press.

Glatthaar, Joseph T. 1990. *Forged in Battle: The Civil War Alliance of Black Soldiers and White Officers.* New York: Free Press.

Grimsley, Mark. 1995. *The Hard Hand of War: Union Military Policy toward Southern Civilians, 1861–1865.* New York: Cambridge University Press.

Gutman, Herbert G. 1976. *The Black Family in Slavery and Freedom, 1750–1925.* New York: Vintage Books.

Holcomb, Julie. 2002. "Eyewitness to War: Samuel N. Kennerly." *America's Civil War* 15, no. 5 (November): 32.

Jenkins, Wilbert J. 2002. *Climbing Up to Glory: A Short History of African Americans during the Civil War and Reconstruction.* Wilmington, DE: Scholarly Resources Books.

King, Wilma. 2006. *The Essence of Liberty: Free Black Women during the Slave Era.* Columbia: University of Missouri Press.

Litwack, Leon F. 1980. *Been in the Storm So Long: The Aftermath of Slavery.* New York: Vintage Books.

McPherson, James M. 1982. *The Negro's Civil War: How American Negroes Felt and Acted during the War for the Union.* Urbana: University of Illinois Press.

McPherson, James M. 1988. *Battle Cry of Freedom: The Civil War Era.* New York: Ballantine Books.

McPherson, James M. 1992. *Marching Towards Freedom: Blacks in the Civil War, 1861–1865.* New York: Facts on File.

Painter, Nell Irvin. 1996. *Sojourner Truth: A Life, a Symbol.* New York: W.W. Norton.

Schwalm, Leslie A. 1997. *A Hard Fight for We: Women's Transition from Slavery to Freedom in South Carolina.* Urbana: University of Illinois Press.

Silber, Nina. 2005. *Daughters of the Union: Northern Women Fight the Civil War.* Cambridge, MA: Harvard University Press.

Taylor, Amy Murrell. 2005. *The Divided Family in Civil War America*. Chapel Hill: University of North Carolina Press.

Trudeau, Noah Andre. 1998. *Like Men of War: Black Troops in the Civil War, 1862–1865*. Boston: Little, Brown and Company.

Vorenberg, Michael. 2004. *Final Freedom: The Civil War, the Abolition of Slavery, and the Thirteenth Amendment*. New York: Cambridge University Press.

Ward, Andrew. 2005. *River Run Red: The Fort Pillow Massacre in the American Civil War*. New York: Viking.

The Longhouse Divided: Native Americans during the American Civil War

7

Andrew K. Frank

As the secession movement and ensuing war tore the United States apart in 1860–1861, the nation's Indians faced a series of personal and communal struggles that threatened their existence as sovereign peoples and ultimately reshaped many of their communities in devastating ways. Although Native Americans often experienced the Civil War and its causes through unique cultural and political lenses, they quickly learned like all Americans that they could hardly ignore the crisis. Native Americans rarely waited for the war and its accompanying disruptions to come to them. Instead, they attempted to use wartime opportunities to pursue their tribal and individual ambitions. They tried to settle old scores, demonstrate their loyalty to their neighbors, secure financial stability and new trading agreements, and reshape their relationship with federal and state governments. Some saw the war as an opportunity to protect their rights to their slave property; others saw it as a way to transform the racial norms of the nation. Despite their varied and often conflicting motivations, however, Native Americans across the nation discovered the tumults and destruction of the Civil War. The difficulties for Indians often paralleled the experiences of their neighbors. Native American men enlisted as soldiers and suffered alarmingly high mortality rates; Native American refugees fled their farms and homes to avoid invading armies; and wartime shortages and inflation affected every community. Perhaps most important, the war split many Native American nations, villages, and clans. Tribal factions frequently coalesced into pro-Union and pro-Confederate divisions that had rather tenuous ties to either government or cause. In many cases, the longhouse, wigwam, earth lodge, or council house was literally divided.

A Multitude of Causes and Experiences

A singular wartime experience did not unite Native Americans, with tribal and regional distinctions creating a cacophony of causes, perspectives, decisions, and results. Most Native Americans actively participated as members of tribal nations, whose leaders forged formal treaties and alliances with the Confederacy and Union. In many cases, the decision to enter the Civil War exacerbated preexisting divisions within tribes and the resulting schisms lasted for generations. Other Native Americans, especially those in the east, participated in the war as individuals whose Native identities went largely unrecognized by wider society. These Native Americans experienced the war in ways that often paralleled the experiences of their black and white neighbors. For western tribes, often with little or no direct interest in political events to the east, the Civil War simply continued trends that began decades or centuries earlier, with additional warfare with the United States and their ultimate dispossession from their lands. Although many western Indians fought against the United States, they were hardly allied with the Confederates.

Despite the spectrum of experiences across tribes and regions, the destruction of the Civil War cut across tribal affiliations. The American Civil War often divided Indian nations in self-destructive ways. Creeks, Cherokees, and many other tribes fought bloody battles among themselves—with members of the same clan even choosing different diplomatic paths. With Native Americans of many nations and political loyalties often living in proximity to one another, the war also resulted in Native Americans frequently waging war on soldiers from other tribal nations. The results were often brutal. In 1862, for example, a mixed Unionist unit of Delaware, Shawnee, and Caddo Indians killed more than half of the Tonkawa Indians in a single raid. Even when Native Americans did not have an active role in the war, they discovered that the United States failed to live up to its earlier treaty obligations and that local militias caused tremendous upheaval. As a result, western Indians suffered some of the most horrific massacres in their history during the war. Finally, Indian reservations and communities became enveloped by the war, as homes and property were frequently destroyed or stolen. Thousands of Native Americans lost their homes, approximately 10,000 became refugees, and thousands more suffered from lack of food and other supplies.

Enlistment and the Military

From the very beginning of the war, many Native Americans joined the fight in the most formal way. An estimated 20,000 Indians joined the Union and Confederate armies, with more joining the Confederate than the Union Army. Death rates for Native Americans enlistees were similar to non-Indians, with about one-fourth of the enlisted soldiers from some tribes dying from battle wounds. Native American soldiers fought in many of the widely known battles in the east—including Second Bull Run,

Ely S. Parker, a Seneca Indian, is pictured (sitting, third from left) among other members of Gen. Ulysses S. Grant's staff (ca. 1864). Parker served as Grant's military secretary. (*National Archives*)

Antietam, the Wilderness, and Petersburg. In the trans-Mississippi western theater, fighting was virtually nonstop as Indian warriors faced each other as well as Union and Confederate soldiers in formal battles and recurring raids. Many Native Americans joined the armies as part of Indian regiments; others enlisted in colored units. Some—like the Seneca Ely Parker—became trusted aids to white officers. In Parker's case, he served as aide-de-camp of Union general Ulysses S. Grant, and wrote the terms of surrender that formally ended the war at Appomattox Court House. Others served as guides and scouts, capitalizing on their tracking skills and knowledge of local terrain. Most Native American soldiers, however, served in the armies' infantries where they fought in largely segregated or tribally affiliated units.

On several occasions, officers praised Native American soldiers for their abilities. Union officer A. C. Ellithorpe, for example, asserted that he had instilled in his Indian troops

> a good state of military discipline. You would be surprised to see our Regt. move. They accomplish the feat of regular time step equal to any white soldier, they form in line with dispatch and with great precision. . . . That they will make brave and ambitious soldiers I have no doubt. Our country may well feel proud that these red men have at last fell into the ranks to fight for our flag, and aid in crushing treason. (Abel 1919/1992b, 73)

Ely Samuel Parker (1828–1895)

Born near the Tonawanda Seneca Indian Reservation in New York, Ely Parker (or Donehogawa) became one of the most influential Unionist Indians during the Civil War. As a child, Parker attended a Baptist mission school and then continued to receive a nontraditional education at the Yates and Cayuga Academies. Although he studied law, his lack of American citizenship prevented him from joining the bar and practicing law. Instead, Parker used his education as a lobbyist for the Tonawanda Reservation and then as an Iroquois sachem. In 1857, Parker helped negotiate the purchase of two-thirds of their lands from the U.S. government.

With the onset of the Civil War, Parker concluded that his and the Senecas' best hopes were as Unionists. At first his offer to raise and lead an Iroquois regiment was rejected by the Union Army. By 1863, however, the United States abandoned its opposition to Parker's assistance and appointed

Other soldiers were more skeptical of Indian soldiers. Indeed, the mixture of Native Americans in the regular army did not always go smoothly. During the Battle of Pea Ridge, drunken Confederate Cherokees, who were urged on to the battlefield with ample amounts of whiskey, directed their weapons at Union as well as a few Confederate soldiers.

> An Arkansan, who had been wounded and partially scalped by one of the Cherokees is so enraged against them as to be in danger of apoplexy when their name is mentioned. . . . He intended to kill every Indians he could find

Native Americans served at almost every significant battle during the Civil War. Here, wounded Indian soldiers nurse their wounds. (*Library of Congress*)

him a captain of engineers and adjutant-general in the U.S. Army. Parker would serve with General Ulysses S. Grant at the Battle of Vicksburg and then as his aide-de-camp during the battle against the Army of Northern Virginia. In 1865, Parker helped write the articles of surrender that Confederate General Robert E. Lee signed at Appomattox Court House.

When the war ended Parker continued to use his unique skills to negotiate treaties on behalf of the Senecas and otherwise help the Indian nations. In 1869, he became the first Native American to serve as the Commissioner of the Bureau of Indian Affairs. He helped create Grant's controversial "Peace Plan," which abolished the treaty system and advocated the assimilation of Native Americans. Although he would eventually be exonerated, accusations of fraud resulted in his resignation in 1871. Parker embodied the goals of assimilation, moving to Connecticut and then New York. He died of complications from diabetes in 1895.

hereafter, no matter where and under what circumstances. ("Battle of Sugar Creek or Pea Ridge" 1862, 7)

Union and Confederate soldiers were equally "incensed against the savages, and talk of hunting them to death" ("Battle of Sugar Creek or Pea Ridge" 1862, 7). Indian atrocities—whether real or rumored—reinforced the stereotypes of Indians for decades to follow.

Enlisted Native Americans often fought for reasons typical of non-Indian soldiers. Sometimes their decision to join the military stemmed from the rationales that led white inhabitants in Border States to choose their loyalties. The desire of members of the Five Civilized Tribes (Cherokees, Creeks, Choctaws, Chickasaws, and Seminoles) to protect their slave interests certainly shaped the decision of some; the desire to maintain loyalty to the United States and continue a policy of accommodation shaped the Catawbas' and other Indians' enlistments in the Union Army. As one Seneca Indian in the Union Army recalled, "we are all prepared to fight for our country to the last extremity" (Hauptman 1995a, 73). For others, enlistment provided a means to demonstrate beyond a shadow of doubt the loyalty of a tribe to their white neighbors—especially important in the Confederate South. Almost all eligible Catawba men in South Carolina enlisted in the Confederate Army, where they served primarily in the Fifth, Twelfth, and Seventeenth South Carolina Volunteer Infantry regiments. The Catawba, who had a long history of accommodation to local concerns and were economically dependant on white society, maintained this multigenerational survival strategy during the war. The Ojibwa—like many Indians in the Great Lakes region—similarly concluded that loyalty to the United States in the war would provide security and a better bargaining position after the war. By saving the Union, they hoped to save their homelands.

Decisions to engage in the military conflict also had their origins in Native American cultural norms and socioeconomic conditions. For many Native American men, especially in the West, enlistment allowed them to prove their manhood at a time when hunting and other forms of sanctioned violence were limited. Young Indian men could finally engage in the coming of age hunting rituals that marked their status in their communities. Others discovered that their skills as guides and scouts allowed them to gain prominence and respect. The offer of lucrative bounties further lured Native Americans into the Union and Confederate armies. In New York, one observer concluded that Indians joined for many reasons. "About twenty-five [Onondoga] Indians have been induced by bounties, whisky, and martial music, all of which they are very fond, to enlist on some of the many regiments of volunteers" (Kneeland 1864, 453). Some of the Onondogas served as guides and river pilots, leading Union troops to their desired destinations and tracking Confederate movements. Some Catawbas also may have been threatened into enlisting—with one soldiers later stating that a white neighbor declared that he "would have to enlist or the white would come down and kill them" (Hauptman 1995a, 93).

The Five "Civilized" Tribes

The experiences of the Five Civilized Tribes epitomized the divisiveness and disruptions of the war. Located in Indian Territory (present-day Oklahoma), these tribes were among the most active participants in the Civil War. As slaveholding and market-oriented communities, these five nations all struggled to maintain their cohesiveness when the war began. As Cherokee leader Thomas Pegg explained, "Our wisest men knew not what to do" (McLoughlin 1993, 201). Indecision, however, did not last long and many chiefs advocated forging formal allegiances with the Confederacy. At the same time, however, many Native Americans expressed concerns about the dangers of entering the conflict. Cherokee chief John Ross said, "We do not wish our homes to become battlegrounds between the states and our soil to be rendered desolate and miserable by the horrors of civil war" (Confer 2007, 42). As support for the Confederacy in Indian Territory became stronger, thousands of Native Americans fled from their homes and their Confederate opposition took notice.

In November 1861, Confederate soldiers marched to the Deep Fork River in the Creek Nation, where Opothleyoholo had created a haven of neutrality for about 8,000 Native American men, women, and children as well as for hundreds of Indian-owned African slaves. Opothleyoholo, an elderly leader who fought in a devastating civil war among the Creek Indians decades earlier, personally experienced the tragedies of war and optimistically hoped Native Americans could avoid the horrors of another war. Loyalty to the Union, he optimistically decided, would ensure that various treaties would remain intact with the United States and that Union soldiers would continue to protect their communities from squatters and other intruders. Opothleyoholo's call for neutrality, however, quickly became the minority position in Indian Territory. Native Americans, who frequently worried that the Republican Party's free soil ideology would lead to the further opening of the west, increasingly cast their lot with their slaveholding chiefs and the Confederate cause. Their fears were exacerbated by party leaders like William H. Seward, who announced in 1860 that the lands "south of Kansas must be vacated by the Indian" (Bailey 2006, 32). Within a few months, even John Ross, the Cherokees' elder statesmen, deviated from his early neutrality and supported the Confederacy. Much of Indian Territory, in essence, became part of the Confederacy.

Opothleyoholo, however, did not stand alone in his opposition to the war and the Indian alliance with the Confederacy. With the support of thousands of like-minded Native Americans, he maintained his stance and appealed to President Abraham Lincoln to continue the federal protection of Indian lands. "Keep off the intruder," he demanded of the new president, "and make our homes again happy as they used to be" (Warde 1999, 59). Lincoln could hardly give Opothleyoholo and his followers his full attention, and Confederate Indians used and threatened armed force to forge a united Indian front. Rather than acquiesce, Opothleyoholo and thousands of other Indians took flight to Kansas. His multitribal group of exiles came from across Indian Territory and included Caddos, Creeks, Seminoles, Cherokees, Osages, Wichitas, Quapaws, and various African Americans. His defiance was hardly seen as an act of neutrality, and he was quickly branded a traitor and Unionist. As Creek Confederate David McIntosh noted, "It is now *certain* that he has combined with his party all the surrounding wild tribes and has openly declared himself the enemy of the South. Negroes are fleeing to him from all quarters" (McLoughlin 1993, 192). In the ensuing battles at Round Mountain and Chusto Talasah, Opothleyoholo and his allied Native Americans soldiers repelled the Confederate Indian Calvary. Confederate reinforcement came in December, encircled the camp, and captured most of the supplies, livestock, and wagons of the refugees. Opothleyoholo's refugees scattered and many of the survivors regrouped in Kansas. With a stance of neutrality no longer desirable or possible, they reformed as the 1st and 2nd Indian Union Brigades and marched back for retribution against their Confederate enemies.

As much as Native Americans suffered from engagements with Union and Confederate soldiers, the intertribal warfare may have been more devastating. For example, Stand Watie, a Confederate Cherokee, obtained a reputation for waging a hard and brutal war against his Indian enemies. As Agent Justin Harlin explained, "In the rebel Indian raids, everything which could be found, and which could be eaten by an Indian—every article of clothing that could be worn by men, women and children, and every article of bedding and blankets—was eagerly seized upon and carried away by them." Farming almost ceased in the nation, and most Unionists fled their homes. He continued, "From being the once proud, intelligent, and wealthy tribe of Indian, the Cherokees are now stripped of nearly all. . . . This is a sad picture, not overdrawn, and which no good man can see and not feel real sorry for their condition" (McLoughlin 1993, 211). Even Watie's wife recognized the tremendous damage that Watie's raids caused to the tribe. "This war—it will ruin a great many good people," she feared. "They will not only lose all their property but a great many will lose their character, which is [of] more value than all their property. . . . I am almost ashamed of my tribe" (McLoughlin 1993, 215). In many ways,

Stand Watie (1806–1871)

Stand Watie was born to a prominent and affluent Cherokee family in the village of Oothcaloga in what would later become part of Georgia. His life epitomized how decisions and tensions in the east continued to shape Native American society after removal and decades later during the Civil War.

Many of Watie's kin had embraced recent innovations to Cherokee society, and they became active participants in the modern centralized Cherokee government. Brother Elias Boudinot, for example, founded the first Native Americans newspaper, the *Cherokee Phoenix*, and uncle Major Ridge was one the most powerful chiefs in the Cherokee Nation.

Watie would rise to prominence in the era of removal, serving as the clerk of the Cherokee Supreme Court and Speaker of the Cherokee National Council. He was one of the signers of the controversial Treaty of New

Cherokee Stand Watie helped form the First Regiment of Cherokee Mounted Volunteers for the Confederacy. He was the last Confederate general to surrender. (*National Archives*)

General William T. Sherman and other practitioners of hard war may have learned this strategy from watching affairs in the west.

When the war ended, Opothleyoholo and other Unionist Indians were hardly rewarded for their loyalty. Although the federal government discussed granting them just compensation for their service and reimbursement for the damage done to their property on account of their loyalty, the Unionist Indians were sorely disappointed. Despite frequent rhetoric to the contrary, Native American soldiers received less than their white counterparts and Native American families did not receive reparations for their destroyed property. As in the past, divisions within Native American communities were ignored and residents of Indian Territory were uniformly punished as conquered enemies. The United States took retribution through a series of postwar treaties that paid little attention to the variety of experiences and loyalties within Native North America. Several tribes were compelled to sell their lands far below their value, while other tribes had their lands reallocated for reservations designated for other culturally diverse Indian nations. In addition to its disastrous diplomatic effects, the Civil War also brought high mortality rates and widespread physical destruction to many Native American communities. These social costs of the war would shape Indian society for decades to follow. As a result, Native Americans were among the biggest losers of the Civil War.

Echota (1835), the land cession that directly led to the forced removal of the Cherokees out of the southeast. Many of the other signers of the treaty were close relations of Watie.

The tensions within Cherokee society that emerged during removal continued in Indian Territory (modern-day Oklahoma). His uncle (Major Ridge), cousin (John Ridge), and brother (Elias Boudinot) formed a political faction in the decade that followed the Treaty of New Echota, and Watie emerged as a leader of this political alliance. In the following years, Cherokee politics could in many ways be seen as a competition between the Watie and the Ross factions.

These divisions within Cherokee society continued through the Civil War. When the war began, Chief Ross allied the Cherokees with the Confederacy. Watie, himself a prominent slaveholder, raised a cavalry regiment in the cause. He became colonel of the First Cherokee Mounted Rifles in October 1861, engaged in many small battles and skirmishes, and helped with the Confederate retreat at the Battle of Pea Ridge in March 1862. The united front of Cherokees gradually eroded and Ross would later lead a Unionist faction of Cherokees to Kansas. His performance resulted in his promotion to brigadier general.

Watie would not surrender to Union forces until June 1865, making him the last Confederate general to surrender.

The war caused more than political and physical destruction; it also reshaped cultural institutions within their communities. The Presbyterian Church among the Seminoles in the Indian Territory saw its influence wane in the early part of the war, especially as it was associated with abolitionism in a nation that largely sided with the Confederacy. As Unionists fled to Kansas, the Baptist Church and its less-defined stance on slavery became the prominent form of Seminole Christianity. Other Native American groups experienced renewals in more traditional forms of religion, with the use of sweat baths, black drink, and various war dances. Among the Delawares, for example, many Baptists returned to the ceremonial cycle of the Big House religion. As one leader proclaimed, "We wish to live together as a Nation according to our former customs" (Hauptman 1995a, 31).

The Tribes of the Southeast

Native Americans who lived in the Confederate states faced a series of disruptions and threats during the Civil War. On the eve of secession, approximately 25,000 Indians lived in the 11 Confederate states. With its population drastically reduced by generations of disease and warfare and a policy of forced removal, the Indians who remained in the southeast lived in a rather precarious position. They were, not surprisingly, also split into Unionist and Confederate camps. Part of the issue resulted from various forms of intermixture and alliances with Maroons and free black people. Those whose fates were closely linked with the concerns of free blacks typically risked either formal support for the Union or waged an informal war of resistance to Confederate interests.

Most Indians in the South did not have the luxury of choosing whether they would be a part of the war. Instead, they became involved when soldiers marched through their territory and their homes became battlefields. The Pamunkey Indians in Virginia, for example, suffered at the hands of both Union and Confederate troops whose supply lines cut across their reservation. As their lives and livelihoods were disrupted by the confiscation of valuables, the Pamunkeys were also forced into becoming active participants in the war. Local Confederate recruiters and officers who passed through their territory tried to impress as manual laborers many Pamunkeys, who they conflated with all "people of color" in the region. These threats convinced many Indians in Virginia to become refugees. Many found temporary homes in the Union states of Maryland and Delaware. Others went even farther, where they found permanent homes among the Great Lakes Indians.

The Choctaws of Mississippi had a similar experience. For much of the war, for example, the relatively small Choctaw tribe in Mississippi went largely ignored. For a while, their peculiar social standing as free people of color and social isolation allowed them to escape conscription and direct confrontation with invading Union soldiers. Even then, however, the Choctaws faced challenges that were created by the war. Most important, they suffered from a shortage of trade goods and basic supplies, and they struggled as the federal government failed to issue the bond payments that were due to them on account of earlier treaties. As demands for manpower increased, they cast their lot with the Confederates and formed the First Battalion of Choctaw Indians. Formed in early 1863, the unit saw limited action. A few soldiers were killed and others captured. Most of their action was local, in Louisiana and Mississippi. They also gained notoriety when they served as search and rescue workers when a Confederate troop train derailed into the Chunky River in Mississippi. They rescued 23 people and retrieved about 90 bodies.

The eastern band of Cherokees, who inhabited the mountains of western North Carolina and eastern Tennessee, were some of the most ardent Native American supporters of the Confederacy east of the Mississippi. Like other tribes, the eastern Cherokee were divided by the war, but only 30 joined the Union Army. In comparison, more than 400 eastern Cherokees enlisted in the Confederate Army where one Confederate colonel concluded they did "good work and service to the South" (Mooney 1900, 170). The eastern Cherokees also served as home guards, helping suppress Unionist activities in the region. Cherokees who did not support the Confederacy fell out of favor with their community, even getting blamed for the onset of smallpox and other problems that plagued the community in later years. According to anthropologist James Mooney, "their tribesmen [were] so bitterly incensed against them that for some times their lives were in danger" (Mooney 1900, 171). The Cherokees also worked to limit Unionist or antiwar sentiment in eastern Tennessee.

The eastern Cherokees, like many Native Americans, fought the Civil War according to the culture and traditions that guided their behavior. They performed war dances before marching off to battle, wore traditional paints and feathers during some battles, and participated in highly ritualized ball games while deployed. Their taking of scalps as war trophies incensed Union soldiers, who utilized these acts of "barbarity" to rally support for the war in the North. On several occasions, Northerners condemned Confederate soldiers who "butchered [Unionists] in cold blood . . . , hunted them with Indians, and permitted scalping" (*The Friend, a Religious and Literary Journal* 1863, 282E).

A Race War

As the Civil War threatened the region's racial hierarchy, Native Americans in the American South frequently became the victims of race-based violence and of the general chaos that characterized the region. Most notably, the Lumbee Indians in Robeson County, North Carolina, fought a long guerilla war with white supremacists in the area. Without a reservation land of their own and surrounded by a general population that denied their Indian identities and treated them as free blacks, the Lumbees and other North Carolina Indians faced constant threats to their lives and livelihoods from their white neighbors. The need for labor in Southern society added to the Lumbees' general lack of security, especially as Confederates conscripted local Indians to build a network of earthen works and forts around Wilmington.

The Lumbees did not passively watch the war destroy their sense of security. Many Native Americans found refuge in local swamps. There, they united with a motley group of African Americans, poor whites, and Union soldiers who escaped from Confederate prisons. Henry Berry Lowry, who became a folk hero among the Lumbees, led these men to wage a retaliatory war against the Confederacy. His men raided neighboring areas, stealing food and supplies from their prominent and more affluent neighbors. Lowry's Gang became local heroes, especially as they obtained a reputation for sharing the spoils of their raids with others who needed it and targeting those with surplus supplies. Lowry was captured on several occasions, but always found a way to escape. North Carolina's Home Guard took matters into its own hands and raided the home of Lowry's father in early 1865. They stole whatever they could from the house, and then arrested him, his wife, and several other family members and friends. When Lowry's father and uncle tried to escape, a 12-man firing squad executed them. The home guard also captured other Indians suspected of aiding the Unionist cause and causing unrest in the area. Lowry and the Lumbees continued to cause havoc until the end of the war. When William Tecumseh Sherman's Union troops arrived in the area in early 1865, local Indians guided them and their heavy artillery through the swamps.

As was too often the case, North Carolina Indians were hardly compensated for their assistance. Instead, they discovered that Sherman's bummers often took the Indians' mules, horses, and supplies for their own use (Oakley 2005, 19–21).

New England

In New England, matters were even more individualized and complex. There, Native American communities were believed to have disappeared, but instead they had eluded detection by outsiders and had intermixed with Africans on the margins of society. Often poor members of fishing and whaling communities, the Indians of New England suffered from the economic turmoil of the war. As shipbuilding turned to the needs of the Union Navy and private owners sold their boats to the navy, the seafaring community suffered. Without sufficient land to provide a self-sufficient existence, New England's Native Americans suffered. As a result, many desperate Native Americans were lured into the army to receive enlistment bounties and wages.

Without widely recognized tribes or nations, these Indians participated in the war in ways that were comparable to their African American neighbors. Native Americans in New England, for example, enlisted as individuals and usually in colored regiments. As a result, their presence in the war effort has often been overlooked. In 1863 and 1864, for example, several Mohegans and Mashpees enlisted in Connecticut's two colored Union regiments. Several Pequot soldiers also enlisted in segregated Union regiments. As in the South, the racial ambiguity of the Indians complicated the participation of Indians in the North. They received "colored" wages that were typically half of what white soldiers received, and they often were relegated to manual labor. They guarded important wagon trains and railroads, built trenches, and otherwise performed support tasks behind the front lines. As time passed, however, Native Americans saw extensive action on the front lines of the war, as the role of colored units expanded.

The Far West

The Civil War hardly provided a respite from the recurrent warfare that had plagued the Southwest and Plains in the 1850s. Instead, the Indian wars of the antebellum era continued "while public attention has been completely absorbed with the Rebellion" ("The Sioux War" 1863, 695). There, the formal and informal wars waged by the United States and its citizens on Native Americans had little to do with the central issues that elsewhere defined the era of the Civil War. Instead, recurring acts of reciprocal violence resulted as American ranchers, miners, and settlers intruded on Native American territory. The onslaught of new settlers to California and the west in 1849, after the discovery of gold, brought untold disruptions to Native American societies who suffered as western settlers looted their way through their lands and coerced others into providing labor or supplies. In 1866, the Apache leader Cochise remarked that

A large number of Navajo Indians were imprisoned at Fort Sumner in New Mexico from 1863 until 1868. (*Courtesy Palace of the Governors Photo Archives, NMHM/DCA, 038194*)

> When I was young I walked all over this country, east and west, and saw no other people than the Apaches. After many summers I walked again and found another race of people had come to take it. How is it? Why is it that the Apaches wait to die—that they carry their lives on their finger nails? (Calloway 2008, 311)

Although most Americans were preoccupied by events to the east, several of the worst massacres took place in the west. In 1863, California Volunteers used the pretext of the war and depredations committed against recent settlers to attack a Shoshoni-Bannock village in Idaho. They killed about 200 men, women, and children. In 1864, the Cheyennes discovered that the war would not ease the pressure they felt from the onslaught of settlers who coveted the gold on their lands. While under the protection of the U.S. government, Colonel J. M. Chivington and the 3rd Colorado Calvary attacked a camp at Sand Creek. Black Kettle raised white and American flags, but they were to no avail. More than 270 Indians were killed, many of them "mutilated in the most horrible way" (Calloway 2008, 303). Chivington's actions were widely condemned, but the damage was done. The Sand Creek Massacre, as it became known, devastated the Cheyenne, who saw one-fifth of their council and many of their most vocal spokesmen for accommodation killed. The Navajo similarly suffered during the war. In 1864, responding to retaliatory raids between the Navajos and recent settlers in New Mexico, Christopher (Kit) Carson, his California Volunteers, and some Ute allies burned villages and orchards, killed livestock, and otherwise ravaged their communities. The Navajos then suffered the "Long Walk"—a brutal journal to the Bosque Redondo reservation in the southeastern part of New Mexico.

The Dakota Uprising

During the American Civil War, Native Americans also dealt with long-standing frustrations with the United States. This was abundantly clear in the 1862 Dakota Uprising. Big Eagle, a Dakota warrior who later converted to Christianity, recalled that there were many causes of the war. The struggle and anger over acculturation policies epitomized much of the problems. "Then the whites were always trying to make the Indians give up their life and live like white men—and the Indians did not know how to do that, and did not want to anyway." Their anger, he explained, was natural.

> If the Indians had tried to make the whites live like them, the whites would have resisted. . . . The Indians wanted to live as they did before the treaty of Traverse de Sioux—go where they pleased and when they pleased, hunt game wherever they could find it, sell their furs to the traders and live as they could. (Nichols 2003, 23)

Indeed the Dakota uprising had many causes. In addition to anger over mistreatment by government officials, a general failure to live up to treaty agreements helped lead the Dakotas to reservations in Minnesota. The Dakotas never received adequate schools, and the food and supplies they should have received as allotments were frequently sold in stores at inflated prices. A poor 1861 harvest and harsh winter ensured that hunger was a reality for many Dakotas—they lived on roots. Matters worsened with the indifference of the Indian agents and traders, one of whom stated that if the Indians were "hungry let them eat grass or their own dung" (Nichols 2003, 134). Indifferent Indian agents and acculturation programs that divided Native Americans further magnified the internal tensions within Dakota society. In July 1862, even as the Dakotas hoped for a better forthcoming harvest, they decided that the time was ripe to retain their ancestral lands and otherwise restore their sovereignty. The Dakotas may have been further emboldened by the relative lack of white men in the region, as they were fighting the war in the east.

In August 1862, the Dakotas attacked the Redwood Indian Agency and the surrounding white settlements. Much of the fighting was particularly brutal, as towns were largely burned, several hundred settlers were killed, an unknown number of women were raped, and a few hundred whites were taken captive. The actions of the Dakotas were widely condemned in the United States and calls for vengeance were common. An article in *Harper's Weekly*, for example, declared that "It will be long before the frontiers of Minnesota will recover from this tragedy, and many of the sufferers will seek justice with their ready rifles, and will range the vast plains west to the Missouri until they have hunted every Indian into the mountains" ("The Indian Murderers in Minnesota" 1862, 807).

When the bloody uprising was finally put down, a hasty trial condemned 303 to death. Lincoln ordered the execution of 39 participants, singling out those who were known to be murderers or rapists. An accused

Dakota warrior received a reprieve from the sentence, but 38 hanged together for their actions. The rest remained captive for four years, during which time about one-third of them died. As a nation, the Dakotas also suffered for the rebellion—their reservation was abolished, their treaties declared null and void, and they were confined to an internment camp at Pike Island near Fort Snelling in Minnesota. The United States offered a $25 bounty for the scalp of any Dakota Indian found in the state and out of the camp. In May 1863 the survivors were removed from the disease-stricken camp and shipped to Crow Creek in the Dakota Territory and then in 1866 moved again to the Santee Reservation in Nebraska.

The Western Delaware

The western territories also included Indians who were long-standing residents as well as recent migrants. Most of these newcomers were forced there by government policies and were still adjusting to their new homes when the Civil War began. For these Native Americans, the war ironically provided opportunities to secure a semblance of stability. The Delaware Indians in Kansas and the Indian Territory saw supporting the Union as the means to their survival as a people. At the beginning of the war, several chiefs sent

> their Grandchildren of other Nations their friendship, and ask of them not to quarrel and shed blood about the condition of the country. Let none of the Tribes war against the Union. . . . If there should be any division in any Nation, and any part of a Tribe attempt to assail and war against the others because they are for the preservation of the Union. ("The Missouri Imbroglio" 1861, 671)

They pledged "to lead the whole power of the Nation to aid and protect such Tribes as may be invaded." Their pledge was not merely an offer to support potential allies, but also a warning to "our Creek Friends, and to all other Nations, that we will stand and die by the Great Father" ("The Missouri Imbroglio" 1861, 671).

The Delaware Indians lived up to their rhetoric as loyal Unionists. Delaware men served as scouts and home guards, protecting the area from incursions by other Indians and Confederate sympathizers. Enlistment rates for the Delawares were remarkable, with 170 of the eligible 210 men volunteering for service by 1862. The Delaware Indians did more than volunteer. Black Beaver, for example, used his decades of experience as a guide and a scout when the war broke out. Black Beaver helped with diplomatic negotiations with various Indian tribes and helped on the battlefield. He provided advance scouting of Confederate troops and led a dangerous expedition to Kansas, in which several hundred Union troops and their Confederate prisoners traveled 500 miles unscathed through dangerous terrain. Black Beaver received the ire of Confederates who razed his ranch at the Wichita Agency, causing an estimated $5,000 in damage.

The interest of the Delaware Indians in the war, however, was entirely local. Supporting the Union, they believed, allowed them to achieve "the interests of his own tribe" (Hauptman 1995a, 23). As elsewhere, the Delawares' strategy did not work out as planned. Just as Black Beaver's efforts to get compensation for his losses from the federal government failed, the Delawares hardly survived the war unscathed. Land speculators, railroadmen, squatters, and non-Delaware Indians who were fleeing Indian Territory all overran the Delawares' tribal lands. Disease killed many of those who survived exposure to the elements and endured the lack of food and other supplies. Confederate troops also created widespread damage and chaos, as William Quantrill and his raiders ransacked Indian and other towns, destroying property, stealing horses, and killing civilians. As one Indian agent explained, "the Delawares are affected by the unsettled condition of the country. Many of them are in the army. Their families are consequently left without male assistance. The large children are withdrawn to labor at home" (Hauptman 1995a, 36). According to their claim for compensation from the federal government, white raiders caused $17,588.25 in damage.

The Costs of War

The human costs of the war devastated many Native American communities. During the war, for example, the Cherokees' western population declined from about 21,000 to 13,566. An estimated 1,500 Creeks lost their lives during the war. Mortality rates only tell part of the story. The physical upheaval of the war also left many communities divided and geographically dispersed. At the end of the war, for example, there were about 2,000 Native American refugees in Kansas and another 7,000 at Fort Gibson in Indian Territory. During the war, the U.S. government estimated that there were almost 14,000 Indian refugees. They included an estimated 2,906 Cherokees at Tishomingo, 574 Seminoles near Fort Washita, and about 5,200 Choctaws and Chickasaws who were scattered in Indian Territory. One-quarter of the nation's Indian children were technically orphans. Rebuilding Native American communities, like other communities elsewhere in the war-torn nation, also proved difficult, especially as the Indian Territory was virtually overrun by deserters near the end of the war. Gangs of lawless soldiers—from the Union and Confederate armies and from Indian and non-Indian backgrounds—indiscriminately looted, burning homes, barns, and stores and stealing cattle and other assets. The property of many Native Americans was destroyed or looted, there was little in the way of wartime harvests, and approximately 300,000 head of cattle were killed or stolen from their Native American owners. One Creek Indian commented that their land was all they had left "and that was because, of all Creek property, only the land was immovable" (Bailey 2006, 45).

The Costs of Victory and Defeat

At the end of the war, many Native Americans pleaded for a return to normality. In early 1866, John Cupco, principal chief of the Unionist

Seminoles, wrote that "we asked [our] Southern brethren to return to homes and live again in peace and we wished some laws to govern us as before the war" (Micco 2006, 132). These pleas went largely unheeded as the United States treated the Indian nations in Indian Territory—regardless of their internal divisions—as conquered enemies. Tensions within the Native American communities, those that predated the war and those that were caused by it, also remained.

As the war progressed and ended, Indians increasingly felt the long arm of the American government and its policies. Central to this was emancipation and Reconstruction. Socially and culturally, emancipation provided one of the most notable changes in Native American society, especially among the southeastern tribes. Through a series of treaties between the United States and the Five Civilized Tribes in 1865 and 1866, for example, African slaves were emancipated and obtained citizenship in their respective tribes. Despite these gains, African Americans in Indian Territory received many of the same mixed messages that were communicated elsewhere. Although Reconstruction would take a different form in Indian Territory, slaves in Indian communities frequently complained that they enjoyed "few, if any of the benefits of freedom." Instead, they were in a "helpless condition" and suffering "many ills and outrages, even to the loss of many a life" (Krauthamer 2006, 112).

Diplomatically, the Civil War also resulted in a new landscape for Native American peoples. Even Unionists could hardly enjoy the fruits of victory. The United States punished tribes—even if they were divided during the war—for rebellious behavior. The Seminole Nation, for example, was required to sell its reservation at $0.15 an acre and buy new land from the Creeks at $0.50 an acre. Other tribes were compelled to cede half their territory in the Indian Territory. This land would become reservations for the Arapahos, Caddos, Cheyennes, Commanches, Iowas, Kaws, Kickapoos, Pawnees, Potawatomis, Sauk and Foxes, and Shawnees. Adding insult to injury, the United States also saw to it that the postwar treaties would ensure that Indian nations would allow railroads and western settlers to cut across their lands.

Conclusion

The American Civil War had disastrous results for most Native Americans. Just as secession divided the United States, the war tore Indian nations apart. As much as Indian tribes attempted to use the Civil War to pursue their own ambitions, few tribes achieved their diplomatic ambitions. Instead, the war exacerbated internal divisions in most Indian communities, physically destroyed their homes, fields, and herds, and limited the ability of most Indians to control their own borders and communities. Slaveholding Indians saw their property rights ignored, while enslaved black Indians often discovered that their freedom would not be protected. The United States forced many recognized tribes—whether Unionist or

Confederate allies—to cede lands and authority in the postwar world. Individual Indian soldiers, who suffered heavy mortality rates and served at many important battles, similarly saw themselves treated as marginal players and second-class soldiers. Perhaps most important, the tensions over land, power, and culture that predated the war continued in the postbellum era as the United States turned its military and unified attention to conquering the Indians of the West.

References and Further Reading

Abel, Annie Heloise. 1915/1992a. *The American Indian as Slaveholder and Secessionist*. Lincoln: University of Nebraska.

Abel, Annie Heloise. 1919/1992b. *The American Indian in the Civil War, 1862–1865*. Lincoln: University of Nebraska.

Anderson, Gary Clayton, and Alan R. Woolworth. 1988. *Through Dakota Eyes: Narrative Accounts of the Minnesota Indian War of 1862*. St. Paul: Minnesota Historical Society Press.

Bailey, Anne J. 2006. *Invisible Southerners: Ethnicity in the Civil War*. Athens: University of Georgia Press.

"Battle of Sugar Creek or Pea Ridge." *Saturday Evening Post*, March 29, 1862, 7.

Calloway, Colin G. 2008. *First Peoples: A Documentary Survey of American Indian History*. 3rd ed. Boston: Bedford/St. Martins.

Confer, Clarissa W. 2007. *The Cherokee Nation in the Civil War*. Norman: University of Oklahoma Press.

Cunningham, Frank. 1998. *General Stand Watie's Confederate Indians*. Norman: University of Oklahoma Press.

"Domestic Intelligence." *Harper's Weekly*, September 30, 1865, 611.

The Friend, a Religious and Literary Journal, May 8, 1863, 282E.

Gibson, Arrell Morgan. 1985. "Native Americans and the Civil War." *American Indian Quarterly* 9: 385–410.

Hatch, Thom. 2003. *The Blue, the Gray, and the Red: Indian Campaigns of the Civil War*. Mechanicsburg, PA: Stackpole Books.

Hauptman, Laurence M. 1995a. *Between Two Fires: American Indians in the Civil War*. New York: Free Press.

Hauptman, Laurence M., ed. 1995b. *A Seneca Indian in the Union Army: The Civil War Letters of Sergeant Isaac Newton Parker, 1861–1865*. Shippensburg, PA: Burd Street Press.

"The Indian Murderers in Minnesota." *Harper's Weekly*, December 20, 1862, 807.

Johnston, Carolyn Ross. 2003. *Cherokee Women in Crisis: Trail of Tears, Civil War, and Allotment, 1838–1907*. Tuscaloosa: University of Alabama Press.

Kneeland, Jonathan. 1864. "Remarks on the Social and Sanitary Condition of the Onondoga Indians." *Ohio Medical and Surgical Journal* 16, no. 5: 453.

Krauthamer, Barbara. 2006. "In Their 'Native Country': Freedpeople's Understandings of Culture and Citizenship in the Choctaw and Chickasaw Nations." In *Crossing Waters, Crossing Worlds: The African Diaspora in Indian Country*, edited by Tiya Miles and Sharon P. Holland, 100–120. Durham, NC: Duke University Press.

McBride, Lela J. 2000. *Opothleyaholo and the Loyal Muskogee: Their Flight to Kansas in the Civil War*. Jefferson, NC: McFarland and Co.

McLoughlin, William Gerald. 1993. *After the Trail of Tears: The Cherokees' Struggle for Sovereignty, 1839–1880*. Chapel Hill: University of North Carolina.

Micco, Melinda. 2006. "'Blood and Money': The Case of Seminole Freedmen and Seminole Indians in Oklahoma." In *Crossing Waters, Crossing Worlds: The African Diaspora in Indian Country*, edited by Tiya Miles and Sharon P. Holland, 121–144. Durham, NC: Duke University Press.

"The Missouri Imbroglio." *The Independent*, October 10, 1861, 671.

Mooney, James. 1900. *Myths of the Cherokees*. In *Nineteenth Annual Report of the Bureau of American Ethnology 1897–98, Part I*. Washington, D.C.: Smithsonian Institution.

Nichols, David A. 1999. *Lincoln and the Indians: Civil War Policy and Politics*. Urbana: University of Illinois Press.

Nichols, Roger L. 2003. *American Indians in U.S. History*. Norman: University of Oklahoma Press.

Oakley, Christopher Arris. 2005. *Keeping the Circle: American Indian Identity in Eastern North Carolina, 1885–2004*. Lincoln: University of Nebraska Press.

Parker, Arthur C. 1919. *The Life of General Ely S. Parker: Last Grand Sachem of the Iroquois and General Grant's Military Secretary*. Buffalo, NY: Buffalo Historical Society.

"The Sioux War." *Harper's Weekly*, October 31, 1863, 695.

Warde, Mary Jane. 1999. *George Washington Grayson and the Creek Nation, 1843–1920*. Norman: University of Oklahoma Press.

White, Christine Schultz. 1996. *Now the Wolf Has Come: The Creek Nation in the Civil War*. College Station: Texas A&M University Press.

Becoming American: Catholics, Jews, and Mormons during the American Civil War

8

Sarah K. Nytroe

On March 4, 1865, following his second inauguration as president of the United States, Abraham Lincoln stood before a crowd of thousands who had gathered near the east side of the Capitol building to watch the ceremony, having braved morning rains and muddy streets to attend. Four years into the conflict that had torn the country apart, and just over a month before the surrender of the Confederate Army at Appomattox Court House, Lincoln used his second inaugural address to reflect upon the Civil War since it began in 1861. Although embroiled in a conflict that emphasized their differences, Lincoln pointed out that the two sections were similar in certain ways. Neither the North nor the South, Lincoln said, had anticipated the length or magnitude of the war. Moreover, the North and the South studied the same Bible, prayed to the same God, and implored Him in their struggle against the other. Lincoln considered further that in the continued appeals to God and religion throughout the war, neither the North nor the South could know what God intended.

> It may seem strange that any men should dare to ask a just God's assistance in wringing their bread from the sweat of other men's faces; but let us judge not, that we be not judged. The prayers of both could not be answered; that of neither has been answered fully. The Almighty has his own purposes. (White 2002, 18–19)

Pondering the Almighty's purposes, Lincoln suggested that slavery was an offense committed by the nation and that God may have intended the war to wipe away the sins of the nation. If that was the case, and God willed the conflict to continue, it was only right to carry on the fight and "bind up the nation's wounds" (White 2002, 18–19). Lincoln's references to the divine would have resonated not only with the thousands of civilians and soldiers who attended the inauguration, but also with the general population of the North and South. During the antebellum period, a majority of Northerners and Southerners possessed a worldview shaped by their religious beliefs. This belief was heightened by religious revivals, and it informed social and political movements and debates, including reform efforts of temperance and abolition, slavery, and the split between the Northern and Southern factions of the Methodist, Baptist, and Presbyterian Churches. The preoccupation with religion spilled over into the Civil War as Northerners and Southerners of all religious backgrounds appropriated religion to provide justification, explanation, and inspiration for the war. Religion pervaded the daily experiences of both the soldiers on the battlefield and in the daily life of civilians on the home front.

Protestant Christianity dominated the religious scene in the antebellum period, with Methodism as the largest religious denomination, followed by Baptist and Presbyterianism. The Methodist, Baptist, and Presbyterian Churches had large membership numbers and church leaders who shaped their religious denominations, respectively, but also influenced society culturally and politically. During the antebellum period, however, several religious minorities experienced increased denominational growth and presence on the American religious scene, albeit sometimes an unwelcome presence. For American Catholics, their minority status was primarily defined by their social and cultural differences from the Protestant majority. For Jews and Mormons their minority status was primarily defined by their limited numbers, although social and cultural differences heightened that status. From the 1830s through the 1850s, Catholics and Jews migrated to the United States in growing numbers, while the emergence of Mormonism offered another religious alternative to that of the Protestant establishment. In the decades preceding the Civil War, with smaller membership numbers and limited institutional presence, these religious minorities focused on establishing themselves both institutionally and religiously, while often facing prejudice and animosity from the religious majority. Perceived as outsiders and foreigners, Catholics, Jews, and Mormons all faced negative public perception and prejudice. The circumstances of the war provided Catholic, Jewish, and Mormon religious communities with the space to address their supposedly tenuous relationship with the nation by addressing issues of loyalty and to shore up their institutional presence in the United States by addressing the spiritual needs of their flock in the army and on the home front.

The Relationship between Politics and Religion

Politics and religion intersected frequently during the Civil War. Early in the war, Secretary of State William H. Seward approached Catholic Archbishop John Hughes and sought Hughes's assistance in advocating the Union cause in Europe. As the first archbishop of New York, a city that possessed the largest Catholic population in the United States, Hughes not only held a strong influence among the Catholics of the city and with the American Catholic hierarchy, but also had been keeping papal officials abreast of the growing conflict in the United States. Although Hughes, and most Catholics, did not support abolitionism, a movement he believed needed "a strait jacket and the humane protection of a lunatic asylum," he remained a stalwart supporter of the Union cause (Blied 1945, 32). He made sure the American flag was displayed from the city's cathedral and supported the draft. Hughes accepted Seward's request and set sail for Europe, making stops in France and in Rome in late 1861 and early 1862. In his discussions with ambassadors, as well as government and church officials in France, Hughes touched upon a variety of issues, including slavery, tariffs, and the blockade. His aim was political—bend European opinion in favor of the Union and gain assurance that the pope would not recognize the Confederacy diplomatically. When he finally arrived in Rome in May 1862, he spoke with papal officials and other clerics about the war. Hughes's diplomatic efforts in Europe, as a representative of the Catholic Church in the United States, were potentially beneficial for two parties. On the one hand, the federal government wanted to gain the support of foreign opinion, whether with of Great Britain, France, or the papacy, and to keep foreign opinion from favoring the Confederacy. On the other hand, Hughes believed that his selection by Seward paid a compliment to American Catholics and their ability to actively support the nation.

As illustrated by Hughes's advocacy of the Union during the war both at home and abroad, and the activity of American Catholics in the war, the Civil War served as a period of transition in the relationship between American Catholics and the nation. In the antebellum period, Irish and German Catholics migrated to the United States, primarily to the North, and did so in significant numbers, enough to cause anxiety on the part of the Protestant majority. The 1830s through the 1850s witnessed many instances of prejudice toward Catholicism and Catholics in the United States. This prejudice was primarily rhetorical, but it also could erupt into violence. Nativists questioned the ability of immigrants to integrate fully into American society and feared the dual allegiance of Catholics to both their country and the papacy. With the rise of the Republican Party and the election of Abraham Lincoln to the presidency in 1860, Irish Catholics, in particular, were wary of associating with a party that they saw as tainted with anti-Catholicism, abolitionism, and pro-Protestantism. The actions of Catholic soldiers, chaplains and religious women, and the hierarchy went far to displace apprehensions about the ability of Catholics to be both Catholic and American.

Catholicism and the War

As an institution, the Catholic Church in the United States did not provide a church position on the war. However, individual bishops, Catholic newspapers, and prominent laity in both the North and the South offered their opinions about the war and the proper role of Catholics and the Church in the war. Unlike such Protestant churches as the Methodists and Baptists, which split across sectional lines over the issue of slavery in the 1850s, the

Claude Paschal Maistre (1820–1875)

A Catholic priest residing in New Orleans during the war and an exception rather than the rule, Claude Paschal Maistre supported the abolition of slavery and equal rights for blacks, a position that gained him the confidence of free African Creoles and earned him the ire of his bishop. By alienating Southern social convention and his religious superior through his radical political and social positions, Maistre and his African Creole congregants were part of a conflict that meshed religion and politics.

Born in France and ordained in the late 1840s, Maistre was embroiled in religious controversy that brought him to Chicago, Illinois. Maistre's religious superiors charged him with blessing marriages and baptisms of non-Catholics, and blessing burials of suicides and Protestants for a fee. Maistre arrived in New Orleans in 1855, where he became the pastor of a developing parish that included free blacks, to whom he immediately began to minister. Although Maistre and his bishop, Archbishop Jean-Marie Odin, fell into disagreement over finances and church property, it was the priest's radical political position and cultivation of religious and social equality for

bishops and archbishops actively affirmed the unity of the Catholic Church, while simultaneously supporting differing political positions on the war. Some bishops sought to avoid political participation at all levels. Bishop Martin Spalding of Louisville, Kentucky, for example, chose not to vote. He wanted his parishioners, however, to form their own opinions, and he maintained a private correspondence regarding the war with his colleague, Archbishop John Purcell of Cincinnati, Ohio. Other bishops chose to use the pulpit and their position of religious authority in a more public manner. Several bishops chose to display the American flag from their cathedrals, including Hughes and Purcell, along with Bishops Michael Domenec (Pittsburgh, Pennsylvania), John Martin Henni (Milwaukee, Wisconsin), and James Wood (Philadelphia, Pennsylvania). Archbishop Francis Patrick Kenrick of St. Louis, Missouri, however, taking a pro-Southern stand, refused to display the American flag from his cathedral. Finally, like his counterpart Archbishop Hughes in New York City, Bishop Patrick Lynch of Charleston, South Carolina, traveled to Europe in 1864 at the request of Confederate officials to cultivate the support of European governments and the papacy. More often than not, the geographic residency of the Catholic hierarchy and their parishioners, like their Protestant counterparts, determined which side they supported during the war.

Catholic loyalty was most clearly addressed when Catholics enlisted in both the Union and Confederate armies. In Massachusetts, Irish regiments were formed, including the Ninth and Twenty-Eighth Massachusetts, and the First Missouri Confederate Brigade included a large number of Irish Catholics. Those Irish who enlisted in the Union Army articulated carefully that they fought in the war to uphold the constitution and the Union; they did not fight to end slavery. The ability to fight hard and well gained some Irish regiments a positive reputation, which often translated into eased blacks that led to the conflict between the two.

Odin, who accepted slavery as a part of Southern society, was upset by Maistre's interaction with free blacks and contraband slaves. Maistre provided contrabands with refuge in his church, refused to use separate registers for the sacraments administered to black and whites, and consistently condemned slavery and praised the Emancipation Proclamation in his sermons. As tensions mounted, Odin revoked Maistre's priestly faculties, placed his parish under suspension, and stated that no Catholics should partake in the sacraments administered by Maistre. In defiance, Maistre continued to serve the spiritual needs of free blacks. Making appeals to Rome, the stalemate between Odin and Maistre continued well after the war and after slavery had been abolished by the Louisiana state convention in 1864. In 1870, Maistre wrote a letter of apology for his disobedience and the subsequent scandal, but not for his radical political and social positions regarding equal rights for blacks. He died five years later in 1875.

anti-Catholic prejudice at home. When the objectives of the war shifted with the issuing of the Emancipation Proclamation in 1862, the passing of a conscription law in 1863, and the recruiting of African Americans into the Union Army, Irish Catholics grew disenchanted with the federal government. In July 1863, anger among Irish Catholics erupted in violent riots, specifically in New York City in the wake of the draft law, and prompted fears that violence would take place in other cities with large Irish populations. In New York City, Hughes invited rioters to his home and attempted to calm them down and deter them from further rioting. In Boston the attack of a policeman by two women prompted Catholic priests to patrol the parish neighborhoods to ensure that the laity stayed out of trouble.

The hierarchy was concerned about two particular issues when it came to Catholics who served in the armies: (1) their conduct on the battlefield and how that conduct reflected upon Catholics in general, and (2) their spiritual state while on the battlefield and living among Protestants. To tackle both of these issues, Catholic chaplains provided a much-needed moral and spiritual role. The number of Catholic chaplains was minimal, with only 40 priests serving in a Union Army that had 400 chaplains. The number of Catholic chaplains in the Confederate Army was even smaller. Military chaplaincy was a work in progress throughout the war for both the Union and Confederate armies. Although the Union Army continually clarified the role and status of chaplains over the course of the war, the Confederacy initially did not provide an official order to meet the religious needs of the troops. Irish regiments often had access to their own chaplains, but many Catholic soldiers had limited access to a Catholic priest. Moreover, the sparse distribution of priests in the North and South, in general, placed greater strains on the Church to meet the religious and spiritual needs on both the

Irish-American soldiers celebrate mass at Camp Cass, Virginia, in 1861. (*Library of Congress*)

home front and the battle front. Because a priest's primary duty lay with his parish, many chaplains served only briefly before being called back by their bishop.

Addressing the spiritual and moral needs of Catholic soldiers proved to be a challenge for chaplains because of the chaos and instability of military life. Accompanying soldiers who were always on the move, chaplains needed to improvise the tools they used to celebrate the Mass, often using whatever was at their disposal. In addition to the Catholic chaplain's role in the most important ceremony of the Catholic faith in the Mass, they heard confessions—in large numbers on the eve of battles—and administered last rites to soldiers in hospitals or on the battlefield. The presence of a chaplain also provided a moral center within a regiment to temper the rowdiness, drinking, and carousing that took place in the camps.

The chaplaincy service of Father John Bannon demonstrates the centrality and difficulty of being a chaplain during the war. Bannon, an Irish immigrant during the early 1850s and a parish priest in St. Louis, Missouri, served as the chaplain to the St. Louis militia before the war. When the war began, Bannon fully immersed himself in the duties of a chaplain with the 1st Missouri Confederate Brigade from 1861 to 1863. Interpreting the war through a religious lens, Bannon believed that Northern aggression threatened a religious way of life, and he supported Southern self-determination. Bannon continually offered his religious services, hearing confessions on the eve of battles, offering the Mass, and advancing with the army when they went into battle. Moreover, while serving with the brigade, Bannon earned a reputation as the "fighting chaplain" for aiding the artillery during dire situations in battle.

Many chaplains remained behind the lines during battles, opting to stay at a military hospitals. Recognizing that this latter option often contributed to negative images of chaplains, Bannon placed himself directly in the line of fire and danger to offer religious and moral support to his men from beginning to end. Bannon entered into a battle carrying only a crucifix and a Bible, and with only a red cloth cross on his arm to indicate his status as a chaplain. When downtime was available, Bannon continued to carry out his priestly functions, often tending to the religious needs of local civilian communities. This dedication became most apparent during the siege of Vicksburg, Mississippi, by the Union forces under Ulysses S. Grant during the spring and summer of 1863. Bannon worked with the city's parish priest to serve the 700 Catholics who lived there. In addition, he worked at the hospital full time and visited the breastworks where the troops were stationed on a daily basis. Bannon's wartime activities became political when he undertook a diplomatic mission for the Confederacy to the Vatican and traveled to Ireland to temper the exodus of Irish to the North and the Union Army. Although Bannon may have been the exception rather than the rule, his ardent support of the Confederacy and his devotion to his religious responsibilities illustrate the compelling presence of Catholics during the war.

Much like chaplains and the fighting ability of Catholic soldiers, the activities of Catholic Women's Religious Orders and the contact between these women and soldiers helped to break down anti-Catholic prejudice existing in both the North and the South. Women religious provided a necessary service during the war in their capacity as nurses. Antebellum anti-Catholic literature often focused on women religious, publishing stories of rampant sexuality or targeting them for their vows of celibacy. However, their ability to tackle the demanding tasks of providing medical care and administering hospitals on a daily basis, and the daily contact they had with doctors and soldiers altered opinions about these Catholic women. Nearly 3,200 women worked as nurses during the war, and more than 600 of those women were Catholic sisters from a variety of religious communities in both the North and the South. Upon entering a religious community, Catholic sisters took vows of poverty, chastity, and obedience, all of which made them desirable for the demanding and chaotic work of taking care of the wounded and dying and for helping to run the hospitals. Requests for their services came from several arenas, including government officials of the Union and the Confederacy, bishops, and doctors, and they often came without warning. These women demonstrated a willingness to go where their services were needed by not only working as nurses in hospitals, but also by tending to the wounded on the battlefield, visiting prison camps, and aiding the wounded on transport ships. Women religious from the Sisters of the Holy Cross of Notre Dame remained in the service of the transport ship, the *Red Rover*. In dangerous conditions and cramped quarters, these women ministered to the needs of nearly 2,400 patients on the transport ship that traveled back and forth on the Mississippi River between Memphis, Tennessee, and Mound City, Illinois, over the course of the war.

United institutionally, individual Catholic archbishops, bishops, and laypersons presented a diversity of viewpoints on the war and the proper role of Catholics in the war. Amid this diversity of opinion between Catholics of the North and the South, the patriotic and diplomatic work undertaken by the Catholic hierarchy, the taking up of arms by Irish and other Catholics, the spiritual and moral support offered by chaplains, and the tending to the wounded by Catholic sisters all altered the negative perceptions of and prejudice toward Catholics in the United States.

Judaism and the War

The Civil War also influenced the experiences of American Jews. A noted foot specialist and British immigrant, Isachar Zacharie settled in Washington, D.C., in 1862. Some of Washington's top federal authorities and politicians sought out Zacharie's medical expertise for treatment, including Abraham Lincoln. In the process of treating Lincoln, Zacharie became a close friend and confidant, and became the trusted recipient of important political and military information from Lincoln and other federal officials in the capital. In January 1863, the doctor traveled to New Orleans on an assignment to assess public opinion toward the commander of the Department of the Gulf, General Nathaniel P. Banks. As in the instances when he lent a learned and willing ear to federal officials during medical treatment, Zacharie did the same with residents in New Orleans as an intermediary between the military government and the civilian population. Shortly after the Battle of Gettysburg in July 1863, Lincoln enlisted Zacharie to explore peace talks with the Confederacy. As illustrated with the political experience of Zacharie, some Jews found themselves interacting with the highest officials of a government at war. At the same time, however, the experience of Jews during the war, both in the North and the South, was shaped by long-held stereotypes against Jews, the challenge of addressing questions of their loyalty, and access to equitable treatment before the law religiously and ethnically.

Approximately 150,000 Jews lived in the United States on the eve of the Civil War, with 25,000 of them residing in the South. The decade leading up to the war witnessed a significant jump in the Jewish population because of immigration, with Jewish communities in major Northern cities like New York, Philadelphia, Boston, Pittsburgh, and Detroit, and in Southern cities like Memphis, Nashville, Mobile, New Orleans, Richmond, and Charleston. New York City was home to 15 congregations alone, Louisiana was home to approximately 8,000 Jews, and New Orleans possessed the largest Jewish community in the South at the beginning of the war. The Jews immigrating to the United States in the 1850s were primarily Ashkenazi, from areas of Eastern and Central Europe, and they quickly outnumbered the Sephardic Jews who had immigrated in the early 19th century and who were descended from Spanish and Portuguese Jews. Sephardic Jews assimilated into American society much more readily than their Ashkenazi counterparts, through intermarriage and a tendency to drift away from the faith. Although these different national origins, periods of immigration, and approaches to Judaism had a profound effect on the experience of Jews within their own communities, the public of the North and South viewed Jews as a whole.

When the war started, Jews living in the North and South faced the challenge of breaking down the stereotype that foreigners were incapable

In September 1862, President Lincoln made Rabbi Jacob Frankel the first commissioned Jewish chaplain in the U.S. Army. (*The Jacob Rader Marcus Center of the American Jewish Archives*)

of demonstrating patriotism. In particular, the stereotype of the "wandering Jew" suggested that Jews were citizens of no country, were cowards, and were disloyal. Although accused in both the North and the South of avoiding military service and deemed untrustworthy, Jews enlisted in both armies. Moreover, Jewish companies were organized in Chicago, Illinois; Syracuse, New York; and in West Point and Macon, Georgia. As much as the organization of Jewish specific regiments could demonstrate Jewish patriotism, the limited number of these kinds of regiments pointed to a desire on the part of Jews to avoid segregating themselves. Many fought for some of the same reasons as did their Protestant and Catholic counterparts in the Union and Confederate armies—that is, for liberty and freedom, defense of home, and duty and obedience to the established government, which had been a strong influence in Jewish tradition.

As with Catholic soldiers, meeting the needs of Jewish soldiers on the battlefield proved to be a difficult task on the practical level. Often without the guidance of a rabbi or a Jewish religious leader on the battlefield, soldiers were left on their own to follow Jewish religious practices and observances. In the absence of a rabbi, soldiers sought each other out for

Judah P. Benjamin (1811–1884)

The first acknowledged Jew in the United States Senate, Judah P. Benjamin served in three cabinet positions—attorney general, secretary of war, and secretary of state—within the Confederate executive administration and became a confidant of Jefferson Davis during the war. Throughout his early legal career and his political career as a senator from Louisiana and in cabinet posts, Benjamin faced the challenge of being both a Jew and a public figure. Although not religiously observant, Benjamin became an easy target for anti-Semitism.

Born in the British West Indies and descending from Sephardic Jews, Benjamin settled with his family in Charleston, South Carolina, where a sizable Jewish community existed. At the age of 14, Benjamin started attending Yale University in New Haven, Connecticut, but left and settled in New Orleans, where he worked as a teacher and in a

Judah P. Benjamin, a Jewish senator from Louisiana, served as the Confederacy's attorney general, secretary of war, and secretary of state. (*National Archives*)

religious practice, while others attended Christian services because some kind of religious service was deemed to be better than none at all. When soldiers were camped near a city with a synagogue or Jewish community, they attended the local services, but while in the field, soldiers found it difficult to keep track of the dates during which they needed to observe the High Holidays and festivals. Other Jewish soldiers sought furloughs during High Holidays and festivals to attend religious services. In addition, soldiers found it difficult to gain access to the kosher foods, like unleavened bread, necessary for religious observances like Passover.

Meeting the spiritual needs of Jewish soldiers in the Union Army became a heated issue within the Northern Jewish community when the federal government did not recognize Jewish chaplains. As the military began mobilizing at the beginning of the war, the position of the chaplain was created to conduct religious services and meet the spiritual needs of soldiers. The first general order regarding the chaplaincy stated that a chaplain needed to come from a Christian denomination and be an ordained minister. The provisions of the order automatically denied Jewish soldiers equal access to leaders of their faith and the satisfaction of their spiritual needs on two levels. First, the phrasing excluded rabbis from obtaining a chaplaincy position in the army because it referred to mercantile house before beginning an apprenticeship with a notary connected to a local commercial law firm. After studying law, Benjamin was admitted to the bar, established a thriving law practice, and traveled in the major social and political circles of the city. A persuasive speaker and reputable commercial attorney, Benjamin was elected to the U.S. Senate in 1852. Although offered a position on the U.S. Supreme Court, Benjamin turned down the position to continue in the Senate.

While holding three cabinet positions in the executive administration of the Confederacy, Benjamin became a convenient target for anti-Semitic attacks. Criticized for his decisions while serving as secretary of war, Benjamin, along with Richmond, Virginia, Jews were targeted as the source of the Confederacy's military and economic troubles as the war progressed. Moreover, the Richmond

and Northern press consistently kept Benjamin's Jewishness at the forefront of their coverage of the politician. Having sent secret service spy rings into Canada, having contemplated and formulated a Confederate equivalent to the Emancipation Proclamation, and having been implicated in the conspiracy that assassinated Lincoln, Benjamin escaped the country at the conclusion of the war. Settling in England, Benjamin became a successful commercial lawyer in the 1870s. He died in 1884 while in Paris.

Christians only, and second, only a limited number of rabbis were officially ordained in the United States in the mid-19th century. It took the visit of a worker with the Young Men's Christian Association (YMCA) to a military camp in Virginia in September 1861 to spark a challenge to and a debate over the government's policy toward wartime chaplains.

Michael Allen, a member of a Pennsylvania regiment and the most educated Jew in the regiment, was the target of the YMCA worker's complaint to the army. Allen was not an officially ordained rabbi and, even though a large number of the men were Jews, his regiment was not specifically Jewish. Allen was forced to resign his position as chaplain. Subsequently, the commander of the regiment, Colonel Max Friedman, and his officers chose an officially ordained rabbi to be their chaplain. Arnold Fischel, who had not enlisted as a soldier, was selected from a synagogue in New York City. Secretary of War Simon Cameron, remaining within the law and the dictates of the general order on chaplains, rejected the application. The rejection, however, only served to agitate the Northern Jewish community, including religious leaders and the Jewish press, to pressure the federal government to change its policy on chaplains to afford Jewish soldiers equal access to their religious leaders while they served. The Jewish press circulated a parade of stories and editorials that examined the legal and ethical components of the issue, and many secular newspapers of major cities provided editorial support to the Jewish position. Meanwhile, petitions of appeal were lobbied before Congress and the president by the rejected chaplaincy applicant, Fischel, under the direction of the Board of Delegates of American Israelites. Less than a year after the incident in the camp in Virginia, Congress responded to Lincoln's changes to the chaplaincy laws. By July 1862, the language of the law was altered to include chaplains of some kind of denomination, not only Christian denominations.

Debate over the issue of wartime chaplains was not the only instance in which Jewish concerns regarding equal treatment before the law came to national attention. Although the issue of chaplaincy stemmed from the spiritual needs of soldiers on the battlefield, the second issue focusing on Jews as a class stemmed from the social and economic positions of Jewish civilians. Many Jews living in the North and South took up occupations in or ownership of small businesses and other economic enterprises like clerks, peddlers, merchants, or shopkeepers. In these positions, Jews were often stereotyped as thieves and people lacking in scruples. With the prolongation of the war and the downturn of the economy, Jews became easily targeted as the source of the sour economy and increasingly became the subject of anti-Semitism in both the Northern and Southern press. In the Northern press, Jews were labeled as subversive elements who supplied the South with the goods needed to fight a war. In the Southern press, where the economic troubles hit hardest, Jews were blamed for inflated prices and the shortage of goods. Once again, however, the issue of equality before the law came to the attention of the federal government with release of General Order Number 11 in December 1862.

By then, speculation and profiteering, particularly in cotton, was looked down upon by military commanders. Union military commanders Grant and William Tecumseh Sherman saw speculators who sold cotton for gold as dangerous to their military aims, especially if that gold could be used to purchase arms for the Confederate Army. In December, Grant issued General Order Number 11, stating that as a class Jews had violated the trade regulations set down by the Treasury Department and, therefore, were expelled from the Department of the Mississippi. They had 24 hours to obey the order.

Many Jews responded with anger and shock over the order, but also with an appeal to change the process of American law. Although Jews believed that individuals should definitely be tried for breaking the law, they did not feel that there was room within American law to assign communal responsibility for violating the law.

Cesar Kaskel, a Jew from Paducah, Kentucky, with friends who were subject to Grant's order, quickly traveled to Washington, D.C., to petition the administration for a recall of the order. As he was passing through Cincinnati, Ohio, Kaskel gained the assistance of Rabbi Isaac Wise, and the two were able to gather together petitions and protests to present to the president. The cooperation of Northern Jews with Kaskel in support of Southern Jews succeeded in gaining the repeal of the order. With no knowledge of Grant's action, Lincoln repealed General Order Number 11 in early January 1863.

The origins of the controversies over chaplaincy and the class status of Jews in American society, coupled with the agitation of the Jewish community and sometimes the larger public at a political level for equal treatment before the law, demonstrated the precarious position of Jews during the Civil War as a religious minority and as a community with long-established stereotypes. At the same time, however, the experience of Jews during the war as soldiers, civilians, and religious leaders illustrated their desire to undermine those stereotypes and to be seen not only as Jews but also as Americans.

Mormonism and the War

American Mormons faced stereotypes and prejudices despite their involvement in the war efforts. It was a momentous occasion one fall day in 1861, when the completed transcontinental telegraph lines linked the war-torn East with the developing Western territories. In the throes of war, the completion of the telegraph assumed added significance for a federal government that needed to maintain control over the lines of communication between the East and the West. With the transcontinental telegraph line passing through the territory of Utah and Salt Lake City, the first message sent East was penned by Brigham Young, the religious leader of the Mormon Church and de facto political leader of the territory. Young sent a brief, but politically important, message affirming the status of Utah in relation to the Union. In the years leading up to the war and during the war, Young and other Mormon leaders continually made questionable statements about the fate of the nation, which left federal authorities in Washington wary of Young and the Mormon population. The telegraphed message, however, stated, "Utah has not seceded but is firm for the constitution and laws of our once happy country" (Arrington 1985, 294). Utah citizens, who were overwhelmingly Mormon, and the territorial government, which was increasingly run by non-Mormons hostile to Mormonism, stood by this statement throughout the duration of the war. At the same time, however, Mormons were caught in a contentious relationship with the territorial government and the federal government, exacerbated by questions of loyalty, agitation for statehood, military presence in the territory, and polygamy. Although the issues that contributed to the tenuous relationship between the federal government and the Mormons had no direct bearing on the course of the war, the war provided the catalyst for reevaluating the status of Mormons and the Utah Territory to the nation.

On the fringes of both the American religious scene and the tensions between the North and South, Mormons and the Church of Jesus Christ of the Latter-day Saints attempted to exist quietly and independently of the rest of the nation since their overland trek from Illinois to Utah in the late 1840s. From the beginning of Mormonism under the guidance of Joseph Smith in the 1820s, Mormons faced considerable resistance and criticism from the American public. Anti-Mormonism exhibited itself in public policy, in literature attempting to expose the falsehood of the religion, and in violence. This increasing hostility prompted Mormons to migrate to the West, where they continued to experience opposition from the American public and the federal government. By 1860, more than 42,000 people lived in the Utah Territory. The increased presence of the United States in territories of the West, however, drew Mormons and Utah into the orbit of national political affairs. In addition, the country's negative perception of Mormons, particularly their practice of polygamy, caused further troubles for the Church during the war.

Keeping a close eye on the political developments taking place in the east, Young spoke for the Mormon community throughout the war and offered an opinion that simultaneously affirmed and undermined Mormon loyalty. In communicating a Mormon religious interpretation of the war, Young's early opinion did not lend itself to easing the mind of the federal government regarding Mormons' loyalty to the nation. The religious interpretation of the war—an interpretation that lost staying power as the war drew to a close—offered by Young fit within the larger Mormon belief in millennialism, which suggested that the return of Jesus to earth was imminent. Part of Jesus' return to earth included the destruction of the nation. The war itself, as interpreted by Young and other Mormon leaders, would serve as the means by which the political organization of the nation would be destroyed, and the Church of Jesus Christ of the Latter-day Saints would be the outlet for the rule of God on earth. In addition, Young and other Mormon leaders believed that the war was an act of revenge on the federal government and the American public for their rejection and hostility toward Mormons.

Prophetic statements made by Mormon founder Smith also pointed to the signs of things to come. Smith prophesied that war would come to the nation starting with a rebellion in South Carolina, and in 1843 he stated that "[t]he commencement of the difficulties which will cause much bloodshed previous to the coming of the Son of Man will be in South Carolina. It may probably arise through the slave question" (Holzapfel 1994, 94). The firing on Fort Sumter off the coast of Charleston, South Carolina, in April 1861 seemed to provide a solid confirmation of Smith's prophecy. Interpretations and opinions of the war offered by Young and Mormon leaders, and consistent criticism from Utah newspapers of the government over non-Mormon territorial administration, however, did not sit well with the federal government or the territorial officials in Utah. Although Young affirmed the territory's allegiance to the Union in the telegraphed message and Mormon support of the constitution as divinely inspired but imperfect, statements relating to the destruction of the nation threw into question the loyalty of Mormons and their wartime political positions. The greatest anti-Mormon agitation and question of loyalty within the confines of the Utah Territory was espoused by Colonel Patrick E. O'Connor, commander of the Third California Volunteers, who was sent to the Utah Territory to protect the overland mail routes and the telegraph lines.

O'Connor's anti-Mormonism, coupled with Mormon frustration with the territorial and military administration of the Utah Territory, contributed to a tense relationship between Mormons and O'Connor's troops, a tension that reached the brink of violent confrontation. When the war started, the federal government pulled out the military presence at Camp

A fort, later known as Camp Douglas, is in the foreground of this photograph of Salt Lake City, Utah. This Union outpost was largely outfitted by local volunteers, often members of the Church of Latter-day Saints. (*Library of Congress*)

Floyd near Salt Lake City in July 1861, much to the happiness of Young and the Mormon leaders. Federal authorities did not ask for troops from Utah and Utah did not volunteer regiments, although some individual Mormons chose to go East and fight. In the fall of 1862, however, after a militia was organized by Young at the request of Lincoln to temporarily protect the stage routes and telegraph lines, federal troops from California under the command of O'Connor were sent to Utah. O'Connor was not shy about expressing his opinions about the Mormons to his superiors in San Francisco, California. In an early report to his superiors, O'Connor argued that the Mormons could not be trusted and were traitors, and that they rejoiced in the knowledge that the war could destroy the government. He not only targeted the Mormons as a whole for their disloyalty, but he also railed against Young, whom he believed ruled as a despot. With the memory of the last time the federal government sent troops to Utah, which resulted in the Utah War in the late 1850s, Young and Mormon leaders were wary when O'Connor opted to locate his 750 soldiers at Camp Douglas on a bluff overlooking Salt Lake City, rather than at Camp Floyd. O'Connor's continued belief that Mormons were disloyal, which seemed to be affirmed when Young expressed animosity toward a loyalty oath demanded of those merchants selling goods to the military, and his suspicions that Mormons aided Indians in their raids, served only to create greater animosity between the two.

Watching with a concerned and worried eye back in Washington, the federal government witnessed a near eruption of violence between O'Connor's troops and the Mormons in the summer of 1863. O'Connor's policy toward the Mormons became enmeshed with the Mormon dislike of the political administration of the territory. Mormons faced the latest hostile territorial governor, Stephen S. Harding, who derided the local government, targeted Mormons for their disloyalty to the Union, and attempted to undermine the powers of the local courts. Believing that Mormons were planning an armed resistance against the military, O'Connor placed Captain Charles Hempstead in Salt Lake City as provost marshal, effectively placing military authority above that of territorial authority. O'Connor's activist policy toward the Mormons during this crisis was tempered by his superior in San Francisco, Major General Irvin McDowell, who reminded O'Connor that his orders were merely to protect the mail and telegraph routes. McDowell communicated to O'Connor that his actions in attempting to resolve the larger territorial disputes between the Mormons and the territorial officials would lead to war, weaken the strength of the troops, and leave Utah vulnerable to attacks by secessionists. Agitating Mormons to the point of violence ultimately would undermine the war effort. The Mormon delegate in Washington submitted petitions to the federal government seeking replacements for Harding and two territorial judges, who they claimed undermined the principles of republicanism and liberty, while O'Connor and his officers submitted counterpetitions seeking to retain the governor and the judges. Although orders came down from the secretary of war to O'Connor's superiors to provide him with reinforcements in Utah, the potentially violent situation was resolved when Lincoln removed Harding and two territorial judges from their positions and appointed a governor more suitable to the position.

Over the course of the war, Young and the Mormon community maintained an active presence in Washington, D.C., campaigning for statehood, while Congress worked to undermine the Mormon religious practice of polygamy, indicating a clash between religion and politics. In the wake of continued tensions with the territorial governments, Young and Mormon leaders started the process of seeking statehood for Utah. With a constitutional convention, the adoption of the State of Deseret, and the appointment of Young as governor of that state in early 1862, the state constitution was presented before the Congressional Committee on Territories in the summer. The petition for statehood sat unaddressed in the committee until December, when the committee ruled against it. With a refusal to approve the petition of statehood, however, the State of Deseret continued to exist during the course of the war functioning as a "ghost" government run by Mormons. At the same time that the Committee of Territories sat on the petition for Utah statehood, an antipolygamy bill presented by Vermont congressman Justin Morrill made its way through Congress and to the desk of the president. Unlike the petition for statehood, the bill was pushed through Congress quickly and Lincoln signed the legislation in July 1862. The bill stated that the practice of polygamy was a federal crime and could result in a fine or jail time. In addition, the congressional legislation sought to undermine the legislation of the territory that favored Mormons. The bill annulled territorial legislation from 1851 that gave the Church rights over the regulation of marriage, and prohibited religious or charitable organizations from holding property valued at more than $50,000 in any given territory. To Mormons the legislation indicated the continued prominence of anti-Mormonism not only in American society but also within the federal government and in its policies. An unstable territorial government and the presence of the "ghost" government in the form of the State of Deseret, however, did not provide an environment conducive for enforcing the legislation. Both Mormons and law-enforcement officials largely ignored the act.

Geographically distant from the war back East, the hostility within the Utah Territory between territorial officials, military commanders, and the Mormons, and fragile relations between Mormons and the federal government over statehood and polygamy prompted tenuous relations and potentially violent situations. Amid these tensions and disagreements, however, Mormons remained loyal to the Union.

Conclusion

Between 1861 and 1865, while the governments and people of the North and the South were entangled in a brutal war that threw into question the state of the nation and the issue of slavery, the prominence of religion and religious impulses influenced the populations of the North and South, and their relationship to and interpretation of the war. For American Catholics, Jews, and Mormons, the war provided the opportunity to demonstrate their loyalty and relationship to the nation. For the larger Protestant society and federal government, the war provided a ripe context to question the loyalty of these religious communities and manifest prejudices that contributed to tenuous relationships between church and state. The wartime experience of religious communities as institutions and as religious leaders and laity lent itself to repositioning these religious minorities in a more positive relationship with the American religious scene and society. Opposition and prejudice continued to be a prominent part of the experience of being a Catholic, Jew, or Mormon in the United States through the remainder of the 19th century and in some cases well into the 20th century. At the same time, however, the relationship between American Catholics, Jews, and Mormons and the nation became less tenuous because of their activities and positions during the war. By the turn of the 20th century, American Catholicism was the largest and fastest-growing religious denomination in the country. Jewish immigration continued into the postwar period, while Jewish communities faced a growing debate over orthodox versus reform religious practice. The end of the war, the growing number of migrants to the West, and increased mining in the region clearly indicated that the attempts by Mormons to live an independent and isolated existence could not be achieved, although Utah statehood finally came 40 years later in 1896. The institutional and individual experiences of Catholics, Jews, and Mormons during the war demonstrate that the relationship between loyalty to the nation and religious and political rights served as an underlying factor in their wartime activity and in the public perception of these religious minority communities.

References and Further Reading

Arrington, Leonard. 1985. *Brigham Young: American Moses*. New York: Alfred A. Knopf.

Blied, Benjamin J. 1945. *Catholics and the Civil War*. Milwaukee, WI: Bruce Publishing Company.

Carter, Kate B. 1956. *Utah during Civil War Years*. Salt Lake City: Daughters of Utah Pioneers, Central Co.

Heathcote, C. W. 1919. *The Lutheran Church in the Civil War*. New York: Fleming H. Revell Company.

Holzapfel, R. N. 1994. "The Civil War in Utah." In *Utah History Encyclopedia*, edited by A. K. Powell. Salt Lake City: University of Utah Press.

Jones, Kelsey. 2005. *Battlefields, Bibles, and Bandages: Portraying an American Civil War Nun*. Westminster, MD: Heritage Books.

McPherson, James M. 1997. *For Cause and Comrades: Why Men Fought in the Civil War*. New York: Oxford University Press.

Shattuck, Gardiner H. 1987. *A Shield and Hiding Place: The Religious Life of the Civil War Armies*. Macon, GA: Mercer University Press.

Simonhoff, Harry. 1963. *Jewish Participants in the Civil War*. New York: Arco.

White, Ronald C. Jr. 2002. *Lincoln's Greatest Speech: The Second Inaugural*. New York: Simon & Schuster.

Young, Mel. 1991. *Where They Lie: The Story of the Jewish Soldiers of the North and South Whose Deaths—[Killed, Mortally Wounded, or Died of Disease or Other Causes] Occurred during The Civil War, 1861–1865: Someone Should Say Kaddish*. Latham, MD: University Press of America.

The Urban Civil War | 9

Clinton Terry

The vast literature on the American Civil War pays scant attention to the lives of the nation's urban dwellers. With the exception of a small number of important incidents, such as the occupation of New Orleans, the Richmond bread riots, or the New York City draft riots, students of the Civil War can read volumes without encountering any significant mention of the effect of the war on urban life. Civil War historians have tended to focus on the military conflict of American against American and no battle between the Union and the Confederacy took place in any of the nation's major cities. Even siege activity, such as that experienced by Vicksburg, Mississippi, and Petersburg, Virginia, was the exception rather than the rule. On those occasions when the Union Army occupied a Confederate city, such as New Orleans, occupation came as the result of military activity outside the city, not fighting within the city itself. No Northern city of any size suffered occupation by the Confederacy, although President Abraham Lincoln always kept a substantial part of the Army of the Potomac between Washington, D.C., and the Confederate Army of Northern Virginia. Conflict in Missouri early in the war threatened St. Louis for a time, and the Confederate advance of September 1862 briefly threatened the cities of Cincinnati, Ohio, and Louisville, Kentucky, although the actual threat to those cities seemed more real at the time than in retrospect. A small body of work is devoted to individual cities. Historians have studied cities like New York, Chicago, Philadelphia, Boston, and Cincinnati, but no single volume addresses the war's general effect on the nation's cities. Most of the literature that considers the home front encompasses the effect of the war on both urban and rural Americans.

The Rise of Industry and the War

The nature of urban settlement in America does much to illustrate the fundamental differences between the Union and the Confederacy. Of the 31 million people living in the United States, according to the Census of 1860, approximately 20 percent lived in urban areas of 2,500 persons or more. Only 14 of the 100 most populous cities in the United States were in states that seceded from the Union. Only one of those cities, New Orleans, the sixth-largest city with a population of 168,675, ranked in the top 20. The second-largest city in the Confederacy was Charleston, South Carolina, with a population of 40,500. In addition to the vast disparity in population, Northern urban centers tended to be centers of manufacturing production, while Southern cities tended to be market centers. Cincinnati, Ohio, which ranked just behind New Orleans with 161,000 residents in 1860, produced four times the manufactured goods of its Southern counterpart.

The rise of the industrial city in America reflected the conflict that produced the Civil War and many of the secondary issues surrounding the war depended very much on how the nation would respond to industrialization. The free labor ideology of the new Republican Party reflected the shift away from craft and toward mechanized production. This new concept of labor relations insisted that workers be paid wages in cash for work performed and protected employers from having to provide for the daily well-being of their workers. This new ideology of how laborers should work and be compensated flew directly in the face of bound labor arrangements in which workers received little or no cash for their efforts. Under bound labor arrangements, employers had to provide food, clothing, and shelter in exchange for work performed and restrictions on the independence of the worker. The most egregious of these bound labor arrangements, of course, was the enslavement of Africans, in which individuals were both laborers and property. Whether or not the United States should retain the institution of slavery had become the single most important cause for war.

Industrialization and the change in labor arrangements that accompanied it affected all aspects of urban life. It was not simply a change of employment status or of work performed, but in the social and family life of the workers. As owners and managers accumulated capital and profit, they had begun the process of separating themselves from the working classes and distancing themselves from social interaction with those classes. This process was well under way in the eastern cities by 1860, less so as one traveled west. But the war, and the opportunities it would provide to accumulate capital from the business of making war, accelerated the process and offered new opportunities for urban settlement.

The Civil War then, changed American cities and affected their residents just as much as the war changed every other aspect of American life. As is the case in any period of dramatic change and high conflict, the war caused significant hardship for many of the nation's urban dwellers and at the same time provided other urbanites with opportunities to advance their economic and social station. Much of the estimated $5.2 billion spent by both the Union and Confederate governments to fight the war found its way into the pockets of urban merchants and manufacturers who provided the subsistence and material to sustain the armies in the field. This great influx of new capital and the new financial mechanisms employed to fund the enormous cost of war allowed for the creation of many new fortunes, to be sure, but also made capital much more available in the urban North. For the Confederacy, defeat brought bankruptcy, which would in many ways define the differences between North and South for the rest of the 19th century and beyond.

Though not a part of this assessment, it should also be recognized that the Union and Confederate armies themselves represented vast mobile cities. These armed urban centers generally encamped, maneuvered, fought, disengaged, and returned to camp to prepare for the next encounter. At any given time in central Virginia between 1861 and 1865, anywhere from 100,000 to 300,000 Americans collectively resided in the temporary cities known as the Army of Northern Virginia and the Army of the Potomac. While in camp and on the march, these American armies consumed all the goods and required all the services any other city might require: food, clothing, shelter, water, sanitation, transportation, medical care, social interaction, and religious services. The list could be extended indefinitely. Yet these vast mobile cities produced almost none of the needed goods and services. It would be for the rest of the nation to produce and funnel those resources through its permanent cities to its mobile cities in the field, cities that consumed rather than produced.

The War and Urban Americans

As the news of the attack on Fort Sumter spread throughout the country, urban Americans quickly accepted war as the answer to the latest expression of sectional crisis. Like their rural counterparts, urban Americans expected a quick resolution and rallied quickly and en masse to the cause. An army of around 15,000 in 1860 swelled to more than 1 million at its peak as suppressing the rebellion became the business of the nation. Rather than enroll volunteers directly in the United States Army, President Lincoln called on the governors of the respective state to raise volunteer regiments. The nation fought the Civil War with regiments raised at the state level, for the most part, validating to some small degree the importance the Confederacy placed on the state in the federal union.

In every city, young men volunteered for service. In New York, rallies that turned Union Square into "a red white and blue wonder" produced six regiments in a matter of days, including the Seventh New York, a collection of merchants, bankers, clerks, and other professionals. Philadelphians answered the call to the tune of eight full regiments. Cincinnati's German Turner Society, an exercise and gymnastics club of German immigrants, organized what would become the Ninth Ohio Volunteer Infantry, an all-German regiment. "Die Neuner," as the regiment came to be called, received its orders from an officer of long-standing American heritage in German translation. Although the spirit of volunteerism ran high, not all new soldiers enlisted because of a sense of duty and honor. Many urban workers also sought employment in the volunteer regiments hastily being prepared for war. Unable to find work as intersectional commercial links disintegrated, military service became the option of last resort.

Such a vast increase in the size of the army required an equally large increase in the number of officers. At the beginning of the conflict, volunteer regiments elected their own officers. Those with previous military or political experience were likely candidates for these positions. A full 85 percent of the volunteers for service in the well-connected Seventh New York Volunteers, which never saw service in the field after the first month, filled the ranks of other regiments as officers. Some served with distinction, though many proved unable to command effectively. The extraordinary success of Ulysses S. Grant is well-known, but others followed similar paths to fame and glory. George McClellan, a West Point graduate who served as a railroad president in Cincinnati, went from captain of a company of volunteers to major general of Ohio volunteers in one day, thanks to his combined experience. Also from Cincinnati, Rutherford B. Hayes left his law practice and duties as city solicitor to lead a regiment with the rank of colonel. Even before the war ended, many of these officers began political careers that would extend through the end of the century.

African American residents had to wait two years before the nation was ready for them to advance the cause of emancipation. It was not until Congress authorized the president to recruit black soldiers in the Militia Act of 1862 that they could hope to serve. Even then, the Fifty-fourth Massachusetts, the first African American regiment to serve, was not fully organized until months after the Emancipation Proclamation had made it clear to the Confederacy that a Union victory would end slavery in the United States. Emancipated slaves and African Americans from all across the North made their way to Massachusetts to fill the ranks. Frederick Douglass himself helped recruit volunteers from as far away as Philadelphia. The reluctance of white officers to accept black recruits diminished only slowly, but by the time the Union had eventually prevailed, some 175,000 black Americans had served the cause.

For many Americans, the onset of war caused severe economic hardship as the North and the South severed long-standing trading relationships. Since the earliest days of settlement, an internal triangle trade had grown to be one of the country's important trading cycles. Cotton grown in the South traveled to the Northeast to be spun and woven into thread and cloth. Manufactured goods from the Northeast moved to the West by way of wagon, river, canal, and increasingly, rail. Demand for Western agricultural products and manufactured goods in the South completed this cycle. Interruption of this important commercial cycle meant many urban Americans would have to scramble to find other sources of income. In Cincinnati and New York, newspaper editors grumbled that grass actually "grew in the streets." Business failures for 1861, as reported by R. G. Dun & Co., a New York company that provided information on the credit worthiness of distant customers, became epidemic. Only when the nation successfully organized itself for war did the panic of 1861 recede, to be replaced by wartime prosperity.

The Effects of War on the Economy

How the Union and Confederacy paid, or did not pay, for this war played an important role in the nation's economic recovery after secession as well as how urban Americans experienced the war. The federal government that had to that point intruded little on the lives of its individual citizens suddenly became the largest and most dominating economic entity. For the Union, dealing successfully with an economic enterprise never imagined even a year before meant reshaping how the government raised revenue. Secretary of the Treasury Salmon P. Chase, with the help of Philadelphia financier Jay Cooke, developed a play by which the United States would finance the war through the sale of bonds, issuing paper currency known as greenbacks, increasing tariffs and excise taxes, and instituting the nation's first income tax. The Thirty-seventh Congress approved Chase's financial plan and extended the basic framework for the Republican economic program, which was in large part an updated version of Alexander Hamilton's original vision for the new nation and Henry Clay's American system. Economic expansionists in the Republican Party pushed through a legislative agenda that included new national banking legislation, a homestead act, government support for a transcontinental railroad, and a new system of land grant colleges.

Along with the general economic reorganization provided by Congress, the food, clothing, shelter, and arms consumed by the Union and Confederate armies in the field proved to be a tremendous economic boom for American cities. The federal government, following the traditional organization of the army, divided the military procurement process into the Ordnance Department, which provided the weapons to fight the war; the Commissary of Subsistence Department, which provided the daily ration for the troops; and the Quartermaster's Department, which provided everything else and arranged for transportation. The Commissary and Quartermaster's departments entered into contracts with private individuals and companies to supply the armies in the field. Both departments established a system of supply depots that awarded contracts, received the goods, examined the quality, arranged for payment to be made, and distributed the goods to armies. Prior to 1860, a single supply depot in Philadelphia and the two national armories in Harpers Ferry, Virginia, and Springfield, Massachusetts, provided most of the equipment used by the army. But as the war quickly escalated, in less than one year, the military supply process went from being a small adjunct of the economy of several cities to being the most important business enterprise in the nation. Supply officers at the various depots struggled to acquire the vast quantities of goods needed to keep the armies fed, clothed, and ready to fight. Early on there was a considerable amount of fraud as some contractors sought quick profit by providing "shoddy" or substandard goods. But in a short period of time, local supply officers came to rely on contractors they knew would provide acceptable quality at a reasonable, but not necessarily the lowest, price. For the contractors, the contracting system provided a tremendous opportunity to earn great wealth. On occasion, the army tried its hand at trying to manufacture uniforms at several of the supply depots with mixed results. Employing local residents and dependents of soldiers who had been injured or killed, the government saved some of the profit while providing some relief for soldiers' families.

For the Union then, adding billions of dollars to the urban economy accelerated the process of industrialization, directly and indirectly. The net effect of the war on the American city and its residents was to stimulate an economic environment that fostered industrial development. For the Confederacy however, the economic expansion required to fight the war produced no such stimulating effect. The military supply process was even more critical for the South than it was for the Union, but it had almost no long-term effect. The Confederate government, which organized its procurement process in much the same way as the Union, made contracts with Southern urban businesses to supply the Confederate armies, while the government also tried to encourage smuggling of military items through the Union blockade. Without an extensive base of existing industries to rely on, the Confederacy had to develop its own sources. By 1863, government-owned and -operated factories supplied much of the arms and equipment consumed by the army. Women used the government-owned facilities to sell homespun cotton and receive cloth to be sewn into uniforms. Small towns and cities such as Richmond, Virginia; Selma, Alabama; and Atlanta, Georgia, saw their wartime population rise dramatically as people flocked from the countryside to work in the factories. For this brief period then, the cities of the Confederacy mimicked the cities of the Union. But as the Union troops advanced deeper into the Confederacy, troops destroyed much of the infrastructure built to support the Confederate war effort. During the Atlanta campaign, troops under William T. Sherman destroyed clothing mills at Roswell and Sweetwater Creek, Georgia, sending the female operatives to Louisville, Kentucky, by train, as he would have sent prisoners of war. But the long-term effect on the prosperity of Southern cities was quite different. Instead of enjoying strong postwar economic expansion, bankrupt Southern cities struggled to advance without the influx of capital enjoyed by their Northern counterparts. This was offset somewhat by Northern investment in Southern cities, but no Southern city could match the postwar growth of the great urban centers of the North.

Changes to the urban landscape in the Confederacy brought about by the business of war had a much smaller effect than in the Union. The South tried to pay for the war through a combination of bonds and paper money, which lost all value when the war ended. Consequently, Southern efforts to build an independent economy had little long-lasting effect on Southern cities except to guarantee their poverty. Investors in the Confederacy lost everything. Cash investments were worthless. Many of the South's manufacturing facilities lay in ruin. Railroads, the connecting link between Southern cities, had been destroyed by the advancing Union armies. The forthcoming Fourteenth Amendment would prohibit the payment of any Confederate debt. The Thirteenth Amendment emancipated all labor capital. The war left Southern cities in a state of tremendous disadvantage compared to their Northern counterparts. No systematic program of economic reconstruction reversed the devastation. Some Northern capitalists saw great opportunity in rebuilding Southern economic institutions. Carpetbaggers, as those who traveled South for profit were often labeled, invested in banks, stores, land, and every other opportunity they could identify. Urban Southerners resented the profit these Northern investors took from their Southern investments, but without the influx of Northern capital, rebuilding urban economic institutions would have taken longer than it did. Still, Southerners suffered from a lack of available capital to expand the region's economy well into the 20th century.

From the secession crisis through the First Battle of Manassas, most Americans believed the war would be short, with one or at most several pitched battles that would decide the issue of secession. President Lincoln's first call for volunteers envisioned 90 days of service and a quick return to civilian life. Most urban Americans concurred with this assessment. But when the first battle at Manassas settled nothing, both Union and Confederate officials began to prepare for a longer conflict.

The Media Reports on the War

The nation's urban residents learned of Shiloh and what they knew about the war from the nation's newspapers. As the mass media of the day,

The *New York Herald's* wagon in the field near Bealton, Virginia, in August 1863. Newspapers provided one of the only consistent ways of obtaining the current information that civilians frequently craved during the war. (*Library of Congress*)

Murat Halstead (1829–1908)

Murat Halstead, editor of the *Cincinnati Daily Commercial*, along with other editors introduced urban Americans to the Civil War. Newspapers represented the nation's window to the world in the 19th century. Their editors wielded tremendous power and considerable political influence as they interpreted the narrative of daily events. In addition, newspapers were everywhere. At any given moment, a city the size of Cincinnati could have as many as 10 daily as well as up to two dozen weekly papers in English and, in the case of Cincinnati, German. Reading a local paper aloud in a tavern was often a daily ritual. Editors were unabashedly partisan, reporting the news from their own ideological perspective and that of their political party. Halstead earned the respect of his readers and his contemporaries for his aggressive reporting and biting commentary.

By the onset of the Civil War, Halstead had already become a fixture in the

Author and journalist Murat Halstead owned part of the *Cincinnati Daily Commercial* during the Civil War. (*Library of Congress*)

newspapers brought a daily stream of news from the front via telegraph, filtered through the lens of the local editor who served his loyal constituents. During the Civil War, editors published approximately 2,000 newspapers each week in the United States, almost 400 of them daily. New York had as many as 17 daily newspapers during the war. Richmond, Virginia, had four. Cincinnati had no fewer than six, two published in German, one Republican, and the other Democrat. Generally four pages of copy and advertisements, each newspaper reflected the political voice of the Republican or Democratic parties or the editorial voice of the publisher. Anxious to sell copies, editors sought to one-up each other in a competitive environment. Accuracy often gave way to an approaching press deadline and a good story, but by reading the newspaper, and listening to the newspaper being read in the neighborhood taverns, Americans kept up with the progress of the war on the battlefield and the political situations in the nation's capital. With rare exceptions, opposition newspapers such as the *New York World* and the *Cincinnati Enquirer* continued to publish throughout the war. As long as Democratic editors took a pro-Union stance, they were generally free to criticize the administration, almost at will.

Reporting on the Battle of Shiloh in April 1862 brought the horrors of war to the home front, particularly for Western cities. In the bloodiest

Cincinnati publishing community. Born to a farm family in rural Butler County, Ohio, some 20 miles north of Cincinnati, Halstead contributed to several newspapers while a student at Farmers' College. The *Cincinnati Daily Commercial* hired Halstead as a reporter in 1853 and his hard work quickly earned him a partnership.

Halstead paid close attention to national politics, earning national recognition for his reports. He attended the execution of John Brown and reported from seven of the eight political conventions that led to the election of Abraham Lincoln in 1860. As the secession crisis deepened, Halstead proposed that a national convention be appointed to reach an appropriate compromise. Like many other Northerners, including the president, Halstead only became an abolitionist as the war progressed.

Although Halstead represented a nominally Republican paper, he took Republicans to task as well as Democrats. He waged editorial war with the local Democratic mouthpiece, the *Daily Enquirer*, but no individual was safe from his scathing attacks. He asserted that Abraham Lincoln "could not be a more inefficient man," and that Secretary of War Simon Cameron "attends to the stealing department." Halstead helped spread the rumor that General William T. Sherman was "insane" and that General Ulysses S. Grant had a serious drinking problem. He witnessed the Battle of Fredericksburg, which left him profoundly disgusted with the federal war effort.

Over time, Halstead became a much stronger supporter of Lincoln and the war effort, rejoicing in the victory and mourning the loss of the president. But for the duration, he remained a strong voice that constantly reminded Cincinnati and the nation of the dire consequences of waging civil war.

battle on record in the Western Hemisphere to that date, more than 3,400 soldiers died on the field and another 2,000 succumbed to their wounds. Correspondents reported the carnage. Many families experienced the pain of losing a loved one for the first time as the three-year regiments recruited in 1861 fought their first major battle. Because many of these regiments had been formed from young volunteers from the same locale, reports of multiple casualties from the same regiment devastated many small towns and urban neighborhoods.

Battle on this scale demonstrated just how unprepared the nation was to care for wounded and disabled soldiers. The cities of the Ohio and Mississippi river valleys responded in the fashion of the 19th century, through the voluntary association, to treat the wounds of those injured at Shiloh. The citizens of Cincinnati quickly outfitted a hospital ship, sending it down the Ohio to the Tennessee to aid the shelter tent hospital hastily set up to tend to the wounded. The most severely wounded had died before significant help arrived, but voluntary service became a way of life for the nation's urban residents.

In American cities of this time, the voluntary association was the most important agent of social action. Citizens bound themselves together to

George Templeton Strong (1820–1875)

The diary of George Templeton Strong, a 40-year literary exercise by a prominent New York lawyer, offers readers a view into the mind and soul of the New York elite and the way they experienced the Civil War. A lifelong New Yorker who was educated at Columbia College and later a trustee, Strong was also a member of the Episcopal Trinity Church Wall Street, a cofounder of the Union League Club of New York, and during the Civil War, the Treasurer of the U.S. Sanitary Commission. In his endeavors, Strong represented the engaged, public-minded citizen of the era. Strong's sense of volunteerism reflected the contemporary view that citizens improved their society through

voluntary association, which proved essential to the Union war effort.

The Sanitary Commission, a semi-official agency that was staffed by women but led by men, became Strong's all-consuming, unpaid vocation during the war. Reacting to women's relief efforts at the beginning of the war, the federal government established the commission in July 1861 to coordinate relief efforts around the nation. It helped soldiers in need, trained and provided nurses to military hospitals, and cared for wounded and disabled soldiers. The Commission served a public purpose with private funds. Early on, his work on the Commission often left Strong

form schools, literary societies, fire companies, orphanages, chambers of commerce, and the like to improve their respective cities. From this spirit of volunteerism among women arose the U.S. Sanitary Commission and a number of affiliated organizations. Although men held the positions of authority, the impetus for the Sanitary Commission was women's response to war. Abhorring the violence, death, and injury of battle, but equally the disease, sin, and iniquity that accompanied life in a mobile city, women reformers, many of whom had been active in the various reform movements of urban America before the war, used the Sanitary Commission to establish a formal connection between the military and the home front and to effectively distribute supplies to the armies. It is from this voluntary service that the civilian nurses such as Dorothea Dix and Katherine Wormeley earned their reputation as the saviors of the wounded soldier. These women offered their most dramatic service at the front in the immediate aftermath of a battle, but their work in the hospitals established in the nation's cities far from the front proved equally important to the recovery of severely wounded and ill soldiers. Local branches of the Sanitary Commission engaged in a variety of fund-raising activities, the most successful of which was the sanitary fair. A combination of circus, exhibition, and auction roughly based on the Great Exhibition in London of 1851, these Sanitary Fairs quickly became the preferred method of fund-raising in American urban areas. In all, Northern cities organized more than 30 fairs and raised more than $4 million in the process, although New York's Metropolitan Fair and Philadelphia's Central Fair contributed more than 75 percent of the total. In addition, the work of the U.S. Christian Commission supplemented the work of the Sanitary Commission. Together they contributed more than $12 million of relief aid.

and his fellow trustees with a deep sense of frustration. It was often difficult and sometimes nearly impossible to get the government to cooperate with the commission's work, to the point that Strong and the other commissioners nearly disbanded the organization in early 1862. After that crisis and with the support of Secretary of War Edwin Stanton, the Sanitary Commission went on to raise more than $20 million worth of cash and supplies through Sanitary Fairs across the Union. The New York Fair of 1864 raised more than $1 million in cash.

Strong's diary and his work for the Sanitary Commission revealed a deep-seated, internal conflict over the nature of the war that existed in many Americans. A staunch Republican who put saving the Union above all else, Strong often wondered early in the war whether Lincoln could lead the nation to victory. During the tumultuous summer of 1863, which included the infamous Draft Riots, Strong had no sympathy for Irish strikers who sought increased wages in response to wartime inflation. Only late in the war was he convinced that Lincoln had taken the correct path. Despite his misgivings, Strong, and other citizens like him, helped preserve the Union through their voluntary contribution of time and money to the cause.

The War and the American Worker

For urban workers the war proved to be a curse, then a modest blessing that turned increasingly toward hardship. The economic downturn of 1861 left many workers without any source of income. Male workers could and did enlist in the volunteer regiments, although female workers and families often suffered. More than one newspaper complained of the economic disruption that accompanied the outbreak of war. Once the nation settled in for the long war, and it became clear that the war on the battlefield would not be won by an overwhelming display of force, urban workers, especially in the major cities of the Union, enjoyed a period of prosperity, thanks to full employment rather than an increase in wages. Many workers enjoyed a rise in wages as employers competed for their services as the labor supply diminished, predominantly because of the drain of men taken by the military but also to a lesser extent to a reduction in new immigrant labor. As the war progressed however, inflation eroded much of the economic prosperity gained by full employment for many workers. Military demand for the necessities of life meant workers competed with the government for goods, food, and clothing in particular, and prices rose to the point at which working men and women had trouble sustaining themselves on wages that did not keep pace.

Few American workers enjoyed the protection of organized labor and most of that organization had been at the local level. Only highly specialized trades, such as the iron molders, printers, and machinists, had any form of national organization. The economic downturn at the beginning of the war forced many workers to seek employment as volunteer soldiers,

Postcard featuring home workers for the U.S. Sanitary Commission. This card and similar ones were sold to raise money for sick and wounded Union soldiers. (*Miller, Francis Trevelyan and Robert Sampson Lanier, The Photographic History of the Civil War, vol. 7, 1911*)

and those who remained home were most grateful to be employed. As the nation attended to the business of providing for its armies on the battle-fields, laborers found their services in demand on the Northern home front. For a brief period, full employment meant a reasonable wage and an opportunity to accumulate some cash reserves. No sooner had many of the workers recovered from the downturn of 1861 than wartime inflation took over as the government competed with its citizens for the necessities of life. For example, when Jane Hasler complained to President Lincoln in 1864 that seamstresses at the government clothing manufactory in Cincinnati had gone without an increase in the price of their piece-work since the beginning of the war, the president ordered an investigation. In response, the local quartermaster in charge referred to the problems associated with getting funds from the federal government to run the local depot rather than address the fundamental unfairness of stagnant wages in an inflationary economy. The seamstresses did receive modest increases in some piece-work compensation in the fall of 1864, but the problem remained unresolved by the war's end.

Besides writing letters to the president, workers organized and held strikes in attempts to win higher wages, with varying degrees of success. Unions petitioned employers and organized strikes against those who refused to negotiate higher wages. Employers often ignored union requests and bound themselves together to resist the organized workers. In Philadelphia, when iron molders struck in late fall 1862, employers agreed secretly to hold out as one until the strike had been broken. In the end, neither side won. The union struggled on without any real power and the manufacturers lost their dominance of the stove-making industry.

Tensions Caused by the War

The greatest urban violence of the war occurred in New York in July 1863, when New Yorkers rioted against the inequality of the draft and the increasing effect of inflation on the lives of workers. Racial issues also came into play during the draft riots—many laborers worried that freed Southern slaves would ultimately glut the workplace. Draft resistance was not limited to New York, as many urban workers, from towns as small as Portsmouth, New Hampshire, to cities as large as Boston, Chicago, and Philadelphia, participated in similar riots. Originally a protest by unionized workers, the New York City protest soon gave way to rioting by unskilled and unemployed workers, who redirected their anger away from the draft offices, $300 men who could pay the required bounty to avoid the draft, and a variety of Republican-run businesses, and toward the city's African American residents. Attacked on the streets, in their homes, on the docks, and wherever they had sought shelter, New York's black population absorbed the brunt of the attack. Only when Mayor George Opdyke requested and received state and federal aid to control the situation was order effectively restored. In all, officials confirmed 199 dead and at least 300 injured in the fighting, making the New York City draft riots the most deadly single incident of urban violence in American history.

Although the issue of slavery did not represent the only cause of the Civil War it was certainly the most important. Urban blacks responded to war in much the same way whites did, except that they were not permitted to volunteer for military service until Congress passed the Militia Act in July 1862. But it was not until the Emancipation Proclamation took effect on January 1, 1863, that Northern blacks could rally to the flag in the same way whites did after Fort Sumter. At home, life for free blacks changed in the same way it did for white urbanites, although the stakes were almost always higher. Black workers were almost always the first to let go during troubled times and the last to be rehired as prosperity returned. Generally locked out of many of the skilled trades, their fortunes rested on the need for unskilled and semiskilled labor. A strong undercurrent of racism accompanied the black experience and on more than one occasion put the lives of black urbanites at considerable risk.

To some extent, many whites blamed blacks and the issue of slavery for the war. This misplaced anger often contributed to a higher state of tension between black and white laborers. One event in Cincinnati in the summer of 1862 illustrates how racism, blame for the war, and economic competition contributed to an uncertain present and future for urban free blacks. Steamboat traffic on the public landing in Cincinnati had yet to fully recover to prewar levels by July 1862. Labor gangs, Irish, German, white, and black competed for a chance to load and unload the many boats that did business on the landing. Blacks were often accused of being willing to underbid their white counterparts, which increased tension among the various labor gangs. On the morning of July 10, this competition erupted into violence. As the local newspapers described it, white workers attacked black workers. Some black workers sought shelter on several of the boats at the landing while others returned the violence in kind. All sources agree that what followed might best be described as a knock-down, drag-out brawl. After several hours, an uneasy truce had been restored and several of the most active participants, white and black, were arrested.

With tensions remaining at a heightened state, Mayor George Hatch sent three-fourths of the police force to Kentucky to try to capture Confederate raider, John Hunt Morgan. Hatch believed that Morgan, who had already earned a reputation for his raiding behind Union lines, might threaten Cincinnati if left unchecked. With the police out of the city, local toughs took the opportunity to attack African American residents in their homes and neighborhoods over several evenings of violence. Ultimately, the mayor activated several companies of home-guard militia to restore order.

Weeks later, when a more serious military threat from 10,000 Confederates under Henry Heth approached the city from the south, Cincinnati's African American citizens volunteered their services in defending the city. City and military officials initially refused to accept African American volunteers because they still contended the conflict remained a white man's war. But when it became clear that much of the defensive work would involve digging trenches and erecting breastworks, the same African Americans, whose volunteer service had been refused just a day or two before, were impressed at gunpoint and transported across the river to Kentucky to labor on the fortifications. Finally organized by a local judge into what came to be known as the Black Brigade of Cincinnati, these workers served until the danger had passed. Many of these workers went on to volunteer for the black regiments that would be organized the next year. Ironically, for perhaps the only time in American history, several hundred free blacks were enslaved in a free state and transported to a slave state to work as bound labor, labor they had willingly volunteered to do days earlier, all in an effort to help win a war that would end slavery in the United States.

Middle-class Northern urbanites and capitalists generally did well during the war. After the economic downturn of 1861, the influx of government-supplied capital allowed business owners, even those not directly involved in the business of war, to profit. A general increase in prices over the course of the war allowed those with a low tolerance for risk to see a strong increase in the value of their investments. War contractors who established stable relations with the Commissary and Quartermaster's Depots earned steady if not spectacular profits. Those who found a way to solve problems for the overworked local supply officers found a steady stream of income.

For those who had a higher tolerance for risk and the fortitude to stand uncertainty, the Civil War provided ample opportunity to speculate on the ebb and flow of wartime fortune. Speculators traded in bonds, gold, currency, cotton, corn, and every other commodity, betting on the fortunes of the armies in the field, often on very low margins. Speculators often reaped huge profits simply by anticipating a rise or drop in commodity prices. Early access to news, generally brought to the cities via the relatively new medium of the telegraph, allowed speculators to reduce their risk significantly. The same opportunities to speculate existed for Southern citizens as well, but unless the speculator could somehow turn paper profits into gold or real property, those profits disappeared on the demise of the Confederacy. In the North, however, speculators managed to hold on to their speculative gains postwar. Henry Morford detailed the depravity of the speculator class in *The Days of Shoddy*, a popular 1863 novel of the sins of a wartime speculator in New York. Morford's villain got his just reward in the end, although no such day of reckoning came for most speculators. Much of the newfound wealth was ultimately a result of government-created capital, which increasingly bound urban capitalists to the success of the Union war effort.

Conclusion

Lee's surrender at Appomattox brought a great sense of joy and relief to Northern cities and the people in them celebrated the Union victory. However, the postsurrender celebration was short-lived. No sooner had the news of the ultimate victory been received than people heard the news that President Lincoln had been assassinated. Grief and anger commingled. In New York, known Copperheads were well advised to display appropriate signs of mourning in their windows and on their persons. In Philadelphia, a Democratic newspaper editor was forced to leave the city. Lincoln's body traveled from Washington through Baltimore, Philadelphia, New York, Albany, Buffalo, Cleveland, Columbus, Indianapolis, and Chicago on the way to its final resting place in Springfield, Illinois. At each stop along the way local committees arranged appropriate services in honor of the nation's slain leader. The celebration and mourning culminated with a Grand Review of the Armies in Washington, D.C., on May 23 and May 24, 1865. The two-day affair saw more that 125,000 men parade from Capitol Hill down Pennsylvania Avenue toward the White House. President Andrew Johnson and General-in-Chief Ulysses Grant and a number of congressional dignitaries reviewed the troops. It was the last great

The May 1865 grand review of the victorious armies of generals Ulysses S. Grant and William T. Sherman in Washington, D.C. (*Library of Congress*)

demonstration of the war. In a matter of weeks, the process of disbanding the Union Army was well under way.

In part because historians have paid so little attention to the nation's cities at war they have reached no consensus about the war and its effect on the cities. What consensus there has been is largely tied to the larger question of the economic impact of the war. In fighting the war and then paying for it, the federal government expanded the capital available for a variety of investments. The nation's capitalists seized the opportunities the war provided and a significant number grew rich as a result. The vast bond sale program devised to pay for war expenditures provided new investment instruments and a model for financing new capital-intensive ventures. For Southern cities, certainly, the end of the war produced no such boom. The total war waged by Generals Grant and Sherman in 1864 and 1865 devastated Southern industry, leaving Southern cities even further behind their Northern counterparts than they had been in 1860. Consequently, the war for the Union had also been a war of separation for the nation's cities. Wealth accumulated in the hands of the capitalists while urban workers struggled to hold ground against inflation. Northern cities gained investment capital, new residents, and a rapidly expanding industrial base. Southern cities bet and lost all. By 1870 a full 26 percent of the 38 million Americans now lived in urban places, a trend that would continue over the succeeding decades. Ultimately, the war produced little that was brand new for Northern cities, rather it accelerated existing trends.

For the South, losing the war meant its cities could not compete. It would be well into the 20th century before things changed significantly.

References and Further Reading

Bernstein, Iver. 1991. *The New York City Draft Riots: Their Significance for American Society and Politics in the Age of the Civil War*. New York: Oxford University Press.

Burrows, Edwin G., and Mike Wallace. 1999. *Gotham: A History of New York City to 1898*. New York: Oxford University Press.

Cronon, William. 1991. *Nature's Metropolis: Chicago and the Great West*. New York: W. W. Norton and Company.

Gallman, J. Matthew. 1990. *Mastering Wartime: A Social History of Philadelphia during the Civil War*. New York: Cambridge University Press.

Gallman, J. Matthew. 1994. *The North Fights the Civil War: The Home Front*. Chicago: Ivan R. Dee.

Karamanski, Theodore J. 1993. *Rally 'Round the Flag: Chicago and the Civil War*. Chicago: Nelson-Hall.

O'Connor, Thomas H. 1997. *Civil War Boston: Home Front and Battlefield*. Boston: Northeastern University Press.

Paludan, Philip S. 1988. *A People's Contest: The Union and Civil War*. New York: Harper & Row.

Richardson, Heather Cox. 1997. *The Greatest Nation on Earth*. Cambridge, MA: Harvard University Press.

Scranton, Philip. 1983. *Proprietary Capitalism: The Textile Manufacture at Philadelphia, 1800–1885*. New York: University Press.

Primary Documents

News reports during the Civil War were undependable and often inaccurate. Without accurate reports, newspapers often published unsubstantiated rumors as facts. As a result, those on the home front waited anxiously for letters from soldiers to allay their fears. Soldiers' families, in particular, hoped for frequent letters from their loved ones on the front lines to keep them informed on their whereabouts and situation. Confederate soldier Elisha Franklin Paxton sent numerous letters to his wife. Through his letters, she and others on the home front were given a sense of camp life as well as battle. Paxton also used his letters to reassure his wife about his safety and give her the news about others from their community.

Confederate Soldier Elisha Franklin Paxton's Letters to his Wife

Near Winchester, July 8, 1861.

The last week has been one of patient waiting for a fight. On Monday, the 1st inst., I was ordered by Col. Jackson to go to Martinsburg and burn some engines, at which I was engaged until Tuesday morning, when I received an order to join my company, accompanied with the information that the enemy was approaching and our force had gone out to give him battle. I obtained a conveyance as speedily as I could, and the first intelligence of the fight I received from my regiment, which I found retreating. My company, I was pleased to learn, had fought bravely. On Wednesday morning we took our stand ten miles this side of Martinsburg, and there awaited the approach of the enemy until Sunday morning, when we retired to this place, three miles from Winchester. This we expect to be our battlefield. When it will take place it is impossible to say. It may be to-morrow, or perhaps not for a month, depending upon the movements of the enemy. I look forward to it without any feeling of alarm. I cannot tell why, but it is so. My fate may be that of Cousin Bob McChesney, of whose death I have but heard. If so, let it be. I die in the discharge of my duty, from which it is neither my wish nor my privilege to shrink. The horsetrade was entirely satisfactory. Act in the same way in all matters connected with the farm. Just consider yourself a widow, and, in military parlance, insist upon being "obeyed and respected accordingly." Pay your board at Annie's out of the first money you get. She may not be disposed to accept it, but I insist upon it. I do not wish to pay such bills merely with gratitude. Newman is still in the army, but I have not seen him for a month. I called to see him the other day, but he was not at his quarters.

It is now nearly three months since I left home, and I hardly know how the time has passed. All I know is that if I do my duty, I have but little leisure. I am used to the hardships of the service, and feel that I have the health and strength to bear any fatigue or exposure. Sometimes, as I lie upon the ground, my face to the sky, I think of Matthew's little verse, "Twinkle, twinkle, little star," and my mind wanders back to the wife and little ones at home. Bless you! If I never return, the wish which lies nearest to my heart is for your happiness. And now, my darling, again good-bye. Kiss little Matthew and Galla for me, and tell them Papa sends it. Give my love to Pa and Rachel, and for yourself accept all that a fond husband can give.

Manassas, July 23, 1861.

My Darling: We spent Sunday last in the sacred work of achieving our nationality and independence. The work was nobly done, and it was the happiest day of my life, our wedding-day not excepted. I think the fight is over forever. I received a ball through my shirt-sleeves, slightly bruising my arm, and others, whistling "Yankee Doodle" round my head, made fourteen holes through the flag which I carried in the hottest of the fight. It is a miracle that I escaped with my life, so many falling dead around me. Buried two of our comrades on the field. God bless my country, my wife, and my little ones!

Manassas, July 26, 1861.

I wrote a short note to you on Tuesday, advising you of my escape from the battle of Sunday in safety. Matters are now quiet, and no prospect, I think, of another engagement very soon. When I think of the past, and the peril through which it has been my fortune to pass in safety, I am free to admit that I have no desire to participate in another such scene until the cause of my country requires it. Then the danger must be met, cost what it may. How I wish, Love, that I could see you and our little ones again! But for the present I must not think of it. Just as soon as the public service will permit I will be with you. The result of the battle has cast a shade of gloom over many who mourn husband, brother and child left dead on the field. Of those of our company who went into the thickest of the fight, at least one-half were killed or wounded. Some others escaped danger by sneaking away like cowards. The other companies from our county suffered as severely as ours. It seems, Love, an age since I have heard from you. You must write oftener. Why is it that you have not sent the daguerreotype of yourself and the children? Send me, by the first opportunity, another shirt just like that which you last sent me. I will lay that by—as it has a hole through it made by a ball in the battle—as a memento of the glorious day. Do not send me any more clothing until I write for it, as I do not wish more than absolute necessity requires, having no means of carrying it with me.

I wish you would call upon Mrs. J. D. Davidson for me, and say to her she has reason to be proud of her brave boy. It was by the heroic services of men like him who have sacrificed their lives that the battle was won. He fell just as he and his comrades were taking possession of a splendid battery of the enemy's cannon, and those who defended it were flying from the field. And now, Love, good-bye. I think you need have no apprehension about my safety for some weeks at least. It is not probable that we shall have another battle very soon; and if we do, as our brigade was in the thickest of the fight before, we will not be so much exposed again. Give my love to Pa, Rachel, Annie, and all my friends. Kiss our dear little ones for their absent papa, and for yourself accept a husband's best love.

Source: Elisha Franklin Paxton, Memoir and Memorials: Elisha Franklin Paxton, Brigadier-General, C.S.A.: Composed of his Letters from Camp and Field while an Officer in the Confederate Army, with an Introductory and Connecting Narrative Collected and Arranged by his Son, John Gallatin Paxton (*New York*: Neale Publishing Co., 1907), *10–14.*

Excerpts from Confederate Judith W. McGuire's Diary (1861)

Many elite white Southern women began writing personal journals at the outset of the Civil War, knowing that they were witnessing momentous events and having the time and education to dedicate to this pursuit. Through women's diaries, details on hospitals, volunteer efforts, rumors, and other home front experiences come to light. Virginian Judith McGuire's diary offers her observations on enemy men and women, battles, hospitals, and home front conditions and morale. She also details the volunteer efforts of the women of her Virginia community for the wounded Confederate soldiers.

July 30th [1861]

I have just been conversing with some young soldiers, who joined in the dangers and glories of the battlefield. They corroborate what I had before heard of the presence of Northern females. I would not mention it before in my diary, because I did not wish to record anything which I did not *know* to be true. But when I receive the account from eye-witnesses whose veracity cannot be doubted, I can only say, that I feel mortified that such was the case. They came, not as Florence Nightengales to alleviate human suffering, but to witness and exult over it. With the full assurance of the success of their army they meant to pass over the mutilated limbs and mangled corpses of ours, and to go on their way rejoicing to scenes of festivity in the halls of the vanquished, and to revel over the blood of the slain, the groans of the dying, the wails of the widow and the fatherless. But "Linden saw another sight," and these very delicate, gentle, *womanly* ladies, where were they? Flying back to Washington, in confusion and terror, pell-mell, in the wildest excitement. And where were their brave and honourable escorts? Flying, too; not as protectors to their fair friends, but with self-preservation alone in view. All went helter-skelter—coaches, cabriolets, barouches, buggies, flying over the roads, as though all Fairfax were mad.

> Ah, Fear! Ah, frantic Fear!
> I see—I see thee near.
> I know thy hurried step, thy haggard eye!
> Like thee, I start; like thee, disordered fly!

Each bush to their disordered imaginations contained a savage Confederate. Cannon seemed thundering in the summer breeze, and in each spark of the lighting-bug, glinted and gleamed the sword and Bowie-knife of the blood-thirsty Southerner. Among the captured articles were ladies' dresses, jewels, and other gew-gaws, on their way to Richmond to the grand ball promised to them on their safe arrival. There were also fine wines, West India fruits, and almost everything else rich, or sweet, or intoxicating, brought by the gay party, for a right royal pic-nic on the field of blood. The wines and brandies came in well for our wounded that night, and we thank God for the superfluities of the wicked.

August 1 [1861]

This whole neighbourhood is busy to-day, loading a wagon with comforts for the hospital at Fairfax Court-House. They send it down once a week, under the care of a gentleman, who, being too old for the service, does this for the sick and wounded. The hospitals and Centreville and the Court-House are filled with those who are too severely wounded to be taken to Richmond, Charlottesville, and the larger hospitals. They are supplied, to a very great degree, by private contributions. It is beautiful to see the self-denying efforts of these patriotic people. Everybody sends contributions on the appointed day to Millwood, where the wagon is filled to overflowing with garments, brandy, wine, nice bread, biscuit, sponge cake, butter, fresh vegetables, fruit, etc. Being thoroughly packed, it goes off for a journey of fifty miles.

Source: Judith W. McGuire, Diary of a Southern Refugee During the War, by a Lady of Virginia (*New York: E. J. Hale & Son, 1867*).

Frederick Douglass Criticizes the United States Government for Its Refusal to Enlist Black Men as Soldiers (1861)

Former slave Frederick Douglass became active in the abolition movement and then continued to fight for African American rights once the Civil War began. Although supporting the Union war effort, he publicly and repeatedly disdained President Abraham Lincoln's refusal to make the abolition of slavery one of the war's official aims. In his newspaper, he continually published pieces on the necessity of involving free African Americans in the Union war effort and of ending slavery. In this piece, he highlights the damage caused by the government's refusal to enlist African American men into the U.S. military. Two years later, in 1863, the Union government finally authorized the formation of its first African American regiment, the Fifty-fourth Massachusetts.

''Fighting Rebels With Only One Hand''

What on earth is the matter with the American Government and people? Do they really covet the world's ridicule as well as their own social and political ruin? What are they thinking about, or don't they condescend to think at all? So, indeed, it would seem from their blindness in dealing with the tremendous issue now upon them. Was there ever anything like it before? They are sorely pressed on every hand by a vast army of slaveholding rebels, flushed with success, and infuriated by the darkest inspirations of a deadly hate, bound to rule or ruin. Washington, the seat of Government, after ten thousand assurances to the contrary, is now positively in danger of falling before the rebel army. Maryland, a little while ago considered safe for the Union, is now admitted to be studded with the materials for insurrection, and which may flame forth at any moment.—Every resource of the nation, whether of men or money, whether of wisdom or strength, could be well employed to avert the impending ruin. Yet most evidently the demands of the hour are not comprehended by the Cabinet or the crowd. Our Presidents, Governors, Generals and Secretaries are calling, with almost frantic vehemence, for men.—"Men! men! send us men!" they scream, or the cause of the Union is gone, the life of a great nation is ruthlessly sacrificed, and the hopes of a great nation go out in darkness; and yet these very officers, representing the people and Government, steadily and persistently refuse to receive the very class of men which have a deeper interest in the defeat and humiliation of the rebels, than all others.—Men are wanted in Missouri—wanted in Western Virginia, to hold and defend what has been already gained; they are wanted in Texas, and all along the sea coast, and though the Government has at its command a class in the country deeply interested in suppressing the insurrection, it sternly refuses to summon from among the vast multitude a single man, and degrades and insults the whole class by refusing to allow any of their number to defend with their strong arms and brave hearts the national cause. What a spectacle of blind, unreasoning prejudice and pusillanimity is this! The national edifice is on fire. Every man who can carry a bucket of water, or remove a brick, is wanted; but those who have the care of the building, having a profound respect for the feeling of the national burglars who set the building on fire, are determined that the flames shall only be extinguished by Indo-Caucasian hands, and to have the building burnt rather than save it by means of any other. Such is the pride, the stupid prejudice and folly that rules the hour.

Why does the Government reject the Negro? Is he not a man? Can he not wield a sword, fire a gun, march and countermarch, and obey orders like any other? Is there the least reason to believe that a regiment of well drilled Negroes would deport themselves less soldier-like on the battlefield than the raw troops gathered up generally from the towns and cities of the State of New York? We do believe that such soldiers, if allowed to take up arms in defence of the Government, and made to feel that they are hereafter to be recognized as persons having rights, would set the highest example of order and general good behavior to their fellow soldiers, and in every way add to the national power.

If persons so humble as we can be allowed to speak to the President of the United States, we should ask him if this dark and terrible hour of the nation's extremity is a time for consulting a mere vulgar and unnatural prejudice? We should ask him if national preservation and necessity were not better guides in this emergency than either the tastes of the rebels, or the pride and prejudices of the vulgar? We would tell him that General Jackson in a slave state fought side by side with Negroes at New Orleans, and like a true man, despising meanness, he bore testimony to their bravery at the close of the war. We would tell him that colored men in Rhode Island and Connecticut performed their full share in the war of the Revolution, and that men of the same color, such as the noble Shields Green, Nathaniel Turner and Denmark Vesey stand ready to peril everything at the command of the Government. We would tell him that this is no time to fight with one hand, when both are needed; that this is no time to fight only with your white hand, and allow your black hand to remain tied.

Whatever may be the folly and absurdity of the North, the South at least is true and wise. The Southern papers no longer indulge in the vulgar expression, "free n——rs." That class of bipeds are now called "colored residents." The Charleston papers say:

> The colored residents of this city can challenge comparison with their class, in any city or town, in loyalty or devotion to the cause of the South. Many of them individually, and without ostentation, have been contributing liberally, and on Wednesday evening, the 7th inst., a very large meeting was held by them, and a committee appointed to provide for more efficient aid. The proceedings of the meeting will appear in results hereinafter to be reported.

It is now pretty well established, that there are at the present moment many colored men in the Confederate Army doing duty not only as cooks, servants and laborers, but as real soldiers, having muskets on their shoulders, and bullets in their pockets, ready to shoot down loyal troops, and do all that soldiers may to destroy the Federal Government and build up that of the traitors and rebels. There were such soldiers at Manassas, and they are probably there still. There is a Negro in the army as well as in the fence, and our Government is likely to find it out before the war comes to an end. That the Negroes are numerous in the rebel army, and do for that army its heaviest work, is beyond question. They have been the chief laborers upon those temporary defences in which the rebels have been able to mow down our men. Negroes helped to build the batteries at Charleston. They relieve their gentlemanly and military masters from the stiffening drudgery of the camp, and devote them to the nimble and dexterous use of arms. Rising above vulgar prejudice, the slaveholding rebel accepts the aid of the black man as readily as that of any other. If a bad cause can do this, why should a good cause be less wisely conducted? We insist upon it, that one black regiment in such a war as this is, without being any more brave and orderly, would be worth to the Government more than two of any other; and that, while the Government continues to refuse the aid of colored men, thus alienating them from the national cause, and giving the rebels the advantage of them, it will not deserve better fortunes than it has thus far experienced.—Men in earnest don't fight with one hand, when they might fight with two, and a man drowning would not refuse to be saved even by a colored hand.

Source: Frederick Douglass, "Fighting Rebels With Only One Hand," Douglass' Monthly *(September 1861).*

Union Recruiting Music (1862)

To encourage recruitment and continued support of the war, both the Union and Confederate governments capitalized on all types of prowar propaganda. Individual supporters composed poetry and songs that gave potential soldiers the impetus to join the military and support their nation. In this Union recruitment song, the author stresses the need for American men to avenge the deaths of their countrymen and to support the Union cause. It, like other recruitment literature, plays up the glory and honor that a soldier will be rewarded with after his time on the battlefield.

"Abraham's Covenant"
"We're going to fight in earnest, boys," our foes henceforth shall feel
No tufts of grass nor compromise, but bomb, and lead, and steel!
We'll spare no murderous traitor on the sea, nor on the land,
Nor will we stay the army's march to hound a contraband.

Our brother's on the battlefield are beck'ning us for aid;
Their ranks are thinn'd of thousands who their gory graves have made!
Then rally to their rescue, and with soldiers' might and will
Revenge the blood of Fairfax grounds, and fatal Malvern hill.

Don't dream of intervention, boys, nor England's cotton cry,
That she will risk her all on bales, is only in your eye;
And as for France, let this suffice, your action don't defer;
When she has done with Mexicans we'll have a bone with her.

Then down your names, fill full the ranks, your country needs you now;
Go share a nation's honor, and there seal the patriot's vow;
Trust in God, and mind your powder, and be this your battle cry—
"Our country, we'll defend thee, or with thee, our country, die!"

Heaven save our bleeding Union from the ruthless, deadly foe,
Help us to strike down treason with a speedy, final blow;
God shield our loyal legions who may bear thrice honored scars,
And soon shall victory crown our arms, and peace our nation's stars.

Source: A. Bert Tobey (words and music), "Abraham's Covenant" (Chicago: H. M. Higgins, 1862).

A Northern Paper Discusses Rumors of Southern "Atrocities of the Rebellion" (1862)

Rumors abounded in Civil War America, and those on the home front found it difficult to get accurate information about battles, loved ones, and events. In addition, exaggerated caricatures of the enemy often filled papers and gave those on the home front increased reasons to support their own cause and despise the enemy. This piece, published in a Union paper, depicted the supposedly inhuman and callous nature of the Confederate enemy that Northern soldiers faced. It labels Southerners—soldiers, politicians, and home-front women—as immoral, savage, and willing to do anything. Dehumanizing the enemy was a common tactic in both the North and South.

ATROCITIES OF THE REBELLION

We are not at all disappointed in the moral character of the rebellion or civil war now raging in our country. War in any form, and for any object, is bad enough; but we early foresaw that a war by professedly Christian Slaveholders for the permanent support and extension of slavery—the only true designation of this contest—in such a land and age as ours, would probably be attended with outrages and horrors very like those of the first French Revolution. We deem it our duty to chronicle a few specimens too well attested to doubt their substantial truth.

HIRING INDIANS TO FIGHT US.—Rebel emissaries were early sent to enlist the Indians; and most of the tribes have caught the bait, and promised active aid. A body of 1300 Indian warriors, armed with rifle, bowie-knife and tomahawk, and with their faces painted one half red, and the other black, joined at one time the rebel camp at Arkansas. In our Revolutionary war there were in the British Parliament men brave and humane enough to denounce their own government for employing Indians in their savage warfare; but the South is eager to get such allies, and to bring them, with their barbarous weapons, into the field.

THE REBEL MODE OF WARFARE.—"If, turning from this revolting spectacle, we fix our gaze," says the *Washington Intelligencer*, "upon the kind of war which the secessionists themselves wage in Missouri, and in a greater or less degree wherever they have the power, we shall be brought to the conclusion, that the presence of Indian savages cannot greatly intensify the horrors of the internecine strife into which they willingly plunge every State or community that they cannot entirely control or possess. The condition into which they have brought Missouri is thus described by the St. Louis Republican: 'The Secessionists of Missouri have undertaken to make this State too hot for those who love the Union and the Constitution of our fathers. Pretending to build the edifice of disunion on the doctrine of State rights, they wage war upon the State as well as upon individuals. And their way of waging war! Shooting into passenger trains; lying in wait in ambush and behind stumps, to fire upon some defenceless traveller; placing kegs of powder upon railroad tracks; calling citizens out of their beds at night to tar and feather or hang them; robbing fields of their crops, orchards of their fruits, farms of their stock; burning bridges and depots; setting fire to barns and dwellings, and establishing such a reign of terror as is making women and children frantic, and driving peace-loving inhabitants from their homes by scores and hundreds.'

"The condition of affairs in Southwest Missouri is deplorable. Numberless atrocities and excesses are daily committed by the rebel forces and those in league and sympathy with them. It is estimated that four-fifths of the horses in possession of the rebel troops, who are generally mounted, were stolen. Foraging parties levy their contributions on friends and foes alike. Frequent robberies of stores have been committed. Large quantities of grain have been taken, and all the flouring mills have been pressed to perform a share in the exactions. This system of plunder is but a small part of the aggravations which afflict the inhabitants in the region indicated. Their fears are excited by roving bands of Indians accompanying the rebel horde. It is averred that a Cherokee named Fry has a commission in his deer skin pouch ensuring him a reward of $50 for the scalp usually worn by Dr. Stemmer, of Jasper county."

TREATMENT OF WOUNDED AND PRISONERS.—A writer who "gives only accounts taken from *officers* of what they themselves saw" at Bull Run, avows that "the proofs are overwhelming and incontrovertible, that our wounded men; were *systematically murdered*, that our surgeons were *systematically shot down*, that our ambulances were *systematically blown up by shells*, and that at the last, our hospital, a church building, was charged on by cavalry, who rode up and fired their revolvers through the windows at the wounded men as they lay on the floors, and at the surgeons who were attending to their wants, and that the enemy eventually set fire to the building, and burned it, and in it scores of wounded and dying men."

During the battle "they carried American flags to deceive our men, and when small squads that had got separated from their regiments, approached these flags, they were fired upon and slaughtered. *The Rebels, also, fired upon the wounded, standing them up for targets, and then firing at them. One of the Connecticut men saw this done.* A number of the 2d New York saw the Rebels' sharpshooters *fire upon and kill two vivandieres* who were giving wine and water to the wounded. They also shot at ambulances bring off the wounded, attacked flags of truce sent out to succor the suffering, fired point-blank at the buildings used as hospitals, and it is said by some, that they fired the buildings. Capt. Haggerty was killed in a charge. When his body was found, his throat was cut from ear to ear, and his ears and nose were cut off. Many of the wounded were found thus disfigured. The faces of our dead were found horribly mauled with the butt ends of muskets, and their bodies filled with wounds, evidently inflicted after they had fallen on the field. Poor Capt. Downey, being overpowered by numbers, threw down his arms and surrendered. 'We take no prisoners, d—n ye,' was the reply; and he was literally blown to pieces, no less than sixteen balls entering his body."

"We have had," says the *N. Y. Observer*, "a conversation with a young gentleman who was an active participant in the fight at Bull Run. We have known him well for many years, and have entire confidence in his veracity. He confirms the statements that have been denied respecting the atrocities perpetrated by the rebels on our wounded. His own observation enabled him to testify that our wounded *were* butchered while they were lying helpless, and pleading for mercy. It is painful to repeat such statements; but, when they come to us in a way to compel us to believe them, it is a duty to make them known to the shame of the men who do such deeds, even in the excitement of war.''

FEMALE BRUTALITY.—It would seem as if the rebellion made in some cases monsters even of women. ''A benevolent (!) lady offers in one case a liberal premium for human scalps sufficient to make a bed-quilt!'' The *N. Y. Commercial Advertiser* says on reliable authority, that ''an officer took possession of the valuable trunks of a rebel officer, with his beautiful uniform, linen, watch, bowie-knife, Bible (!) and letters; and one of the letters (opened to find a direction) written by a lady, closed with this sentence, 'If you succeed in killing a Yankee, I wish you would *skin him* and *tan the hide*; I have something in mind that I want to make of it.'''

REWARDS FOR BRUTALITY.—The Southern Congress some time ago offered 'a bounty of twenty dollars for each person on board any armed ship or vessel belonging to the United States, at the commencement of any engagement, which shall be burned, sunk or destroyed by any vessel commissioned as aforesaid, for each and every prisoner by them captured and brought into port.' We believe that such a piece of barbarism as this never before disgraced the statute-book of a professedly civilized people.

Source: Advocate of Peace 14 (*January/February 1862*): 22.

An Account of Indian Involvement in the Union War Effort (1862)

As the following account of the southeastern Indians of the Indian Territory reveals, Native Americans participated as central actors on many Civil War battlefields, especially in the West. The war divided Native American communities as it provided opportunities for them to settle old scores and pursue new interests. Most Native Americans, though, initially tried to remain isolated from the dispute. From the start of the war, however, the United States and the Confederacy both attempted to convince various Native American nations to end their neutrality and become allies. Over the course of the war, fewer Native Americans could or wanted to remain neutral.

THE BATTLES BETWEEN THE LOYAL INDIANS AND THE REBELS

A correspondent of the Cincinnati Gazette, writing from Fort Leavenworth, under date of January 15, says:—

The news from the Indian country is of great interest. On the arrival home of the Indian delegation from Washington, they represented the magnitude of the Federal forces and their vast resources for carrying on the war, to the several tribes, who at once collected a large force and declared themselves in behalf of the Union. This Indian army, numbering nearly four thousand men, was placed under the command of Ho-pothe-yo-ho-la, an aged Creek chieftain, who fought under Jackson in the war of 1812, and is at present well known to the national officers. The principal chiefs under him were Yustenrick-co chokme, Pascofar, Cho-of-lop-haigo, Ah ha-luck, Yuste-migo, and Sun-muckee-micco—mostly of the Seminoles.

This force, armed with common hunting rifles and bows and arrows, and stationed on the Verdigris river, near Coody's Bluffs, was attacked, on Christmas day, but Ben McCulloch's Texan Rangers and a large force of rebel Indians, and, after a desperate conflict, was defeated. Two hundred of the Cherokees stood their ground until every man but one was killed. The Creeks fled before the desperate charge of the Rangers. The Seminoles took advantage of the ground, and acquitted themselves in a manner worthy of the highest praise.

Once incident of this battle for freedom we would fain notice, as the historian may fail to chronicle it: to wit, the heroic conduct of Ho-pothe-yo-ho-la, the silver-haired chieftain in command, who, having been driven from his first position by an irresistible charge of the enemy, sought a second one, and declared his intention of dying rather than retreat further; and he was only prevented from carrying out this declaration by being seized by two of his warriors and carried off the field, whilst a dauntless band of his braves covered his retreat by opposing the pursuing foe in the most unflinching and fearless manner. Three hundred Cherokees (commanded by John Ross) were stationed between the mouths of the Verdigris and Grand rivers. The latest intelligence from that quarter is that they were surrounded by the rebels, and it is supposed they have been entirely cut to pieces ere now.

The result of the war in the Indian Territory has proved very destructive to the loyal tribes, who have been compelled to leave their towns to the mercy of an unsparing foe. It is the belief of the principal chiefs that they would have been able to have stood their ground had they not been destitute of ammunition. General Hunter had ordered 4,500 pounds of ammunition to be loaded into wagons, on yesterday, while Mr. Johnson, agent for the Delawares, secured the services of twenty-five warriors to serve as an escort, and the writer was to accompany the expedition; but before the arrival of the time appointed for our departure, intelligence was received of the total rout of the loyal tribes, and their arrival in Southern Kansas, where some thirteen thousand men, women, and children, are now awaiting assistance from the Government—they being destitute, having to leave their homes in such haste as to prevent them from making the necessary preparation for their comfort. And when we consider that these hapless mortals were, in their destitute condition, forced to travel for eight days through an uninhabited country, we may have a faint realization of the amount of suffering which they must have endured. This news was received on yesterday evening, and on this morning General Hunter despatched sixteen wagons, ladened with ammunition, flour, and bacon, to the relief of the reported sufferers. E. H. Corruth, the celebrated mediator between the Government and the Indians will, by order of General Hunter, start to Southern Kansas on tomorrow, for the purpose of taking the census of all the tribes represented, and at the same time will organize the warriors into regiments, which will at once apply for acceptance into the Government service, and will, no doubt, prove efficient auxiliaries, as Mr. Corruth, who has just arrived from their headquarters, reports them filled with revenge, and desirous of at once being led against an enemy who vanquished them, because destitute of the necessary munitions to enable them to make a successful resistance.

Source: Saturday Evening Post, *February 1, 1862, 3.*

A Confederate Woman Held at the Old Capitol Prison Describes Her Imprisonment (1862)

Despite antebellum preconceptions about women as meek and uninvolved in military matters, many women became spies for the Union and Confederacy during the Civil War. These women took advantage of assumptions about femininity to appear harmless, to hide information and supplies on their bodies, and to coax information out of unsuspecting men. If discovered, these women faced imprisonment and banishment. The Union used the Old Capitol Prison to hold Southern female spies. Those there often wrote extensive letters, journals, and newspaper articles describing their situation and affirming their dedication to the Confederacy. Many, including the woman whose account is published below, refused to be cowed by the reality of imprisonment and instead hoped for release to begin their espionage activities again.

Old Capitol Prison, March 14, 1862

Dear Doctor: I do not know how you are affected by this confinement but to me 'tis intolerable. Within the past two weeks through representations made by the superintendent, to whom we appealed and who I believe has at least a suspicion of a soul, having been born South, we have been permitted to exercise for half an hour three times a day in the filthy yard thronged by contrabands and surrounded by sentries. Still it is in the open air. I do wish you would write, if but two or three lines, and give to the party who hands you this. It can reach me as this is sent.

Day before yesterday we were informed by Superintendent Wood that in all probability we should be sent to some of the Northern fortresses. The idea of being sent north is death to me. I'd rather they'd shoot me at once. The news from Manassas scared a good many of the cowardly fools whom we are well rid of into taking the oath of allegiance to the magnanimous Government, but our men of stamina have rejected their overtures with scorn. Whilst walking in the yard I addressed sotto voce in passing inquiries to several of our Maryland boys who had just been brought in and find as I supposed it (the evacuation) a strategic affair on the part of our Army. The boys looked pretty rough and rusty—a little depressed at their capture but in good health; say we are not whipped and not going to be.

I do not see why they keep you incarcerated; you have done nothing. I am the mischievous rebel that has done all the mischief. They ascribe to me a marvelous power and capacity of mischief. I'll be even with them yet. Why do you not make use of the means in your power to get out and try to reach Dixie? The way is open. True there is risk, but "nothing risked, nothing won." See Doctor Thomas, who would introduce you to the President and Secretary Benjamin; or the better one to see would be Doctor Bealle.

I did write to Seward and since to Stanton, but 'tis useless; they've got too much against me. The commission is not all. Mrs. Rose Greenhow and myself were the first females brought to this old Union rat trap, but our number is gradually increasing. The first accession was Mrs. Morris, still with us; the next a Mrs. J. Barton, alias Mrs. McCarter; [she] still sports her male attire—can't help herself. Then a party were brought here who were released in two or three days. Then Mrs. Morris of Baltimore, who is likely to remain with us; then two young ladies captured at Dranesville or thereabout who said they were sorry, promised amendment, took the oath and God speed them. I am always glad when we get rid of a craven. Colonel Thompson is out at last, Schley will get out this evening. We have quite a sprinkling of Marylanders here and some from Baltimore City. Strange to say every lady now under arrest and with but three or four exceptions have been Marylanders.

Your situation is preferable to mine. You are in Baltimore near your friends where your wants and comforts can be ministered to by friends. Whilst my condition is pitiable in the extreme I almost wish that death would come to my relief; but these devils shall not have the pleasure to know how much I feel. I tax every power and every nerve to bear up, but 'tis indeed a terrible tax. The indignities we are continually subjected to is a disgrace to people calling themselves civilized to permit. But I will not repine; every dog has his day. Our turn will come anon. I'll stick to the old Merrimac while there's a plank to her deck, and when she goes to pieces or sinks I'll go with her. I saw her and examined her thoroughly and felt sure she would be able to weather the gale.

Good night, for as usual I have an intolerable headache
C[atherine] V. B[axley]

Source: The War of the Rebellion: A Compilation of the Official Records of the Union and Confederate Armies, *Series 2, Volume 2 (Washington, DC: Government Printing Office, 1897): 1319–1320.*

Rabbi M. J. Michelbacher's Sermon on a Confederate Day of Prayer (1863)

Religion played an integral part in the lives of 19th-century Americans. Consequently, in both the North and South, the presidents and other political leaders frequently called for days of prayer and fasting for their respective nations. Clergy of all denominations responded to these calls and shaped their sermons accordingly. In this passage, Rabbi M. J. Michelbacher affirms his Jewish congregation's dedication to their nation and their willingness to fight for it. He further encourages them to continue in their efforts for the Confederacy as he leads them in prayer for their nation.

BRETHREN OF THE HOUSE OF ISRAEL:

It is due to you, to whom I always speak of your faults, without fear, favour, or affection, to say, I have carefully investigated your conduct from the commencement of this war to the present time, and I am happy in coming to the unbiassed conclusion, that you have fulfilled your duties as good citizens and as men, who love their country. It has been charged by both the ignorant and the evil-disposed against the people of our faith, that the Israelite does not fight in the battles of his country! All history attests the untruthfulness of this ungracious charge, generated in the cowardly hearts and born between the hypocritical lips of ungenerous and prejudiced foes. The Israelite has never failed to defend the soil of his birth, or the land of his adoption.... In respect to those Israelites who are now in the army of the Confederate States, I will merely say, that their patriotism and valor have never been doubted by such men as have the magnanimous souls of Lee, Johnston, Jackson and others of like manhood. The recorded votes and acts of the Israelites of this Confederacy, amply prove their devotion to the support of its Government. They well understand their duties as citizens and soldiers, and the young men do not require the persuasion of conscription to convert them into soldiers, to defend, as they verily believe, the only free government in North America. Many of our young men have been crippled for life, or slain upon the field of battle, in the service of the Confederate States, and there are several thousands yet coursing the campaigns of war against those enemies of our Confederacy, who are as detestable to them, as were the Philistines to David and his countrymen.

The humanity and providence of the Israelite for the distressed families of the soldiers of our army, have allayed the pangs of poverty and brought comfort to households, wherein before were only seen hopelessness and misery....

PRAYER.

Again, do we approach Thee, O God of Israel—not as a single meeting of a part, but as the whole congregation of all the people of the land, that trust in Thy protection forever, and who do now come before Thee, to seek it in the midst of dangers, yet *more* appalling than those of the past, that Thou didst put aside without harm unto us! ...

O God of our fathers! God of Abraham, Isaac and Jacob! hear our prayers, and listen graciously to our supplications, this day, for our salvation as a people, struggling before Thee for our liberties and independence, now threatened with renewed dangers and calamities, from the combining and concentrating powers of our enemies....

The man-servants and the maid-servants Thou hast given unto us, that we may be merciful to them in righteousness and bear rule over them, the enemy are attempting to seduce, that they too may turn against us, whom Thou hast appointed over them as instructors in Thy wise dispensation!

Because of Thy strength in aid of us, our enemies have failed against us, in all the modes and means of warfare known and adopted among the men Thou hast civilized—*because of Thy strength* they have failed; and, behold, O God, they incite our man-servants and maid-servants to insurrection, and they place weapons of death and the fire of desolation in their hands, that we may become an easy prey unto them; they beguile them from the path of duty, that they may waylay their masters, to assassinate and to slay the men, women and children of the people, that trust only in Thee. In this wicked thought, let them be frustrated, and cause them to fall into the pit of destruction, which in the abomination of their evil intents, they digged for us, our brothers and sisters, our wives and our children.

Our land and our waters are troubled with the presence of the foes of Thy people. Drive them away, O Lord! Let it be, that their boasted ships of terror may come to naught before the breath of our Lord God, as He sendeth it forth upon the waters of the Great Deep.

Bless, O God, the tillage of our fields, that they may bring forth abundantly for the wants of the people! Give unto each one the bread of life, and let the fat of the land be seen in plenty in the home of every family of the Confederate States of America. . . .

We implore Thee to turn the hearts of the people of the Confederate States of America generously and kindly every one to the other, that, in the midst of common tribulation, they may cheer and sustain each other till they shall have safely passed through the troublous flood of war, to the happiness of a peaceful land, regenerated by Thy favoured presence forever and ever! . . .

We believe, O God, that piety cannot subsist apart from patriotism—we love our country, because Thou hast given it unto us as a blessing and a heritage for our children; and, now, O God, we call upon Thee, to bring salvation to the Confederate States of America, and to crown independence with lasting honour and prosperity.

O God! Give cheerfulness to the hearts of our people; and, as a sign of our confidence in Thee and Thy especial protection over us, let the play of the children be seen in the streets of our cities, towns and villages and all places of our country. Let no fear come near our maidens, and be Thou unto our young men a tower of strength, that they may stand with undaunted hearts to shield and sustain the matrons and patriarchs of the people! Drive, O God, the fear of black famine far away from our borders, and open the Omnipotent hand of Thy Heavenly bounty upon all these—the people of this Thy land, which we dedicate anew to Thee this day. And, O God, keep in remembrance this day forever!

Be Thou, O God, with our armies, and inspire the leaders thereof with a pious fear of Thee. Endow them with the faculty of anticipating the designs of the enemy and the wisdom, to thwart every movement of hostility!

Inspire our soldiers with that patriotic courage, which comes from the thought of duty to Thee and to their country. Give unto them, sleepless vigilance, vigorous and active bodies and hands, to wield in victory the weapons of battle. Give unto them, when in pursuit of the flying foe, the swiftness of the eagle, and in the fight, let them be as fierce lions among the prey!

Send, O God, Thy protecting messengers to our ships of war upon the waters of the rivers and of the great deep! Shield our infant navy from all the dangers of storm and battle; and, in all its engagements with the enemy, let the power of the wonderful arm of the God of Israel be its succour, defence and victory! Let the boast of the enemy's naval superiority in numbers over us, be unto Thee, O Lord, their weakness and destruction. And give unto us, Thy people that trust in Thee, O God of Israel, the crown of triumph!

O God! Give counsel and wisdom to Thy servant, Jefferson Davis, President of the Confederate States of America, and grant speedy success to his endeavours to free our country from the presence of its foes.

Be Thou with him and the legislature of the Confederate Government of America, and give unto them Thy care and blessing.

Send us peace, O Lord God, we humbly implore Thee! … Amen! Hallooyah!

Source: Rev. M. J. Michelbacher, A Sermon Delivered On the Day of Prayer, Recommended by the President of the C. S. of A., the 27th of March, 1863, At the German Hebrew Synagogue, *Bayth Ahabah (Richmond, VA: Macfarlance & Furgusson, 1863).*

New York Celebrates the Capture of a Confederate Ship by Robert Smalls (1862)

In May 1862, African American slave Robert Smalls, employed by the Confederate Navy as a deckhand on the Planter, sailed the ship out of Confederate hands in Charleston to the safety of a Northern vessel, the Onward. Smalls turned the Planter and its contents, including ammunition and weaponry, over to the Union Navy. The press in the Union hailed Smalls as a hero and a bill passed by Congress and signed President Abraham Lincoln financially rewarded him. Public ceremonies further lauded his accomplishment. Small's actions revealed the inherent problem of using African Americans as part of the Confederate war effort.

THE HERO OF THE PLANTER

Public Reception of Robert Smalls at Shiloh Church—Addresses by Rev. J. N. Gloucester, Prof. W. J. Wilson, Robert Smalls, Rev. H. J. H. Garnet and Others—Presentation and Resolutions—The Sentiment Against Colonization

The colored people of this City assembled in large numbers, at 8 P.M., yesterday, in the Shiloh Church, on the corner of Mario and Prince streets, to do public honor to Capt. Robert Smalls, their gallant brother, who, "with his comrades, seized a rebel gunboat, rescued his family and those of his companions from Slavery, passing six forts, reaching the Union squadron, and presenting the Government with the trophies of his achievement." Punctually the house was crowded with the most intelligent and respectable portion of the African-Americans of the great Metropolis. The female portion of the audience was very numerous, and remarkable for every visible characteristic that adorns the sex. Neither personal attractions, taste nor dignity were wanting.

Mr. J. H. Townsend presided, and after he had opened the exercises with a few introductory remarks, Rev. John T. Raymond delivered a prolonged and fervent prayer, invoking the most radical and complete change in the condition of the colored race in America.

The first speaker was Rev. J. N. Gloucester who, in a very extended and emphatic address reviewed the present posture of affairs in this country, regretted the ninety days' delay involved in the President's Emancipation edict which, however, he was inclined to look upon as merely a day of grace to the rebels. The speaker was followed in warm and spirited addresses by Prof. W. J. Wilson, of Brooklyn; Rev. H. H. Garnet and others, all of whom commended that unwritten page of the history of the present war which is inscribed with the deeds of the black man, and were equally emphatic and decided in their views against forced colonization. These sentiments continually elicited the most enthusiastic plaudits. The choir alternated the addresses with the very beautiful chanting of "John Brown's Hymn," "There's a Better Time a-Coming," and other favorite Emancipation ditties, and, throughout, the entire audience was wrought up to a high pitch of pleasurable excitement.

While Prof. Wilson was speaking, Robert Smalls entered the house and was received with deafening cheers. A few minutes later, he was presented on behalf of the colored community with a massive and very handsome gold medal, executed by Ball & Black of this City. The medal bore on its face a representation of Charleston harbor, with the steamer *Planter* and Fort Sumpter in the foreground, and the Union squadron in the distance, and, on the reverse side, the following inscription:

"Presented to Robert Smalls by the colored citizens of New-York, Oct. 2, 1862, as a token of their regard for his heroism, his love of liberty, and his patriotism.

Robert Smalls, whose famous escape and personal appearance we have already made familiar, replied, in a very modest and touching address, recounting his desperate venture and expressing the hope, that as he was about to return to his duty as a pilot on the Union fleet at Port Royal, he might yet guide it safely into Charleston harbor. Mrs. Smalls and her little boy Robert were presented, and the whole family were greeted with wild and prolonged cheering.

The following resolutions were then read by Prof. Reagon, and applauded to the echo.

Resolved, That the colored people of the City of New-York cordially welcome Mr. Robert Smalls, of Charleston, S.C., as a representative of the loyal people, comprising four millions of black Unionists now living in the rebel or semi-rebel States.

First—By achieving his own liberty and freedom from the despotism which now broods over the South.

Secondly—By securing the liberty of his wife and children and those of the crew of his vessel, thereby carrying out most gloriously and promptly the doctrine of immediate emancipation.

Thirdly—In that the act of seizing the gunboat and passing successfully the six forts which environ Charleston Harbor, he developed a capacity for military and naval conduct excelled by nothing which has occurred in the present war, and equaled by only a few events in any other war.

Fourthly—By presenting to the Federal Government the valuable prize won by his prowess, he has show in his own behalf and of those whom he represents, a faithful devotedness to the cause of the American Union, which ever has and ever will illustrate the conduct of the black citizens of the United States.

Fifthly—Our brother Smalls has by this one act proven beyond any man's gainsaying the safety, the justice and the easy possibility of the General Government [indecipherable print]

The concourse then, amid general good feeling and cheers for Admiral DuPont, adjourned.

Source: New York Times, *October 3, 1862, 8.*

The Women's Pennsylvania Branch of the U.S. Sanitary Commission's Call for Contributions (1863)

On June 18, 1861, the United States established the U.S. Sanitary Commission (USSC). This organization was created to coordinate the volunteer efforts, mostly of women, throughout the United States on behalf of Union soldiers. The USSC not only guided women's efforts in manufacturing supplies, but it also distributed the gathered materials to the soldiers who needed them the most. Under the auspices of the USSC, Northern women served as nurses, raised money for the soldiers, donated clothing and food, made clothing and blankets, ran hospital ships, and ran sanitary fairs, all for the benefit of the Union Army. In this newspaper excerpt, the local USSC branch in Pennsylvania called on women to join the organization and to donate specific items for the soldiers. Similar calls for aid were published in papers throughout the United States.

WOMEN'S PENNSYLVANIA BRANCH OF THE U.S. SANITARY COMMISSION.

The women of the Pennsylvania Branch of the United States Sanitary Commission, appeal to the women of Pennsylvania, and of the neighboring counties of adjoining States, for assistance in their new enterprise—not as to those who have been unmindful of our sick and wounded soldiers—but fully cognizant of the great amount of supplies which their industry has prepared and sent for distribution to various Aid Societies.

Our appeal is based upon the knowledge that this Commission has greater facilities for doing this work than any State or Local Agency—that out of the thousands of boxes distributed by them, but one has been lost—that their Agents are notified of the time of an army's advance, and permitted to transfer their stores to as near the front as possible—and that they are the only organization authorized by Government to pass within the lines, and administer their supplies on the field of battle for the saving of life and the relief of suffering, knowing no difference between men from any section who are nobly fighting for the preservation of the Union.

This work must be left undone if THE WOMEN of the land do not keep the Sanitary Commission supplied with the means of doing it. For this purpose, some of the women of Philadelphia have organized under the name of the "Women's Pennsylvania Branch of the United States Sanitary Commission," and we invite every loyal woman in the city and State and surrounding counties of other States, to co-operate with us.— A small amount of self-denial, or of exertion on the part of each, would insure to the Commission an exhaustless supply of those needed stores. There is no time to be lost. Let every county, every town organize and put themselves in communication with us without delay. We know not how many lives depend upon our exertions—how much suffering rests with us to relieve. Let us assume these duties solemnly, with the determination that while the war lasts, we will devote our energies to this sacred cause.

LIST OF ARTICLES NEEDED.

Flannel Shirts, ordinary size and make.

Flannel Drawers, " "

Double Calico Wrappers.

Blankets and Quilts for single beds.

Cotton Shirts and Drawers.

Bed Sacks, 7 feet by 3 feet; slit in the middle, with strings.

Carpet Slippers, with stiff soles.

Woolen Sacks, Towels.

Handkerchiefs, made of old chintz or lawn dresses.

Wines, Syrups and Jellies should be packed in separate boxes. Jellies should be covered with cloth, pasted over the mouth of the jar. Bottles should have the cork tied or sealed over. They should be packed in sawdust, as firmly as possible. Every bottle should be labeled.

On the top of the contents of each box, under the cover, a list of what it contains, with the name and address of the donor, should be placed; a duplicate of this list should be sent by mail.

Each box should be marked on the outside with the name of the Society, Town and State from which it is sent. Boxes should be directed:

WOMEN'S PENN. BRANCH, U.S. SAN. COM.

1307 Chestnut Street, Philadelphia.

Source: Saturday Evening Post, *March 28, 1863, 2.*

Media Accounts of Bread Riots in Southern Cities (1863)

Wartime shortages and inflation affected everyone in the Confederacy, but they hit poor women especially hard because these women did not have the resources to combat rising prices and scarcity of food. In the spring of 1863, the crisis had reached a tipping point. Hundreds of women in cities across the South, frustrated with their government's perceived inattention to their plight, publicly protested the high price of bread and other necessities. These primarily poor white women voiced their discontent with a government that asked them to sacrifice for the greater good, but did nothing to help them feed their children and survive. These bread riots should not been seen as expressions of disloyalty or Unionism, but rather as public calls for the Confederate government to do its duty to its citizens—rioting women wanted an end to policies that magnified their economic woes. Although the Richmond bread riot was the largest of its kind, similar protests took place in cities in North Carolina, Georgia, Alabama, and other urban areas. The following excerpts reflect public perception in the North of the various bread riots taking place.

FRUSTRATED WOMEN IN RICHMOND PARTICIPATE IN BREAD RIOT

The Bread Riot which took place in Richmond on Thursday is very significant of the condition to which rebeldom is reduced. If the people of that city are compelled to break open the public stores to obtain bread, what must be the state of the inhabitants of those districts which produce but little food and raise mainly cotton or tobacco? Virginia is the most fruitful grain raising State in the South, and is the Eastern portion of it what Tennessee and Kentucky are to the West, and if the want of food manifests itself in such a demonstrative fashion as to bring out a hungry mob of three thousand women into the streets of the capital, we can readily imagine how dire must be the distress existing in the other States.

Source: The New York Herald, *April 2, 1863.*

THE "WAYWARD SISTERS" DOWN SOUTH

Rebel papers are teeming with reports of the riotous doings of the Southern Female, who as we foretold in our last number, has carried the idea of bread-riots beyond the range of cereals and into the region of dry-goods. The following bit from a Southern paper gives a lively general impression of the Southern Female on the rampage:

"The Atlanta (Ga.) *Confederacy* announces that there was a women's riot at Milledgeville, in that State on the 10th inst. There were about three hundred women engaged.... They pitched into the dry-goods store of Mr. Gans, a Jew, and seized his fine goods. After a frightful flurry the delicate creatures were dispersed by an eloquent appeal from Judge Harris, of the Superior Court. The correspondent says the women 'didn't want anything but the *fine things.*'"

We can hardly conceive anything more appalling than a charge of three hundred rebellious females, hooped with steel, armed with sharp tongues, and determined to wreak their will upon a fellow's dry-goods, or perish in the attempt. The only safety for such an unfortunate dry-goods person as "Mr. Gans, a Jew," would probably arise from the certainty of the Southern females fighting among themselves for the "fine things" so indispensable to their maintenance. The whole fray, indeed, considering its elements, would naturally resolve itself into a bonnet box—that is, in a pugilistic, not modistic, sense. Thus, a diversion being created in favor of the dry-goods man while one half of the Southern females is contending with the other half in wild rushes over a box of *ruches*, the proprietor might be enabled to call in the police and quell the row.

Does not this present a suggestion of the final result to which we are tending? When bacon and boots grow a little scarcer at the South than they now are, Secessia will split upon the food question, and the row will be over—unless General HOOKER anticipates General STARVATION, and carries the revolted bacon back to Uncle Sam by a salt.

Source: Vanity Fair *7, no. 161 (May 9, 1863): 54.*

ANOTHER BREAD RIOT

Another female bread riot is reported to have taken place in Mobile on September 4, on which occasion the Seventeenth Alabama troops were ordered out to put down the disturbance, but refused to do their duty. The Mobile Cadets were driven from the field, or rather streets, by the infuriated women. The rioters openly declared that "if some means were not rapidly devised to relieve their suffering or to stop the war they would burn the city." The suffering in Mobile is said to be very great.

Source: Harper's Weekly, *October 10, 1863, 643.*

A Reporter's View of the New York City Draft Riots (1863)

Like their counterparts in the South, citizens in the North displayed their displeasure with the course of the war and their frustration with its continuation through public protests. Tensions came to a head after the United States instituted a draft in the summer of 1863. Within hours of the publication of names that had been drawn in the New York City draft, hundreds of angry citizens gathered. The protesters, who ultimately numbered around 50,000, were primarily Irish immigrants. After joining up, they rioted in east-side neighborhoods for three days before being stopped by federal troops. In the process, the rioters, who focused their anger on the city's African American population, looted stores, burned down a black church and orphanage, and otherwise terrorized residents. The resulting damage was estimated at more than $1.5 million, and estimates of the killed and wounded range between two dozen and 100 people.

CAPT. THOMAS W. THORNE, CITY HALL.

Early on Monday thousands of excited people were gathered in the Park and Printing-house Square. Incendiary harangues were made, and threats uttered; every colored man met in the vicinity was attacked and beaten. Capt. Thorne detailed five of his force, in citizens' dress, who mingled with the different crowds, and reported every fifteen minutes. At 5 1/2 o'clock P.M. the force with Capt. Warlow's command reported to headquarters, and were sent thence to the First Precinct, through which tour was made. On returning at dusk, met by citizens at the Post-office, who informed them of attack on *Tribune* Building. Started up Nassau Street at double-quick, came on the crowd of five or six thousand, the work of destruction having been commenced, the office entered, gutted, and fired. Capt. Thorne gave the word to his men to keep together. The order to charge was given, and on they went, without waiting to estimate odds, the handful, with a ringing cheer, against the thousands; the first blow was received by the Captain, a bludgeon on the head, knocking him back six feet; down went the man who gave it by the locust of officer Cowen; on went the men, dealing blows right and left, desperately and with fearful effect; the mob, even with its proportions, could not stand the impetuous charge; they fought a few moments, surged back, and then again swung forward, as though to crush out the force; it was too late; on and among them were the command, nearly every blow bringing to the ground a rioter; in one place, six lay so close as almost to touch each other; it was too much for the lawless, and, after hard and hand-to-hand fighting to Frankfort Street, they broke, fleeing in wild confusion. That portion which went up Chatham and Center Streets were closely followed for a while, and severely clubbed by this force; that portion which fled across the Park were met by Inspector Carpenter and his men, and scores knocked down. No mercy was shown, and over a hundred lay in the square and Park, the well-punished victims of their own folly and crime. While the mob were being thus terribly handled in the street, some of the force turned their attention to the *Tribune* Building, fighting their way to and entering it. The fire had but just been lighted, and was readily extinguished. Officer McWaters, on entering the door, was assaulted by a burly ruffian, armed with a hay-rung, who, by a powerful blow on the shoulder, knocked him down; instantly on his feet again, he more than repaid on the heads of the rioters the blow. The building was cleared speedily, and not a man found in it escaped without severe punishment.

This good work being in detail so bravely and thoroughly accomplished, Capt. Thorne ordered his force to cover Spruce Street and the square at Frankfort. Sergeant Devoursney took command. What of the crowd had returned from Chatham Street and Center were pushed back to Frankfort, and the space below entirely cleared. Meantime rumors were constant of mobs accumulating up-town to come down and finish a work which had been so disastrously for the rioters foiled. About eleven o'clock the mob had reassembled above Frankfort Street, though not in the old proportions, and were pressing sharply upon the police thrown across the square. Sergeant Devoursney used every argument to induce them to retire, and these failing, ordered, "Now, men, go in and give it to them!" Go in they did forthwith, and, where moral suasion had failed, the locusts succeeded. It was a quick, severe fight, and a number were so badly punished as to be unable to get away. This was the last serious demonstration in that section, the determined action and success of the police furnishing a lesson which was laid to heart.

After the attack at the *Tribune* those laying in the street were allowed to be carried off by their friends returning for them, and the square looked somewhat like a field of battle. In the charge ordered by Capt. Thorne, very many of the locusts were broken by the men of this precinct; pretty good evidence that when they hit they meant to hurt. When the mob was being driven off, the writer of the "Record" came very near experiencing the locusts while attempting to reach the *Times* Building. But for the prompt recognition of officer Frank Brown, of the Twenty-sixth Precinct, who rushed forward and warded off three well-raised and well-aimed clubs, he would have had a serious and practical experience wherewith to speak of "locusts." Sergeant Devoursney was in the crowd alone and edging his way to the *Tribune* office just before the mob broke into it; he had got on to the sidewalk, and drawing his revolver was about to shoot the man cheering on the crowd, and who was also engaged in breaking in the door; several bold and good citizens were there, endeavoring to dissuade the rioters from their work, and they crowded around the Sergeant, one of them seizing his arm and begging him to desist, that he would do no good, would sacrifice his own life, besides exciting the crowd to a frenzy; heeding the wise advice he forced his way back, got to the station, found Capt. Thorne had been telegraphed to, hurried back, heard the cheer of the gallant force on its charge from Nassau, went in with his locust and fought his way through and to them, joining in the general fight. When it is remembered that the Sergeant was in uniform, his conduct exhibits the truest courage. Officer McCord was in citizen's dress, and going to the assistance of his comrades was hit and hurt by mistake. Officer Gardner received a serious blow from a brick on the leg. An elderly gentleman, who was among those at the *Tribune* office, attempting to dissuade the mob, was hurt on the head by the police, who, of course, were ignorant of his purpose in being there. He was taken to the station-house, had his wound dressed, and asked if it would leave a scar. On being told it would, he said he should wear it proudly. The wounded who were not carried off by their friends were conveyed to the Twenty-sixth Precinct station-house, where Police Surgeon Kennedy, with two assistants and half-a-dozen attendants, were busily engaged in washing, bandaging, sewing and strapping. The room had all the appearance of an army hospital after a battle—the floor covered with blood, bandages, lint, surgical instruments, pails of bloody water, with Surgeon Kennedy, his shirt-sleeves rolled up, examining, dressing, and ordering. His cool, systematic and quick appliances showed him to be master of the situation. There were wounds of all descriptions the incised, contused, lascerated, punctured, and pistol-shot. All were cared for, and the Doctor's kindness of heart glistened through the cool exterior of the skillful surgeon.

Source: David M. Barnes, The Draft Riots in New York. July, 1863. The Metropolitan Police: Their Services during the Riot Week. Their Honorable Record. (*Baker & Godwin, 1863*).

A Patriotic Poem for Northern Children (1863)

The extended war efforts required support from the civilian population, even the children, in the North and South. Consequently, authors of children's literature adapted to the changed circumstances and began promoting war themes in their writing. Wartime children's literature informed children about the war, used the war to teach ethical lessons, and recruited children to work for their nation's cause. This Northern poem features a boy playing at war, but asserting his willingness to join the Union forces like his father and brother. His war games mimic the battles going on between the Union and Confederacy, and demonstrate his knowledge of events around him.

''The Home Guard''
My father's gone down with the army, to fight;
My brother's a sailor, away on the sea;
And now where my mother sits quiet at night,
There's no one to look at but Annie and me.
Rub-a-dub!

Sometimes when I beat an alarm on my drum,
Annie folds her arms tight and declares she won't yield;
For we are at play that the rebels have come,—
But I'd just like to see them come into our field!
Rub-a-dub!

Little Annie's my sister; and though she's a girl,
She's almost as brave and as good as a boy;
And I really believe, if her very last curl
Could help our dear Country, she'd give it with joy.
Rub-a-dub!

We were talking about that one day, she and I,
And trying to make up our minds what to do;
For when father and brother are willing to die,
It seems as if we ought to do something too.
Rub-a-dub!

''You know, Willie,'' said Annie, ''I've hemmed a good deal,
And I've got a grey stocking all nicely begun;
But then I can't knit half as fast as I feel,
And the war may be over before it is done.''

''Yes, Annie,'' said I, ''I dare say it will be;
but all girls can do is the best that they can.
But this is the point—I am sure I can't see
Why a boy shouldn't fight, just as well as a man.''
Rub-a-dub!

"Now if General Burnside would make me his aide,
I'd never give aid to the rebels—not I!
And as to this talk about being afraid,
Why, if the right time came, I guess I could die."
Rub-a-dub!

Then Annie's blue eyes like our spring over flowed,
(Girls' tears come so easy!) "O Willie," said she,
"If you marched away with the men down the road,
Then who would take care of poor mother and me?"
Rub-a-dub!

So we went and asked mother—and mother cried too;
At least for a minute she couldn't just speak;
And then she said, "Children, there's plenty to do,
If work for the Country is all that you seek."
Rub-a-dub!

"But look at these dear little hands—and you'll see
The Lord did not fit them for sabre and gun;
And when we would soldiers and conquerors be,
With arms of his giving the work must be done.

"You cannot go into the battle, my dears,
But kneel down and pray for the hosts that have gone!
That God may give victory unto our tears,
Nor leave our brave soldiers to fight on alone.

"Pray, pray for your Country! that God would be nigh,
And with these deep fires burn out all her dross,
And give to the people his peace from on high,
And joy out of weeping, and gain out of loss.

"In each of our hearts there's disorder to quell,
And rebels enough to be put to flight there;
And none serve their Country so truly, so well,
As those who fight Satan by faith and by prayer.

"So little ones, pray!—even very small hands
Are strong when uplifted to heaven's great King;
some fight for their Country in fierce armed bands,
But we on our knees must the victory bring."

Then mother rose up and went quickly away,
With oh such a sob coming up from her breast!
And I wish I could be with my father to-day,—
And we'd give them a lesson, Jeff, Lee, and the rest!
Rub-a-dub!

Rub-a-dub-dub, Rub-a-dub-dub!
Rub-a-dub, dub-a-dub, dub-a-dub-dub!

Source: The Little American 1 (*July 15, 1863): 159.*

Patriotic Northern Poetry (1863)

Wartime propaganda took many forms. This poem, which was set to music, responds positively to President Abraham Lincoln's July 1862 call for 300,000 more volunteers to help fight the Confederacy and bring the war to a speedy close. This song was published in various outlets, including children's magazines.

"Three Hundred Thousand More"
We are coming, Father Abraham, three hundred thousand more,
From Mississippi's winding stream and from New England's shore;
We leave our plows and workshops, our wives and children dear,
With hearts too full for utterance, with but a silent tear;
We dare not look behind us, but steadfastly before—
We are coming, Father Abraham—*three hundred thousand more!*

If you look across the hilltops that meet the *northern* sky,
Long moving *lines* of rising dust your vision may descry;
And now the wind, and instant, tears the cloudy veil aside,
And floats *aloft* our spangled *flag* in *glory* and in *pride*;
And *bayonets* in the sunlight gleam—and bands brave *music* pour—
We are *coming*, Father Abraham—*three hundred thousand* more!

If you look up all our *valleys*, where the growing *harvests* shine,
You may see our sturdy *farmers* fast forming into line;
And *children* from their mother's knees are pulling at the weeds,
And learning how to *reap* and *sow*, against their country's needs;
And a farewell group stands weeping at every cottage door—
We are *coming*, Father Abraham—*three hundred thousand more!*

You have called us, and we're coming, by *Richmond's* bloody tide
To lay us down for *Freedom's* sake, our *brother's* bones beside;
Or from foul *treason's* savage grasp to *wrench* the murderous blade,
And in the face of *foreign* foes its fragments to parade.
Six hundred thousand loyal men and *true* have gone before—
We are coming, Father Abraham—*Three hundred thousand* more!

Source: The Student and Schoolmate 11 (*September 1863): 312–313.*

Charlotte Forten's Description of "Life on the Sea Islands" (1864)

In 1862 Charlotte Forten, along with other Northern women volunteers, joined the efforts in Port Royal, South Carolina, where they began educating and assisting the newly freed slaves of the area. Forten, an African American from Philadelphia, had long been active in abolitionist causes. She became the first African American teacher assigned to the Port Royal district. She spent two years teaching freed slaves in a school that she and two other volunteers set up in a local Baptist church. During her time in Port Royal, Forten kept extensive and detailed journals. In this excerpt, she described the early days of teaching on the Sea Islands.

''Life on the Sea Islands''

The first day at school was rather trying. Most of my children were very small, and consequently restless. Some were too young to learn the alphabet. These little ones were brought to school because the older children—in whose care their parents leave them while at work—could not come without them. We were therefore willing to have them come, although they seemed to have discovered the secret of perpetual motion, and tried one's patience sadly. But after some days of positive, though not severe treatment, order was brought out of chaos, and I found but little difficulty in managing and quieting the tiniest and most restless spirits. I never before saw children so eager to learn, although I had had several years' experience in New England schools. Coming to school is a constant delight and recreation to them. They come here as other children go to play. The older ones, during the summer, work in the fields from early morning until eleven or twelve o'clock, and then come into school, after their hard toil in the hot sun, as bright and as anxious to learn as ever.

Of course there are some stupid ones, but these are the minority. The majority learn with wonderful rapidity. Many of the grown people are desirous of learning to read. It is wonderful how a people who have been so long crushed to the earth, so imbruted as these have been, — and they are said to be among the most degraded negroes of the South, — can have so great a desire for knowledge, and such a capability for attaining it. One cannot believe that the haughty Anglo Saxon race, after centuries of such an experience as these people have had, would be very much superior to them. And one's indignation increases against those who, North as well as South, taunt the colored race with inferiority while they themselves use every means in their power to crush and degrade them, denying them every right and privilege, closing against them every avenue of elevation and improvement. Were they, under such circumstances, intellectual and refined, they would certainly be vastly superior to any other race that ever existed.

After the lessons, we used to talk freely to the children, often giving them slight sketches of some of the great and good men. Before teaching them the ''John Brown'' song, which they learned to sing with great spirit, Miss T. told them the story of the brave old man who had died for them. I told them about Toussaint, thinking it well they should know what one of their own color had done for his race. They listened attentively, and seemed to understand. We found it rather hard to keep their attention in school. It is not strange, as they have been so entirely unused to intellectual concentration. It is necessary to interest them every moment, in order to keep their thoughts from wandering. Teaching here is consequently far more fatiguing than at the North. In the church, we had of course but one room in which to hear all the children; and to make one's self heard, when there were often as many as a hundred and forty reciting at once, it was necessary to tax the lungs very severely.

My walk to school, of about a mile, was part of the way through a road lined with trees,—on one side stately pines, on the other noble live-oaks, hung with moss and canopied with vines. The ground was carpeted with brown, fragrant pine-leaves; and as I passed through in the morning, the woods were enlivened by the delicious songs of mocking - birds, which abound here, making one realize the truthful felicity of the description in ''Evangeline,'' —

''The mocking-bird, wildest of singers, Shook from his little throat such floods of delirious music

That the whole air and the woods and the waves seemed silent to listen.''

The hedges were all aglow with the brilliant scarlet berries of the cassena, and on some of the oaks we observed the mistletoe, laden with its pure white, pearl-like berries. Out of the woods the roads are generally bad, and we found it hard work plodding through the deep sand.

Source: Charlotte Forten, "Life on the Sea Islands," Atlantic Monthly *13 (May 1864): 587–596.*

Eliza Frances Andrews Describes the Destruction Visited upon Georgia by William Tecumseh Sherman's Troops (1864)

In late 1864, Union general William Tecumseh Sherman marched his 60,000 soldiers through Georgia, as he moved them from Atlanta to Savannah in his famous "March to the Sea." Throughout the march, Union soldiers lived off the land and looted the homes that they encountered. Georgian Eliza Frances Andrews witnessed much of the damage as she traveled between her homes in Washington, Georgia, and Macon, where they went for safety from Union troops. In this diary entry, Andrews described the damage to homes, fields, and farms that Union soldiers caused as they made their way across the area.

December 24, 1864

About three miles from Sparta we struck the ''Burnt Country,'' as it is well named by the natives, and then I could better understand the wrath and desperation of these poor people. I almost felt as if I should like to hang a Yankee myself. There was hardly a fence left standing all the way from Sparta to Gordon. The fields were trampled down and the road was lined with carcasses of horses, hogs, and cattle that the invaders, unable either to consume or to carry away with them, had wantonly shot down to starve out the people and prevent them from making their crops. The stench in some places was unbearable; every few hundred yards we had to hold our noses or stop them with the cologne Mrs. Elzey had given us, and it proved a great boon. The dwellings that were standing all showed signs of pillage, and on every plantation we saw the charred remains of the gin-house and packing-screw, while here and there, lone chimney-stacks, "Sherman's Sentinels," told of homes laid in ashes. The infamous wretches! I couldn't wonder now that these poor people should want to put a rope round the neck of every red-handed "devil of them" they could lay their hands on. Hay ricks and fodder stacks were demolished, corn cribs were empty, and every bale of cotton that could be found was burnt by the savages. I saw no grain of any sort, except little patches they had spilled when feeding their horses and which there was not even a chicken left in the country to eat. A bag of oats might have lain anywhere along the road without danger from the beasts of the field, though I cannot say it would have been safe from the assaults of hungry man. Crowds of soldiers were tramping over the road in both directions; it was like traveling through the streets of a populous town all day. They were mostly on foot, and I saw numbers seated on the roadside greedily eating raw turnips, meat skins, parched corn—anything they could find, even picking up the loose grains that Sherman's horses had left. I felt tempted to stop and empty the contents of our provision baskets into their laps, but the dreadful accounts that were given of the state of the country before us, made prudence get the better of our generosity.

The roads themselves were in a better condition than might have been expected, and we traveled at a pretty fair rate, our four mules being strong and in good working order.... Our next halt was near a dilapidated old house where there was a fine well of water. The Yankees had left it, I suppose, because they couldn't carry it away. Here we came up with a wagon on which were mounted some of the people we had seen on the cars the day before. They stopped to exchange experiences, offered us a toddy, and brought us water in a beautiful calabash gourd with a handle full three feet long. We admired it so much that one of them laughingly proposed to "capture" it for us, but we told them we didn't care to imitate Sherman's manners....

Before crossing the Oconee at Milledgeville we ascended an immense hill, from which there was a fine view of the town, with Gov. Brown's fortifications in the foreground and the river rolling at our feet. The Yankees had burnt the bridge, so we had to cross on a ferry. There was a long train of vehicles ahead of us, and it was nearly an hour before our turn came, so we had ample time to look about us. On our left was a field where 30,000 Yankees had camped hardly three weeks before. It was strewn with the *débris* they had left behind, and the poor people of the neighborhood were wandering over it, seeking for anything they could find to eat, even picking up grains of corn that were scattered around where the Yankees had fed their horses. We were told that a great many valuables were found there at first,—plunder that the invaders had left behind, but the place had been picked over so often by this time that little now remained except tufts of loose cotton, piles of half-rotted grain, and the carcasses of slaughtered animals, which raised a horrible stench. Some men were plowing in one part of the field, making ready for next year's crop.

Source: Eliza Frances Andrews, The War-Time Journal of a Georgia Girl, 1864–1865 (*New York*: D. Appleton and Company, 1908), *32–38.*

Poet Walt Whitman's Tribute to Slain President Abraham Lincoln, ''O Captain! My Captain!'' (1865)

President Abraham Lincoln's assassination by Southerner John Wilkes Booth on April 14, 1865, and his death the next day shocked the citizenry. Outpourings of grief abounded, including several poems by Walt Whitman. Whitman, a great admirer of the president, first publicly mourned Lincoln with "Hush'd Be the Camps To-Day," which he published on May 4, 1865. He further mourned the slain president in 1865 and 1866 with his elegiac poem "When Lilacs Last in the Dooryard Bloom'd," and "O Captain! My Captain!" both of which were published in *Drum Taps*. "O Captain! My Captain!" became one of Whitman's most popular poems.

''O Captain! My Captain!''
O Captain! my Captain! our fearful trip is done,
The ship has weather'd every rack, the prize we sought is won,
The port is near, the bells I hear, the people all exulting,
While follow eyes the steady keel, the vessel grim and daring;
But O heart! heart! heart!
O the bleeding drops of red,
Where on the deck my Captain lies,
Fallen cold and dead.

O Captain! my Captain! rise up and hear the bells;
Rise up—for you the flag is flung—for you the bugle trills,
For you bouquets and ribbon'd wreaths—for you the shores a-crowding,
For you they call, the swaying mass, their eager faces turning;
Here Captain! dear father!
This arm beneath your head!
It is some dream that on the deck,
You've fallen cold and dead.

My Captain does not answer, his lips are pale and still,
My father does not feel my arm, he has no pulse nor will,
The ship is anchor'd safe and sound, its voyage closed and done,
From fearful trip the victor ship comes in with object won;
Exult O shores, and ring O bells!
But I with mournful tread,
Walk the deck my Captain lies,
Fallen cold and dead.

Source: Walt Whitman, "O Captain! My Captain!" Saturday Press, *November 4, 1865.*

Reference

Abolitionism   Movement to end the institution of slavery. Although abolitionists agreed that the institution of slavery needed to be eliminated, they differed in their tactics as well as in their definition of African American freedom.

Aid Societies   Groups formed at the outset of the Civil War to raise money as well as to make clothes, blankets, bandages, flags, and other supplies for soldiers. Northern aid societies organized under the umbrella of the U.S. Sanitary Commission, but Southern societies worked independently.

American Colonization Society (1817–1912)   Antislavery organization formed to resettle freed slaves in Africa. Established an American colony, Monrovia (later named Liberia), in Africa for freed slaves.

Andersonville (Camp Sumter)   Military prison in Georgia open from 1864 until 1865. Designed to hold 10,000, it was severely overcrowded with captured Union soldiers, most of whom had no protection from the elements. At one point, the population rose to almost 33,000 prisoners. Approximately 13,000 prisoners of war died while detained at Andersonville.

Antietam/Sharpsburg, Battle of (September 17, 1862)   The bloodiest daylong battle and the first Civil War battle on Union soil in Maryland. A Union victory led President Abraham Lincoln to issue the preliminary Emancipation Proclamation. Approximately 23,000 soldiers died or were wounded on this day, more American casualties than had occurred in the combined wars up to this point in U.S. history.

Army of the American Eagle   Aid organization formed by Alfred L. Sewell as a means for children to help the Union war effort. Designed to raise money for the Northwestern Sanitary Fair. More than 12,000 children raised more than $16,000 for the Union through this organization.

Association for the Relief of Maimed Soldiers   Aid society organized in Richmond in 1864 that operated throughout the Confederacy. Supplied artificial limbs to replace soldiers' amputated ones.

Atlanta, Evacuation of (Special Field Order Number 67)   Called for the evacuation of all civilians from Atlanta, Georgia, after its capture by Union general William T. Sherman in September 1864. Resulted in the evacuation of approximately 1,600 civilians, most of whom were women or children.

Barton, Clara (1821–1912)   Civil War nurse from Massachusetts who was famous for her battlefield work for the Union Army. Barton would later establish the American Red Cross in 1881.

Bickerdyke, Mary Ann Ball "Mother" (1817–1901)   Union nurse from Ohio who initially went to the battle front to care for the wounded on her own and was later made an agent of the U.S. Sanitary Commission.

Blackwell, Elizabeth (1821–1910)   First woman to earn a professional medical degree in the United States. Helped establish the Women's Central Association of Relief and the U.S. Sanitary Commission.

Blockade   The Union blockade of Confederate seaports began in 1861. It prevented the bulk of goods from coming in or out of the South and contributed to the shortages of basic necessities throughout the war.

Blockade Running   Confederates used private ships to find ways around the Union blockade of Southern ports. Blockade running was profitable for the few who managed to avoid capture, and the goods garnered high prices.

Booth, John Wilkes (1838–1865)   President Abraham Lincoln's assassin and ardent Confederate. Booth shot Lincoln, who was attending a play at Ford's Theater in Washington, D.C., in the back of his head on April 14, 1865. Booth was cornered in a Virginia farmhouse on April 26. He refused to surrender and was shot and killed.

Border States   Missouri, Kentucky, Maryland, and Delaware played roles in the Confederate and Union war efforts. Although Border States remained in the Union, they often had significant populations of Confederates and African American slaves.

Bounty Jumpers   Men who joined the Union Army under a false name to collect the monetary bounties that were often given to new recruits. Jumpers waited until the bounty was paid before deserting and then often repeating the process.

Bread Riots   Southern protests of shortages and lack of foods in several Confederate cities throughout 1863. Women demanded fair prices and food for their families. The largest occurred in Richmond, Virginia, on April 2, 1863. Others occurred in Mobile, Alabama, and in the Georgia towns of Macon, Atlanta, and Augusta.

Buchanan, James (1791–1868)   President of the United States when South Carolina seceded from the Union in December 1860. Democrat who did little to calm the sectional crisis that grew during his administration.

Bull Run/Manassas, First Battle of (July 21, 1861)   First major battle of the Civil War. Civilians gathered on the surrounding fields in Virginia with picnic baskets to watch what they assumed would be a quick and bloodless skirmish. The Confederates routed the Union in a rather disorganized affair that resulted in approximately 1,200 casualties.

Bull Run/Manassas, Second Battle of (August 29–30, 1862) Part of the Union attempt to take the Confederate capital at Richmond, Virginia. Confederates ultimately forced a Union retreat back to Washington, D.C. The second Union defeat at Manassas resulted in nearly 16,000 Union casualties and more than 9,000 Confederate casualties.

Butler, Benjamin F. (1818–1893) Northern politician and military man. Refused to return captured Southern slaves, instead proclaiming them "contraband of war." Issued the controversial General Order Number 28 (the "Woman Order") during his occupation of New Orleans.

Camp Followers Civilians who followed Civil War armies in any capacity. Some were temporary visitors, while others found employment in the military units as cooks, laundresses, nurses, or prostitutes.

Carpetbaggers Derogatory term used to describe Northerners who came south after the Civil War. It was assumed that these politicians or businessmen came south to take advantage of the locals and to make a profit.

Chancellorsville, Battle of (April 29–May 6, 1863) Confederate victory in Virginia that also resulted in the death of General Thomas "Stonewall" Jackson by friendly fire. The battle resulted in 29,000 casualties.

Chickamauga, Battle of (September 19–20, 1863) One of the bloodiest Civil War battles. This Confederate victory in Georgia resulted in approximately 34,000 casualties.

Civilians Civil War battles in populated areas made many civilians into frontline witnesses, nurses, and aid workers. Civilians helped their war efforts by raising funds, food, and supplies for soldiers. Throughout the war, civilians on both sides dealt with shortages, enemy invasion, and other difficulties.

Confederate Surrender Began with the surrender of Confederate General Robert E. Lee's Army of Northern Virginia at Appomattox Court House in Virginia on April 9, 1865. General Joseph E. Johnston surrendered his Confederate forces to Union general William T. Sherman in North Carolina on April 18. Remaining Southern troops officially capitulated in May.

Confederate Sympathizers, Northern Democrats, Copperheads, anti-emancipationists and others who lived in the United States but supported the Confederacy in some capacity. Some took active roles for the Southern war effort, while others merely opposed the war.

Confiscation Acts (1861–1864) Acts laying out the treatment of enemy property passed by the United States to aid in the war effort. These acts, the first of which was passed in August 1861, liberated slaves captured by Union forces. The second Confiscation Act was passed in July 1862 and was followed by Captured and Abandoned Property Acts in March 1863 and July 1864.

Conscription Drafts designed to swell the ranks of the Union and Confederate armies. Most conscription acts were used to encourage the enlistment of volunteers. The first Confederate conscription acts were passed in April 1862. The Union passed its first conscription act in 1863.

Contraband Relief Association Organization created in 1862 by free African American women in Washington, D.C., to help freedpeople in the area. The name changed to Freedmen and Soldier's Relief Association in 1864.

Contrabands Legal term applied to African American slaves who escaped and took refuge with the Union armies. Benjamin Butler used the term in 1861 to justify his refusal to return slaves that escaped to Fortress Monroe.

Cumming, Kate (ca. 1828–1909) Confederate nurse who was born in Scotland and lived in Mobile, Alabama, when the war began. Her journal detailed her responsibilities and the situations she encountered as a front-line nurse.

Davis, Jefferson (1808–1889) President of the Confederacy. Before the war, he served as secretary of war and as a U.S. Senator from Mississippi. Captured by U.S. troops in 1865 and imprisoned for two years for his role in the Confederate government.

Democratic Party Oldest continuous political party in United States. Split over the issue of slavery at the 1860 convention. Northern Democrats nominated Stephen A. Douglas for president and Southern Democrats nominated John C. Breckenridge.

Desertion Soldiers on both sides of the Civil War left their posts for various reasons. Although some left temporarily and returned of their own volition, as the war progressed, both the Union and Confederate armies instituted harsh punishments for deserters.

Disease Leading cause of death for Civil War soldiers. Epidemics as well as diseases caused by unsanitary camp conditions weakened military units, and twice as many soldiers died from diseases as did from battle wounds.

Dix, Dorothea Lynde (1802–1887) Superintendent of the U.S. Army Nurses during the Civil War. Created volunteer female nursing corps for the Union that had strict requirements for training, dress, and professionalism and that would number more than 3,000.

Douglass, Frederick (ca. 1818–1895) Runaway slave and active abolitionist. Published his autobiography in 1845 as an abolitionist tract, began an antislavery newspaper (*The North Star*) in 1847, and lectured for the American Anti-Slavery Society.

Draft Riots Public disturbances over the Union's conscription policies. The largest draft riot occurred in New York City in July 1863.

Dred Scott v. Sandford   The 1856 Supreme Court case debating the citizenship status of African Americans. The 1857 decision held that Scott had no right to sue for his freedom because, as a slave, he was not a citizen of the United States and therefore had no legal rights. The ruling also declared that masters maintained their rights to their slave property when they traveled to free states or territories.

Election of 1860   Resulted in the presidency of Republican Abraham Lincoln and the ultimate secession of 11 states from the Union. The candidates were Lincoln, Democrats Stephen A. Douglas and John C. Breckenridge, and Constitutional Unionist John Bell. Lincoln won less than 40 percent of the popular vote and was only on the ballot in five slaveholding states. He won 180 of the 303 electoral votes.

Election of 1864   In this wartime election, Republican Abraham Lincoln won a second term in office defeating Democrat and former Union general George B. McClellan. Nineteen states allowed absentee voting and others allowed furloughed soldiers to vote at home.

Emancipation Proclamation   Issued by President Abraham Lincoln on January 1, 1863. Provided for the freedom of slaves in the Confederate states and paved the way for emancipation of all African Americans.

Enfield Rifle Musket   British firearm used extensively by both Union and Confederate armies. Weighed more than nine pounds with its bayonet and was accurate at more than 1,000 yards.

Enlistment   Union and Confederate armies depended on volunteers to form the core of their troops. Men joined the armies for many reasons and sometimes were encouraged to do so for the bounties offered to them.

Enlistment Bounties   Monetary rewards offered to men who voluntarily enlisted in the Union and Confederate armies. Amounts varied within both nations.

Fifteenth Amendment   Gave African American men the right to vote. Enacted on March 30, 1870.

Foraging   Soldiers' efforts to live off the land during military campaigns by taking whatever food items they needed from fields and homes they encountered. Foraging was commonly practiced by both armies. Union generals Philip Sheridan in Virginia's Shenandoah Valley and William T. Sherman in Georgia and the Carolinas became known for the destruction caused as their troops foraged to support their armies.

Fort Pillow Massacre (April 12, 1864)   After their capture of Fort Pillow, Confederate general Nathan Bedford Forrest and his men reportedly killed surrendering African American troops who had been stationed at the Tennessee fort with other Union units. Congressional investigations verified that more than 300 African Americans had been killed in this incident.

Fort Sumter (April 12–14, 1861) First hostile engagement between Confederates and the U.S. military. This incident at the garrison in the Charleston, South Carolina, harbor led to President Abraham Lincoln's call for troops and to the secession of the Upper South states of Arkansas, North Carolina, Virginia, and Tennessee.

Fourteenth Amendment Granted citizenship to African Americans and protected their civil rights. Enacted on July 28, 1868.

Fredericksburg, Battle of (December 13, 1862) One of the worst defeats of the Union Army during the Civil War. The Virginia battle resulted in more than 12,500 Union casualties and 5,400 Confederate casualties.

Freedmen's Bureau (Bureau of Refugees, Freedmen, and Abandoned Lands) Established by Congress on March 3, 1865, to aid former slaves in their efforts to adapt to freedom. Oliver O. Howard, Union general, was appointed the head of the Freedmen's Bureau. It resettled, distributed rations to, provided medical care for, helped negotiate labor contracts for, and established schools for the freedpeople and helped African American veterans secure bounties owed them.

Freedpeople Former slaves emancipated during and after the Civil War. Some freedpeople had gained their freedom by running to Union lines, while others became free after the capture of their towns by Union troops. Schools, hospitals, and other programs were set up for freedpeople on the Sea Islands during the Civil War and throughout the South during Reconstruction.

Frémont, John C. (1813–1890) Union officer in the Civil War. Issued unauthorized emancipation orders in August 1861 that Lincoln later rescinded. In 1856, he became the first presidential candidate for the Republican Party. He lost to Democrat James Buchanan.

Fund-raising Efforts by individuals, local aid societies, and national organizations to raise money and gather supplies for the soldiers and their families. Both the Union and Confederacy pursued fund-raising efforts on behalf of their needy.

Garrison, William Lloyd (1805–1879) Radical abolitionist and newspaper publisher of *The Liberator*. Proponent of immediate emancipation of slaves and full equality for freedpeople.

Gettysburg, Battle of (July 1–3, 1863) Bloodiest battle of the Civil War. This Pennsylvania battle ended with a Union victory and approximately 50,000 casualties.

Government Girls Northern women employed as clerks and office workers in federal offices during the Civil War. They worked in the Treasury and War Departments, the post office, and the Quartermaster General's office at lower pay than their male counterparts.

Grand Army of the Republic   Organization formed by Union veterans in 1866 to preserve the memory of the Union war effort. Held annual encampments (reunions) and founded soldiers' homes. Had more than 400,000 members at its height and was dissolved in 1956 with the death of its last member.

Grant, Ulysses S. (1822–1885)   Commander of the U.S. Army beginning in March 1864. Helped lead the Union to military victory and received surrender of Confederate troops at Appomattox Court House on April 9, 1865. Elected president of the United States in 1868.

Greenhow, Rose O'Neal (ca. 1814–1864)   Confederate spy imprisoned first in her Washington, D.C., home and then in the Old Capitol Prison before being banished from Union soil in June 1862. Published a book about her imprisonment while in England to gain support for the Confederacy.

Guerilla Warfare   Irregular fighting by noncommissioned groups who used extralegal violence outside of the battlefield on behalf of their cause. Most guerilla warfare during the Civil War took place in the South and the West and most guerillas were Confederates.

Homespun   Homemade fabric of cotton, linen, or wool worn by Confederates during the Civil War. Became a badge of honor for Confederate women who gloried in their sacrifice for the Confederacy.

Hospital Ships   Mobile hospitals used by the Union to treat sick and wounded soldiers away from the battlefield. In December 1862, the USS *Red Rover* became the first permanent hospital ship.

Hospitals   Battlefield casualties and camp diseases required the establishment of military hospitals throughout the Union and Confederacy. Field hospitals, general hospitals, "way hospitals," and specialized hospitals were all set up to care for the needs of wounded and sick soldiers. Hospitals were sometimes set up in hotels, churches, schools, homes, warehouses, or boarding houses.

Impressment   Term for appropriation of private property—food, horses, slaves, clothing, cattle—and freedmen to aid the military efforts. Property owners received receipts or payment for items that were impressed. In March 1863, the Confederate government passed the Impressment Act to regulate and utilize what previously had been a state issue.

Irish Brigade   Infantry brigade that was formed by mostly Irish immigrants in New York. The 69th New York Voluntary Infantry Regiment brigade was formed in September 1861. Other Irish brigades later formed and included the 63rd New York Voluntary Infantry Regiment and the 88th Voluntary Infantry Regiment.

Ironclads   Armored warships. The first Confederate ironclad was the CSS. *Virginia* and the first Union one was the USS *Monitor*. Both sides produced more ironclads for use throughout the Civil War.

Jackson, Thomas J. "Stonewall" (1824–1863)   Confederate general from western Virginia. Received nickname of "Stonewall" after his performance at the first battle of Bull Run/Manassas. Killed at Chancellorsville.

Johnson, Andrew (1808–1875)   President of the United States after the assassination of Abraham Lincoln and during Reconstruction. The Tennessee Unionist and Democrat became Lincoln's vice president in 1864. Although he was not convicted, he was the first president to be impeached.

Keckley, Elizabeth (ca. 1818–1907)   Former slave and organizer of the Contraband Relief Association. Became Mary Todd Lincoln's dressmaker in 1861. Founded the Contraband Relief Association in 1862 to help freedmen in the nation's capital. Published her memoir in 1868.

Ladies' Memorial Associations   Postwar organizations formed in the South to commemorate the Confederate dead. They reburied dead Confederate soldiers in Southern cemeteries, raised money to erect memorial statues, and decorated the graves of Confederate soldiers.

Lee, Robert E. (1807–1870)   Commander of the Confederacy's Army of Northern Virginia from 1862 to 1865. Virginian and graduate of West Point, Lee originally turned down President Abraham Lincoln's offer to command the U.S. Army. Lee received command over all Confederate armies in 1865. He surrendered his army to Ulysses S. Grant at Appomattox Court House, Virginia, on April 9, 1865.

The Liberator   Abolitionist newspaper published by William Lloyd Garrison from 1831 until 1865. Published weekly in Boston, Massachusetts.

Lincoln, Abraham (1809–1865)   President of the United States during the Civil War. He was the first Republican president. His presidency brought about the emancipation of slaves and the successful Union war effort. Shot by John Wilkes Booth while watching a play at Washington, D.C.'s Ford's Theater on April 14, 1865. He died the next day.

Livermore, Mary Ashton Rice (1820–1905)   An associate manager of the Northwestern Branch of the U.S. Sanitary Commission. Recruited nurses to serve at army posts, raised money for the Union effort, and planned two successful Sanitary Fairs in Chicago.

Lost Cause   Term used to describe an interpretation of the war espoused by former Confederates and sympathizers to describe the Southern war effort. Romanticizes the culture and history of the Old South, minimizes the importance of slavery to the war, and glorifies General Robert E. Lee.

Loyalty Oaths   Union documents aimed at judging the loyalty of citizens and Southerners. Federal employees had to sign a loyalty oath. The July 1862 Ironclad Test Oath forced individuals to swear past and future loyalty to the United States.

Massachusetts Fifty-fourth (Colored) Infantry   First African American unit commissioned to fight for the Union. Led by Robert Gould Shaw and formed in 1863 after the release of the Emancipation Proclamation.

Minié Bullet (Minié Ball)   Standard bullet during Civil War. Its shape and grooves allowed it to travel a long distance accurately. Its range when shot from a rifle was approximately 400 yards. It could shatter the bone of the person it hit.

Morgan, John Hunt (1825–1864)   Leader of a group of Confederate guerillas. A scout in the Confederate Army until 1862, when he was given command of his own squadron. He and his men began raiding Federal camps and destroying Union property and supplies. In 1863, "Morgan's Raiders" attacked areas in Indiana and Ohio.

Mosby, John Singleton (1833–1916)   Head of a band of Confederate guerillas. His independent operations with his "Mosby's Rangers" began in 1863. He and his men regularly raided federal posts in Virginia and Maryland. He initially commanded only nine men on his raids, but "Mosby's Rangers" expanded to eight companies by the end of the Civil War.

National Women's Loyal League (Women's National Loyal League)   Organization formed in 1863 by Northern female reformers who wanted a role in the outcome of the Civil War. Collected approximately 400,000 signatures in support of a constitutional amendment abolishing slavery in the United States.

Nativism   Anti-immigrant and anti-Catholic sentiment that was prevalent before and during the Civil War. Before the war, Nativists formed the American Party (also called the Know-Nothing Party), which eventually was enveloped by the Republican Party.

Nurses   Women first entered the previously male-dominated field of nursing during the Civil War. Female nurses served in home front hospitals, in battlefield hospitals, on hospital ships, and wherever else they were needed. In the Confederacy, many women became nurses because of their proximity to the battles.

Olmsted, Frederick Law (1822–1903)   General secretary of the U.S. Sanitary Commission from 1861 until 1863 who supervised branch offices and the distribution of food, clothing, and medical supplies to soldiers. Also a landscape architect who designed Central Park and other parks both before and after the Civil War, and a travel writer.

Parole   Captured Civil War soldiers were often released after they swore not to take up arms again until officially exchanged. The informal system was formalized with a cartel based on ranks in July 1862. The parole and exchange system broke down in 1863, after the release of the Emancipation Proclamation.

Pensions, Soldiers'   The United States established a pension system for Civil War soldiers in 1862. Union soldiers received discharge pay and a government pension for their service beginning with the war's close. Confederate soldiers did not receive pensions until the end of Reconstruction.

Pensions, Widows' As early as 1862, wives of deceased Union soldiers became eligible to receive government aid as the survivors of men who were entitled to military pensions. Confederate widows received some aid during the war but did not receive pensions until the 1880s, when state governments made provisions for the wives of Confederate soldiers.

Petersburg Campaign (June 1864–April 1865) A 10-month siege that culminated in the capture of Richmond. Nearly 160,000 soldiers ultimately participated in this campaign for the Confederate capital in Virginia. The campaign resulted in almost 70,000 casualties.

Plantations Large rural landholdings in the South operated with slave labor. Southern plantations primarily grew rice, cotton, or tobacco.

Port Royal Sea Island off the coast of South Carolina that was captured by the Union in November 1861. Freedmen and freedwomen took possession and cultivated the lands until their white owners reclaimed their plantations after the war. Schools for freedpeople were set up here, and Northern women came to serve as teachers for the former slaves.

Prisons More than 150 military prisons existed during the war. Many were simply overcrowded camps with little protection from the elements and food shortages. Nearly 410,000 men spent some time in a Civil War prison.

Quantrill, William Clarke (1837–1865) Notorious commander of a band of Confederate guerillas. He and his men were made an official part of the Confederate Army in 1862, with Quantrill as a captain. He led his 450 men in the sacking of Lawrence, Kansas, in 1863. He died during an 1865 raid in Kentucky.

Reconstruction Period of reunification from the Civil War for the United States and of rebuilding for the American South. Events seen as part of Reconstruction date from 1861. The period officially ended in 1877 with the removal of federal troops from the South. During this era, African Americans enjoyed new social, political, and economic freedoms.

Red Rover First Union hospital ship, created in June 1862. It was not only equipped to house and care for wounded soldiers and sailors, but also carried supplies to other navy ships. Nurses from the Sisters of the Holy Cross were the first women to serve on a navy ship.

Refugees Many people left their homes for the presumed safety of cities or the aid of family members during the Civil War. Approximately 200,000 Southerners became refugees as the result of food shortages, disease, impending Union invasion, or destruction of their homes. Slaves became refugees (and contrabands) when they escaped and ran to Union lines.

Republican Party Political party formed in 1854 of former Whigs, antislavery Democrats, Free Soilers, and Know-Nothings. In 1860, Abraham Lincoln was the first presidential candidate to win on the Republican ticket.

Ross, John (1790–1866) Democratically elected principal chief of the Cherokee Nation during the Civil War. He led the Cherokees' resistance to removal before the Trail of Tears and remained a powerful leader until his death in 1866. During the war, he initially advocated Native American neutrality, then sided with the Confederacy, and ultimately became a Unionist.

Sanitary Fairs Fund-raising galas run by the U.S. Sanitary Commission and designed to raise money for the Union war effort. The largest fair was held in Chicago in 1863. Organizers raised more than $70,000 through this venue.

Sea Islands Abandoned plantations on these islands off the coasts of South Carolina, Georgia, and Florida were temporarily redistributed to freedpeople after the Civil War. Schools and hospitals were set up to aid the freedpeople, and Northern women traveled south to staff these institutions. Slaves on these islands had cultivated rice and cotton.

Scalawags Derogatory term used for white Southerners who supported Northern Republicans' plans for the Reconstruction South or who aided the freedmen. The term was applied to white Unionists and to former Whigs who remained in the South throughout the war.

Secession Withdrawal from the Union. In response to Republican Abraham Lincoln's election, South Carolina voted to secede from the Union on December 20, 1860. In 1860 and 1861, 10 other slaveholding states joined South Carolina in seceding and formed the Confederate States of America.

Shaw, Robert Gould (1837–1863) Commander of the Union's first black regiment, the Massachusetts Fifty-fourth. Killed during the assault on Battery Wagner, South Carolina, in July 1863, Shaw was buried in a common grave with his soldiers.

Sheridan, Philip Henry (1831–1888) Union cavalry officer born in New York and raised in Ohio. During his 1864 campaign in Virginia's Shenandoah Valley, Sheridan and his troops systematically destroyed foodstuffs, farm implements, and other civilian items seen as vital to the support of the Confederate armies.

Sherman Land (Special Field Order Number 15) Issued on January 16, 1865, by General William T. Sherman. The order made provisions to redistribute the land on the Sea Islands to freedmen who applied. Each family was entitled to 40 acres of land.

Sherman, William Tecumseh (1820–1891) Union Army officer best known for his march through Georgia and the Carolinas with 60,000 troops. Played prominent roles in the Battle of Shiloh, the fall of Vicksburg, and the Atlanta campaign, as well as in the march to the sea and through the Carolinas. He received the surrender of Confederate Joseph Johnston near Durham, North Carolina.

Shiloh, Battle of (April 6–7, 1862)   Largest and deadliest engagement in the Mississippi Valley campaign. Union forces led by Ulysses S. Grant and Don Carlos Buell and Confederates led by Albert Sidney Johnston and P. G. T. Beauregard met in southwestern Tennessee near Shiloh Church and Pittsburg Landing. The battle resulted in a Union victory and combined casualties of almost 24,000.

Shirkers   Derogatory term applied to men who refused to enlist in the Civil War armies.

Slavery   System of unfree labor employed in the plantation South. Elite white Southern slaveholders considered their black slaves to be chattel property. At the outset of the Civil War, there were approximately 4 million slaves in the United States.

Sons of Confederate Veterans   Organization founded in 1896 to preserve the Confederate version of the Civil War. Members of this hereditary organization participate in preservation efforts and reenactments, among other activities.

Southern Unionists   Those in Confederate territory who supported the Union war effort, either through actions or sentiment.

Springfield Rifle (U.S. Rifle Musket)   Weapons produced at the Springfield Armory in Massachusetts. Used by both Union and Confederate soldiers throughout the Civil War.

Stowe, Harriet Beecher (1811–1896)   Abolitionist author of *Uncle Tom's Cabin; Or, Life Among the Lowly* (1851). The book was first published in serial form and was credited by many as an impetus for the war against slavery.

Strong, George Templeton (1820–1875)   Treasurer of the U.S. Sanitary Commission and founder of the Union League Club in New York City.

Suffrage   The right to vote. African American men received this right with the passage of the Fifteenth Amendment in 1870. American women did not have the right to vote until the enactment of the Nineteenth Amendment in 1920.

Taylor, Susie King (1848–1912)   Former slave who served as a nurse and laundress for the 33rd U.S. Colored Troops in South Carolina. She taught other freedpeople to read and write. Hers is the only memoir of an African American woman who served during the Civil War.

Thirteenth Amendment   Constitutional amendment that abolished slavery. Readmission into the Union required ratification of this amendment. It was incorporated into the Constitution on December 18, 1865.

Treasury Girls   Term used to describe women hired by the Confederate government between 1862 and 1865. They worked in clerical positions for the Treasury Department, Quartermaster Department, War Department,

Post Office Department, and Commissary General. They often filled positions left vacant by the men in the Confederate armies.

Tredegar Ironworks, CSS Richmond, Virginia, iron foundry. Produced much of the artillery and cannon used by Confederate soldiers as well as the armor that lined the ironclad CSS *Virginia*. By 1863, Tredegar's workforce had expanded from 900 to 2,500 and included shoemaking shops, a sawmill, a tannery, and a firebrick factory. It was protected during the fall of Richmond in April 1865.

Truth, Sojourner [Isabella Baumfree] (1797–1883) Abolitionist, former slave, women's rights activist, and preacher. Truth traveled the United States giving lectures on abolitionism, women's rights, religion, and temperance. She helped the Union war effort by fund-raising, nursing, collecting supplies, and aiding former slaves.

Tubman, Harriet [Araminta Ross] (1822–1913) Runaway slave who helped others escape from Southern slavery to the free states. An abolitionist and a suffragist, Tubman aided those on the Underground Railroad. She also became a Union spy and nurse.

United Confederate Veterans (UCV) Organization formed in 1889 by former Confederate soldiers. It served as a benevolent, historical, social, and literary association. The last reunion planned by the UCV was held in 1951.

United Daughters of the Confederacy Organization formed in 1894 by white Southern women. Members work to preserve the Confederate memory of the Civil War as well as to preserve Civil War sites. They promote the ideals of the Lost Cause and generally romanticize the Old South.

United States Christian Commission Organization created by the Young Men's Christian Association in 1861 to raise money and send supplies to Union soldiers. Set up reading rooms at some army camps and distributed more than 1 million Bibles to soldiers.

United States Sanitary Commission Formed in June 1861 to coordinate relief efforts throughout the United States. Inspected and improved sanitary conditions at camps and military hospitals. Provided supplies and nurses to soldiers.

Van Lew, Elizabeth (1818–1900) Virginia spy for the Union. She remained in Richmond throughout the war, entertaining Confederate officers and government officials and then passing on information to Union authorities.

Vicksburg, Siege of (1863) Union forces cut off supplies to Vicksburg in May 1863, causing food shortages and desperation. The Union capture of Vicksburg, Mississippi, on July 4, 1863, cut the Confederacy in two and gave the United States control of the Mississippi River.

Vivandieres Women who accompanied military units to war. They served as laundresses, nurses, and cooks and some fulfilled ceremonial functions.

Wirz, Henry (1823–1865) Confederate commander of the Andersonville Prison in Georgia. Only man executed for war crimes after the Civil War.

"Woman Order" (General Order Number 28) Order issued by Union general Benjamin F. Butler in New Orleans on May 15, 1862. It declared that any woman showing contempt for the occupying Union troops would be "regarded and held liable to be treated as a woman of the town plying her avocation." The order was designed to control the city's hostile female population.

Women's Central Association of Relief Female aid society and precursor to the U.S. Sanitary Commission established in New York City in April 1861. Members provided health services and provisions to Union soldiers.

Wormeley, Katherine Prescott (1830–1908) Union nurse and hospital administrator in 1862 and 1863. Founded the Woman's Union Aid Society in Newport, Rhode Island, in 1861 and became the assistant manager of the New England branch of the U.S. Sanitary Commission. Worked on a hospital ship. Published a history of the U.S. Sanitary Commission and published her Civil War memoir.

Young Men's Christian Association (YMCA) The YMCA's first club in the United States was founded in Boston in 1855. During the Civil War, members created the U.S. Christian Commission to help Union soldiers.

Bibliography

Abel, Annie Heloise. 1915/1992a. *The American Indian as Slaveholder and Secessionist*. Lincoln: University of Nebraska.

Abel, Annie Heloise. 1919/1992b. *The American Indian in the Civil War, 1862–1865*. Lincoln: University of Nebraska Press. (Reprint of *The American Indian as Participant in the Civil War*. Cleveland, OH: Arthur H. Clark.)

Alleman, Tillie Pierce. 1889. *At Gettysburg or What a Girl Saw and Heard of the Battle*. New York: W. Lake Borland.

Alvarez, David J. 1983. "The Papacy in the Diplomacy of the American Civil War." *Catholic Historical Review* 69: 227–248.

Anderson, Gary Clayton, and Alan R. Woolworth. 1988. *Through Dakota Eyes: Narrative Accounts of the Minnesota Indian War of 1862*. St. Paul: Minnesota Historical Society Press.

Arrington, Leonard. 1985. *Brigham Young: American Moses*. New York: Alfred A. Knopf.

Arrington, Leonard, and Davis Bitton. 1979. *The Mormon Experience: A History of the Latter-day Saints*. New York: Alfred A. Knopf.

Ash, Stephen V. 1988. *Middle Tennessee Society Transformed, 1860–1870: War and Peace in the Upper South*. Baton Rouge: Louisiana State University Press.

Ash, Stephen V. 1991. "Poor Whites in the Occupied South, 1861–1865." *Journal of Southern History* 57 (1): 39–62.

Ash, Stephen V. 1995. *When the Yankees Came: Conflict and Chaos in the Occupied South, 1861–1865*. Chapel Hill: University of North Carolina Press.

Ash, Stephen V. 2002. *A Year in the South: Four Lives in 1865*. New York: Palgrave Macmillan.

Ash, Stephen V. 2008. *Firebrand of Liberty: The Story of Two Black Regiments That Changed the Course of the Civil War*. New York: W. W. Norton and Company.

Attie, Jeanie. 1992. "Warwork and the Crisis of Domesticity in the North." In *Divided Houses: Gender and the Civil War*, edited by Catherine Clinton and Nina Silber, 247–259. New York: Oxford University Press.

Attie, Jeanie. 1998. *Patriotic Toil: Northern Women and the American Civil War*. Ithaca, NY: Cornell University Press.

Ayers, Edward L. 2003. *In the Presence of Mine Enemies: War in the Heart of America, 1859–1863*. New York: W. W. Norton and Company.

Bailey, Anne J. 2003. *War and Ruin: William T. Sherman and the Savannah Campaign*. Wilmington, DE: Scholarly Resources, Inc.

Bailey, Anne J. 2006. *Invisible Southerners: Ethnicity in the Civil War*. Athens: University of Georgia Press.

Baker, Paula. 1984. ''The Domestication of Politics: Women and American Political Society, 1780–1900.'' *American Historical Review* 89 (June): 620–647.

Bardaglio, Peter. 1992. ''The Children of the Jubilee: African American Childhood in Wartime.'' In *Divided Houses: Gender and the Civil War*, edited by Catherine Clinton and Nina Silber, 213–229. New York: Oxford University Press.

Bardaglio, Peter W. 2002. ''On the Border: White Children and the Politics of War in Maryland.'' In *The War Was You and Me: Civilians in the American Civil War*, edited by Joan E. Cashin, 313–331. Princeton, NJ: Princeton University Press.

Barton, George. 1898. *Angels of the Battlefield: A History of the Labors of the Catholic Sisterhoods in the Late Civil War*. Philadelphia, PA: Catholic Art Publishing Company.

Barton, H. Arnold. 1975. *Letters from the Promised Land: Swedes in America, 1840–1914*. Minneapolis: University of Minnesota Press.

''Battle of Sugar Creek or Pea Ridge.'' *Saturday Evening Post*, March 29, 1862, 7.

Bercaw, Nancy. 2003. *Gendered Freedoms: Race, Rights, and the Politics of Household in the Delta, 1861–1875*. Gainesville: University Press of Florida.

Berlin, Ira. 1998. *Many Thousands Gone: The First Two Centuries of Slavery in America*. Cambridge, MA: The Belknap Press of Harvard University Press.

Berlin, Ira, Barbara J. Fields, Steven F. Miller, Joseph P. Reidy, and Leslie S. Rowland. 1992. *Slaves No More: Three Essays on Emancipation and the Civil War*. New York: Cambridge University Press.

Berlin, Ira, Joseph P. Reidy, and Leslie S. Rowland, eds. 1982. *Freedom: A Documentary History of Emancipation, 1861–1867. Series II: The Black Military Experience*. New York: Cambridge University Press.

Berlin, Ira, Joseph P. Reidy, and Leslie S. Rowland, eds. 1998. *Freedom's Soldiers: The Black Military Experience in the Civil War*. New York: Cambridge University Press.

Berlin, Ira, and Leslie S. Rowland, eds. 1997. *Families and Freedom: A Documentary History of African-American Kinship in the Civil War Era*. New York: New Press.

Berlin, Jean V. 2001. ''Did Confederate Women Lose the War?: Deprivation, Destruction, and Despair on the Homefront.'' In *The Collapse of the*

Confederacy, edited by Mark Grimsley and Brooks D. Simpson, 168–193. Lincoln: University of Nebraska Press.

Bernstein, Iver. 1991. *The New York City Draft Riots: Their Significance for American Society and Politics in the Age of the Civil War*. New York: Oxford University Press.

Blair, William. 1998. *Virginia's Private War: Feeding Body and Soul in the Confederacy, 1861–1865*. New York: Oxford University Press.

Blanton, DeAnne. 1993. "Women Soldiers of the Civil War." *Prologue: The Journal of the National Archives* 25: 27–35.

Blanton, DeAnne, and Lauren M. Cook. 2002. *They Fought Like Demons: Women Soldiers in the Civil War*. New York: Vintage Books.

Blegen, Theodore, ed. 2001. *The Civil War Letters of Hans Christian Heg*. Northfield, MN: Norwegian-American Historical Association.

Bleser, Carol, ed. 1991. *In Joy and In Sorrow: Women, Family, and Marriage in the Victorian South*. New York: Oxford University Press.

Bleser, Carol K., and Lesley J. Gordon, eds. 2001. *Intimate Strategies of the Civil War: Military Commanders and Their Wives*. New York: Oxford University Press.

Blied, Benjamin J. 1945. *Catholics and the Civil War*. Milwaukee, WI: Bruce Publishing Company.

Blight, David W. 1991. *Frederick Douglass' Civil War: Keeping Faith in Jubilee*. Baton Rouge: Louisiana State University Press.

Blight, David W. 2001. *Race and Reunion: The Civil War in American Memory*. Cambridge, MA: Harvard University Press.

Botume, Elizabeth Hyde. 1968. *First Days amongst the Contrabands*. New York: Arno Press and *New York Times*.

Boyd, Belle. 1865. *Belle Boyd, In Camp and Prison*. New York: Blelock.

Bradley, Mark L. 2000. *This Astounding Close: The Road to Bennett Place*. Chapel Hill: University of North Carolina Press.

Brewer, James H. 1969. *The Confederate Negro*. Durham, NC: Duke University Press.

Brinsfield, John Wesley. 2003. *Faith in the Fight: Civil War Chaplains*. Mechanicsburg, PA: Stackpole Books.

Brockett, L. P., and Mary C. Vaughn. 1867. *Women's Work in the Civil War: A Record of Heroism, Patriotism and Patience*. Philadelphia, PA: Zeigler, McCurdy and Co.; R. H. Curran.

Brown, Alexis Girardin. 2000. "The Women Left Behind: The Transformation of the Southern Belle, 1840–1880." *The Historian* 62: 759–778.

Brown, Thomas J. 1997. *Dorothea Dix: New England Reformer*. Cambridge, MA: Harvard University Press.

Bryan, Charles F., Jr. 1988. "Tories Amidst Rebels: Confederate Occupation of East Tennessee, 1861–1863." *East Tennessee Historical Society Papers* 60: 3–22.

Burrows, Edwin G., and Mike Wallace. 1999. *Gotham: A History of New York City to 1898*. New York: Oxford University Press.

Burton, Orville Vernon. 1985. *In My Father's House Are Many Mansions: Family and Community in Edgefield, South Carolina*. Chapel Hill: University of North Carolina Press.

Burton, Orville Vernon. 2007. *The Age of Lincoln*. New York: Hill and Wang.

Burton, William L. 1980. "'Title Deed to America:' Union Ethnic Regiments in the Civil War." *Proceedings of the American Philosophical Society* 124, no. 6 (December): 455–463.

Bynum, Victoria E. 1992. *Unruly Women: The Politics of Social and Sexual Control in the Old South*. Chapel Hill: University of North Carolina Press.

Bynum, Victoria E. 2001. *The Free State of Jones: Mississippi's Longest Civil War*. Chapel Hill: University of North Carolina Press.

Calloway, Colin G. 2008. *First Peoples: A Documentary Survey of American Indian History*. 3rd ed. Boston: Bedford/St. Martins.

Campbell, Edward, Jr., and Kym S. Rice. 1996. *A Woman's War: Southern Women, Civil War, and the Confederate Legacy*. Richmond, VA: Museum of the Confederacy.

Campbell, Eugene E. 1988. *Establishing Zion: The Mormon Church in the American West, 1847–69*. Salt Lake City, UT: Signature Books.

Campbell, Jacqueline Glass. 2003. *When Sherman Marched North from the Sea: Resistance on the Confederate Home Front*. Chapel Hill: University of North Carolina Press.

Carmichael, Peter S. 2005. *The Last Generation: Young Virginians in Peace, War, and Reunion*. Chapel Hill: University of North Carolina Press.

Carter, Kate B. 1956. *Utah during Civil War Years*. Salt Lake City, UT: Daughters of Utah Pioneers, Central Co.

Cashin, Joan E. 1990. "The Structure of Antebellum Families: 'The Ties That Bound Us Was Strong.'" *Journal of Southern History* 56: 55–70.

Cashin, Joan E. 1996. *Our Common Affairs*. Baltimore, MD: Johns Hopkins University Press.

Cashin, Joan E., ed. 2002. *The War Was You and Me: Civilians in the American Civil War*. Princeton, NJ: Princeton University Press.

Cashin, Joan E. 2006. *First Lady of the Confederacy: Varina Davis's Civil War*. Cambridge, MA: The Belknap Press of Harvard University Press.

Censer, Jane Turner. 1987. *North Carolina Planters and Their Children, 1800–1860*. Baton Rouge: Louisiana State University Press.

Censer, Jane Turner. 2003. *The Reconstruction of White Southern Womanhood, 1865–1895*. Baton Rouge: Louisiana State University Press.

Chesnut, Mary Boykin. 1981. *Mary Chesnut's Civil War*, edited by C. Vann Woodward. New Haven, CT: Yale University Press.

Chesnut, Mary Boykin. 1984. *The Private Mary Chesnut: The Unpublished Civil War Diaries*, edited by C. Vann Woodward and Elisabeth Muhlenfeld. New York: Oxford University Press.

Cimprich, John. 2005. *Fort Pillow, a Civil War Massacre, and Public Memory*. Baton Rouge: Louisiana State University Press.

Click, Patricia C. 2001. *Time Full of Trial: The Roanoke Island Freedmen's Colony, 1862–1867*. Chapel Hill: University of North Carolina Press.

Clinton, Catherine. 1982. *The Plantation Mistress: Woman's World in the Old South*. New York: Pantheon Books.

Clinton, Catherine. 1995. *Tara Revisited: Women, War, and the Plantation Legend*. New York: Abbeville Press.

Clinton, Catherine. 2000a. *Fanny Kemble's Civil Wars*. New York: Simon & Schuster.

Clinton, Catherine, ed. 2000b. *Southern Families at War: Loyalty and Conflict in the Civil War South*. New York: Oxford University Press.

Clinton, Catherine, and Nina Silber, eds. 1992. *Divided Houses: Gender and the Civil War*. New York: Oxford University Press.

Clinton, Catherine, and Nina Silber, eds. 2006. *Battle Scars: Gender and Sexuality in the American Civil War*. New York: Oxford University Press.

Confer, Clarissa W. 2007. *The Cherokee Nation in the Civil War*. Norman: University of Oklahoma Press.

Conyngham, David Porter, and Lawrence Frederick Kohl. 1998. *The Irish Brigade and Its Campaigns*. New York: Fordham University Press.

Cornish, Dudley Taylor. 1987. *The Sable Arm: Black Troops in the Union Army, 1861–1865*. Lawrence: University Press of Kansas.

Cox, LaWanda. 1985. *Lincoln and Black Freedom: A Study in Presidential Leadership*. Urbana: University of Illinois Press.

Creighton, Margaret S. 2002. "Living on the Fault Line: African American Civilians and the Gettysburg Campaign." In *The War Was You and Me: Civilians in the American Civil War*, edited by Joan E. Cashin, 209–236. Princeton, NJ: Princeton University Press.

Creighton, Margaret S. 2005. *The Colors of Courage: Gettysburg's Forgotten History, Immigrants, Women, and African Americans in the Civil War's Defining Battle*. New York: Basic Books.

Cronon, William. 1991. *Nature's Metropolis: Chicago and the Great West*. New York: W. W. Norton and Company.

Cullen, Jim. 1992. "'I's a Man Now': Gender and African American Men." In *Divided Houses: Gender and the Civil War*, edited by Catherine Clinton and Nina Silber, 76–91. New York: Oxford University Press.

Cunningham, Frank. 1998. *General Stand Waite's Confederate Indians*. Norman: University of Oklahoma Press.

Dale, Edward Everett, and Gaston Litton. 1939. *Cherokee Cavaliers*. Norman: University of Oklahoma Press.

Desjardin, Thomas A. 1995. *Stand Firm Ye Boys From Maine: The Twentieth Maine and the Gettysburg Campaign*. New York: Oxford University Press.

Dickens, William Earl. 1998. "The Standardization of the Military Chaplaincy during the American Civil War." PhD diss., Southern Baptist Theological Seminary.

Diner, Hasia R. 1983. *Erin's Daughters in America: Irish Immigrant Women in the Nineteenth Century*. Baltimore, MD: Johns Hopkins University Press.

"Domestic Intelligence." *Harper's Weekly*, September 30, 1865, 611.

Durrill, Wayne K. 1990. *War of Another Kind: A Southern Community in the Great Rebellion*. New York: Oxford University Press.

Dyer, Thomas G. 1999. *Secret Yankees: The Union Circle in Confederate Atlanta*. Baltimore, MD: Johns Hopkins University Press.

Edmondston, Catherine Anne Devereaux. 1979. *Journal of a Secesh Lady: The Diary of Catherine Ann Devereaux Edmondston, 1860–1866*, edited by Beth G. Crabtree and James Welch Patton. Raleigh: North Carolina Division of Archives and History, Department of Cultural Resources.

Edwards, Laura F. 1997. *Gendered Strife and Confusion: The Political Culture of Reconstruction*. Urbana: University of Illinois Press.

Edwards, Laura F. 2000. *Scarlett Doesn't Live Here Anymore: Southern Women in the Civil War Era*. Urbana: University of Illinois Press.

Elmore, Elting, in Old Schoolmates Association. 1910. "Reunion of Former Attendants of Milwaukee University and the Milwaukee High School." *Children in Urban America Project*, Hotel Pfister, September 8, 1910, Marquette University, Milwaukee, Wisconsin.

Elmore, Grace Brown. 1997. *A Heritage of Woe: The Civil War Diary of Grace Brown Elmore, 1861–1868*, edited by Marli F. Weiner. Athens: University of Georgia Press.

Escott, Paul D. 2006. *Military Necessity: Civil-Military Relations in the Confederacy*. Westport, CT: Praeger.

Evans, Eli N. 1973. *The Provincials: A Personal History of Jews in the South*. New York: Atheneum.

Evans, Eli N. 1988. *Judah P. Benjamin, the Jewish Confederate*. New York: Free Press.

Fahs, Alice. 2001. *The Imagined Civil War: Popular Literature of the North & South, 1861–1865*. Chapel Hill: University of North Carolina Press.

Faulkner, Carol. 2004. *Women's Radical Reconstruction: The Freedmen's Aid Movement*. Philadelphia: University of Pennsylvania Press.

Faust, Drew Gilpin. 1988. *The Creation of Confederate Nationalism: Ideology and Identity in the Civil War South*. Baton Rouge: Louisiana State University Press.

Faust, Drew Gilpin. 1990. "Altars of Sacrifice: Confederate Women and the Narratives of War." *Journal of American History* 76: 1200–1228.

Faust, Drew Gilpin. 1992a. "'Trying to Do a Man's Business': Gender, Violence, and Slave Management in Civil War Texas." *Gender and History* 4: 197–214.

Faust, Drew Gilpin. 1992b. *Southern Stories: Slaveholders in Peace and War*. Columbia: University of Missouri Press.

Faust, Drew Gilpin. 1996. *Mothers of Invention: Women of the Slaveholding South in the American Civil War*. Chapel Hill: University of North Carolina Press.

Faust, Drew Gilpin. 1998. "Ours as Well as that of the Men: Women and Gender in the Civil War." In *Writing the Civil War: The Quest to Understand*, edited by James M. McPherson and William J. Cooper, Jr., 228–240. Columbia: University of South Carolina Press.

Faust, Drew Gilpin. 2000. "A Moment of Truth: A Woman of the Master Class in the Confederate South." In *Slavery, Secession and Southern History*, edited by Robert Louis Paquette and Louis A. Ferleger, 126–139. Charlottesville: University Press of Virginia.

Faust, Drew Gilpin. 2005. "'The Dread Void of Uncertainty': Naming the Dead in the American Civil War." *Southern Cultures* 11: 7–32, 113.

Faust, Drew Gilpin. 2008. *This Republic of Suffering: Death and the American Civil War*. New York: Alfred A. Knopf.

Fellman, Michael. 1989. *Inside War: The Guerrilla Conflict in Missouri during the American Civil War*. New York: Oxford University Press.

Fellman, Michael. 1992. "Women and Guerilla Warfare." In *Divided Houses: Gender and the Civil War*, edited by Catherine Clinton and Nina Silber, 147–165. New York: Oxford University Press.

Fellman, Michael. 2000. *The Making of Robert E. Lee*. New York: Random House.

Fisher, Noel C. 2001. *War at Every Door: Partisan Politics and Guerrilla Violence in East Tennessee, 1860–1869*. Chapel Hill: University of North Carolina Press.

Forbes, Ella. 1998. *African American Women during the Civil War*. New York: Garland Publishing, Inc.

Fox-Genovese, Elizabeth. 1988. *Within the Plantation Household: Black and White Women of the Old South*. Chapel Hill: University of North Carolina Press.

Frank, Andrew K. 1999. *The Routledge Historical Atlas of the American South*. New York: Routledge.

Frank, Lisa Tendrich. 2001. "To 'Cure Her of Her Pride and Boasting': The Gendered Implications of Sherman's March." PhD diss., University of Florida.

Frank, Lisa Tendrich. 2005. "War Comes Home: Confederate Women and Union Soldiers." In *Virginia's Civil War*, edited by Peter Wallenstein and Bertram Wyatt-Brown, 123–136. Charlottesville: University of Virginia Press.

Frankel, Noralee. 1999. *Freedom's Women: Black Women and Families in Civil War Era Mississippi*. Bloomington: Indiana University Press.

Franklin, John Hope. 1963. *The Emancipation Proclamation*. Garden City, NJ: Doubleday.

Furman, Jan, ed. 1998. *Slavery in the Clover Bottoms: John McCline's Narrative of His Life During Slavery and the Civil War*. Knoxville: University of Tennessee Press.

Gabaccia, Donna. 1994. *From the Other Side: Immigrant Life in the U.S., 1820–1990*. Bloomington: Indiana University Press.

Gaines, W. Craig. 1989. *The Confederate Cherokees: John Drew's Regiment of Mounted Rifles*. Baton Rouge: Louisiana State University Press.

Gallagher, Gary W., ed. 1996. *Chancellorsville: The Battle and its Aftermath*. Chapel Hill: University of North Carolina Press.

Gallagher, Gary W. 1997a. *The Confederate War: How Popular Will, Nationalism, and Military Strategy Could not Stave Off Defeat*. Cambridge, MA: Harvard University Press.

Gallagher, Gary W., ed. 1997b. *The Wilderness Campaign*. Chapel Hill: University of North Carolina Press.

Gallagher, Gary W. 2006. *The Shenandoah Valley Campaign of 1864*. Chapel Hill: University of North Carolina Press.

Gallagher, Gary W., and Alan T. Nolan, eds. 2000. *The Myth of the Lost Cause and Civil War History*. Bloomington: Indiana University Press.

Gallman, J. Matthew. 1990. *Mastering Wartime: A Social History of Philadelphia During the Civil War*. New York: Cambridge University Press.

Gallman, J. Matthew. 1994. *The North Fights the Civil War: The Home Front*. Chicago, IL: Ivan R. Dee.

Gannon, James P. 1995. *Irish Rebels, Confederate Tigers: A History of the 6th Louisiana Volunteers, 1861–1865*. New York: Cambridge University Press.

Gardener, Sarah E. 2004. *Blood and Irony: Southern White Women's Narratives of the Civil War, 1861–1937*. Chapel Hill: University of North Carolina Press.

Gardenhire, Kibbie Tinsley Williams. 1939. "Memoir." Tennessee State Library and Archives, Nashville.

Gibson, Arrell Morgan. 1985. "Native Americans and the Civil War." *American Indian Quarterly* 9: 385–410.

Giesberg, Judith Ann. 2000. *Civil War Sisterhood: The U.S. Sanitary Commission and Women's Politics in Transition*. Boston, MA: Northeastern University Press.

Ginsburg, Lawrence M. 2001. *Israelites in Blue and Gray: Unchronicled Tales from Two Cities*. Lanham, MD: University Press of America.

Ginzberg, Lori D. 1990. *Women and the Work of Benevolence: Morality, Politics, and Class in the Nineteenth-Century United States*. New Haven, CT: Yale University Press.

Gladstone, William A. 1990. *United States Colored Troops: 1863–1867*. Gettysburg, PA: Thomas Publications.

Glatthaar, Joseph T. 1990. *Forged in Battle: The Civil War Alliance of Black Soldiers and White Officers*. New York: Free Press.

Gordon, Lesley, J. 1998. *General George E. Pickett in Life and Legend*. Chapel Hill: University of North Carolina Press.

Gordon, Lesley J., and John C. Inscoe, eds. 2005. *Inside the Confederate Nation*. Baton Rouge: Louisiana State University Press.

Gottschalk, Phil. 1991. *In Deadly Earnest, The History of the First Missouri Brigade, CSA*. Columbia, MO: Missouri River Press.

Grimké, Charlotte Forten. 1988. *The Journals of Charlotte Forten Grimké*, edited by Brenda Stevenson. New York: Oxford University Press.

Grimsley, Mark. 1995. *The Hard Hand of War: Union Military Policy toward Southern Civilians, 1861–1865*. New York: Cambridge University Press.

Grimsley, Mark. 2002. *And Keep Moving On: The Virginia Campaign, May-June 1864*. Lincoln: University of Nebraska Press.

Grimsley, Mark, and Brooks D. Simpson, eds. 2001. *The Collapse of the Confederacy*. Lincoln: University of Nebraska Press.

Grunberger, Michael W., and Hasia R. Diner. 2004. *From Haven to Home: 350 Years of Jewish Life in America*. New York: George Braziller in association with the Library of Congress.

Guterman, Benjamin. 2000. "Doing 'Good Brave Work': Harriet Tubman's Testimony at Beaufort, South Carolina." *Prologue* 32: 154–65.

Gutman, Herbert G. 1976. *The Black Family in Slavery and Freedom, 1750–1925*. New York: Pantheon Books.

Hall, Richard H. 2006. *Women on the Civil War Battlefront*. Lawrence: University Press of Kansas.

Hatch, Thom. 2003. *The Blue, the Gray, and the Red: Indian Campaigns of the Civil War*. Mechanicsburg, PA: Stackpole Books.

Hauptman, Laurence M. 1993. *The Iroquois in the Civil War: From Battlefield to Reservation*. Syracuse, NY: Syracuse University Press.

Hauptman, Laurence M. 1995a. *Between Two Fires: American Indians in the Civil War*. New York: Free Press.

Hauptman, Laurence M., ed. 1995b. *A Seneca Indian in the Union Army: The Civil War Letters of Sergeant Isaac Newton Parker, 1861–1865*. Shippensburg, PA: Burd Street Press.

Hawks, Esther Hill. 1984. *A Woman Doctor's Civil War: Esther Hill Hawks' Diary*, Gerald Schwartz, ed. Columbia: University of South Carolina Press.

Hays, William Shakespeare. 1863. *The Drummer Boy of Shiloh*. Augusta, GA: Blackmar & Bro.

Hearn, Chester G. 1997. *When the Devil Came Down to Dixie: Ben Butler in New Orleans*. Baton Rouge: Louisiana State University Press.

Heathcote, C. W. 1919. *The Lutheran Church in the Civil War*. New York: Fleming H. Revell Company.

Holcomb, Julie. 2002. "Eyewitness to War: Samuel N. Kennerly." *America's Civil War* 15, no. 5 (November): 32.

Holzapfel, R. N. 1994. "The Civil War in Utah." *Utah History Encyclopedia*, A. K. Powell, ed. Salt Lake City: University of Utah Press.

Horowitz, Murray M. 1978. "Ethnicity and Command: The Civil War Experience." *Military Affairs* 42, no. 4 (December): 182–189.

Horton, James Oliver, and Lois E. Horton. 1979. *Black Bostonians: Family Life and Community Struggle in the Antebellum North*. New York: Holmes and Meier.

Hubbard, George U. 1963. "Abraham Lincoln as Seen by the Mormons." *Utah Historical Quarterly* 31 (Spring): 91–108.

Hunter, Tera W. 1997. *To 'Joy My Freedom: Southern Black Women's Lives and Labors After the Civil War*. Cambridge, MA: Harvard University Press.

"The Indian Murderers in Minnesota." *Harper's Weekly*, December 20, 1862, 807.

Inscoe, John C. 1996. "The Civil War's Empowerment of an Appalachian Woman: The 1864 Slave Purchases of Mary Bell." In *Discovering the Women in Slavery: Emancipating Perspectives of the American Past*, edited by Patricia Morton, 61–81. Athens: University of Georgia Press.

Inscoe, John C. 2005. "'Talking Heroines': Elite Mountain Women as Chroniclers of Stoneman's Raid, April 1865." In *Inside the Confederate Nation*, edited by Lesley J. Gordon and John C. Inscoe, 230–247. Baton Rouge: Louisiana State University Press.

Inscoe, John C., and Robert C. Kenzer, eds. 2001. *Enemies of the Country: New Perspectives on Unionists in the Civil War South*. Athens: University of Georgia Press.

Inscoe, John C., and Gordon B. McKinney. 2003. *The Heart of Confederate Appalachia: Western North Carolina and the Civil War*. Chapel Hill: University of North Carolina Press.

Jabour, Anya. 2007. *Southern Sisters: Young Women in the Old South*. Chapel Hill: University of North Carolina Press.

Jenkins, Wilbert J. 2002. *Climbing Up to Glory: A Short History of African Americans during the Civil War and Reconstruction*. Wilmington, DE: Scholarly Resources, Inc.

Johnston, Carolyn Ross. 2003. *Cherokee Women in Crisis: Trail of Tears, Civil War, and Allotment*. Tuscaloosa: University of Alabama Press.

Joiner, Gary D., Marilyn S. Joiner, and Clifton D. Cardin, eds. *No Pardons to Ask, nor Apologies to Make: The Journal of William Henry King, Gray's 28th Louisiana Infantry Regiment*. Knoxville: University of Tennessee Press, 2006.

Jones, Jacqueline. 1985. *Labor of Love, Labor of Sorrow: Black Women, Work and the Family from Slavery to the Present*. New York: Vintage Press.

Jones, Kelsey. 2005. *Battlefields, Bibles, and Bandages: Portraying an American Civil War Nun*. Westminster, MD: Heritage Books.

Jones, Terry L. 1987. *Lee's Tigers: The Louisiana Infantry in the Army of Northern Virginia*. Baton Rouge: Louisiana State University Press.

Josephy, Alvin M., Jr. 1991. *The Civil War in the American West*. New York: Alfred A. Knopf.

Kaplan, Benjamin. 1973. "Judah Philip Benjamin." In *Jews in the South*, edited by Leonard Dinnerstein and Mary Dale Palsson, 75–88. Baton Rouge: Louisiana State University Press.

Karamanski, Theodore J. 1993. *Rally 'Round the Flag: Chicago and the Civil War*. Chicago: Nelson-Hall.

Kaufmann, Wilhelm. 1999. *The Germans in the American Civil War*, trans. Steven Rowan; Don Heinrich Tolzmann, Wener D. Mueller, and Robert E. Ward, eds. Carlisle, PA: John Kallman Publishers.

Keckley, Elizabeth. 1868/1988. *Behind the Scenes, or Thirty Years a Slave and Four Years in the White House*. New York: Oxford University Press.

Kennedy, X. J., Dorothy M. Kennedy, and Jane E. Aaron, eds. 2008. *The Brief Bedford Reader*. New York: Macmillan.

King, Wilma. 2006. *The Essence of Liberty: Free Black Women during the Slave Era*. Columbia: University of Missouri Press.

Kneeland, Jonathan. 1864. "Remarks on the Social and Sanitary Condition of the Onondoga Indians." *Ohio Medical and Surgical Journal* 16 (5): 453.

Kohl, Lawrence Frederick. 1986. *Irish Green and Union Blue*. New York: Fordham University Press.

Kohl, Lawrence Frederick, ed. 1992. *William Corby, C.S.C.: Memoirs of Chaplain Life: Three Years with the Irish Brigade in the Army of the Potomac*. New York: Fordham University Press.

Korn, Bertram Wallace. 1951. *American Jewry and the Civil War*. Philadelphia, PA: Jewish Publication Society of America.

Korn, Bertram Wallace. 1973a. "American Judaeophobia: Confederate Version." In *Jews in the South*, edited by Leonard Dinnerstein and Mary Dale Palsson, 135–156. Baton Rouge: Louisiana State University Press.

Korn, Bertram Wallace. 1973b. "Jews and Negro Slavery in the Old South, 1789–1865." In *Jews in the South*, edited by Leonard Dinnerstein and Mary Dale Palsson, 89–134. Baton Rouge: Louisiana State University Press.

Krauthamer, Barbara. 2006. "In Their 'Native Country': Freedpeople's Understandings of Culture and Citizenship in the Choctaw and Chickasaw Nations." In *Crossing Waters, Crossing Worlds: The African Diaspora in Indian Country*, edited by Tiya Miles and Sharon P. Holland, 100–120. Durham, NC: Duke University Press.

Larson, Gustive O. 1965. "Utah and the Civil War." *Utah Historical Quarterly* 33 (Winter): 55–77.

Lash, Jeffrey N. 1989. "'The Federal Tyrant at Memphis': General Stephen A. Hurlbut and the Union Occupation of West Tennessee, 1862–1864." *Tennessee Historical Quarterly* 48 (1): 15–28.

Lawson, Melinda. 2002. *Patriot Fires: Forging a New American Nationalism in the Civil War North*. Lawrence: University Press of Kansas.

Lebsock, Suzanne. 1984. *The Free Women of Petersburg: Status and Culture in a Southern Town, 1784–1860*. New York: W. W. Norton and Company.

LeConte, Emma. 1987. *When the World Ended: The Diary of Emma LeConte*, Earl Schenck Meirs, ed. Lincoln: University of Nebraska Press.

Leonard, Elizabeth D. 1994. *Yankee Women: Gender Battles in the Civil War*. New York: W.W. Norton and Company.

Leonard, Elizabeth D. 1995. "Civil War Nurse, Civil War Nursing: Rebecca Usher of Maine." *Civil War History* 41: 190–207.

Leonard, Elizabeth D. 1999. *All the Daring of the Soldier: Women of the Civil War Armies*. New York: W. W. Norton and Company.

Lerner, Gerda. 1998. *The Grimké Sisters from South Carolina: Pioneers for Women's Rights and Abolition*. New York: Oxford University Press.

Levine, Bruce. 1992. *The Spirit of 1848: German Immigrants, Labor Conflict, and the Coming of the Civil War*. Urbana: University of Illinois Press.

Lewis, Lloyd. 1932. *Sherman: Fighting Prophet*. New York: Harcourt, Brace and Company.

Litwack, Leon F. 1980. *Been in the Storm So Long: The Aftermath of Slavery*. New York: Vintage Books.

Lockwood, Lewis C., and Charlotte Forten. 1969. *Two Black Teachers during the Civil War*. New York: Arno Press and *New York Times*.

Long, E. B. 1981. *The Saints and the Union: Utah Territory during the Civil War*. Urbana: University of Illinois Press.

Logue, Larry M. 1996. *To Appomattox and Beyond: The Civil War Soldier in War and Peace*. Chicago: Ivan R. Dee.

Lovoll, Odd S. 1999. *The Promise of America: A History of the Norwegian-American People*. Minneapolis: University of Minnesota Press.

Lowry, Thomas P. 2006. *Confederate Heroines: 120 Southern Women Convicted by Union Military Justice*. Baton Rouge: Louisiana State University Press.

Macaulay, John Allen. 2001. *Unitarianism in the Antebellum South: The Other Invisible Institution*. Tuscaloosa: University of Alabama Press.

Maher, Mary Denis. 1989. *To Bind Up Their Wounds: Catholic Sister Nurses in the U.S. Civil War*. New York: Greenwood Press.

Manning, Chandra. 2007. *What This Cruel War Was Over: Soldiers, Slavery, and the Civil War*. New York: Alfred A. Knopf.

Marcus, Jacob Rader, ed. 1996. *The Jew in the American World*. Detroit, MI: Wayne State University Press.

Marten, James. 1990. *Texas Divided: Loyalty and Dissent in the Lone Star State*. Lexington: University of Kentucky Press.

Marten, James. 1998. *The Children's Civil War*. Chapel Hill: University of North Carolina Press.

Marten, James A. 2003. *Civil War America: Voices from the Home Front*. Santa Barbara, CA: ABC-CLIO.

Marten, James A. 2004. *Children for the Union: The War Spirit on the Northern Homefront*. Chicago, IL: Ivan R. Dee.

Marten, James, and A. Kristen Foster, eds. 2008. *Essays on the Civil War Era*. Kent, OH: Kent State University Press.

Massey, Mary Elizabeth. 1949. "The Food and Drink Shortage on the Confederate Homefront." *North Carolina Historical Review* 26: 306–334.

Massey, Mary Elizabeth. 1952/1993. *Ersatz in the Confederacy: Shortages and Substitutes on the Southern Homefront*. Columbia: University of South Carolina Press.

Massey, Mary Elizabeth. 1964/2001. *Refugee Life in the Confederacy*. Baton Rouge: Louisiana State University Press.

Massey, Mary Elizabeth. 1966/1994. *Women in the Civil War* (Reprint of *Bonnet Brigades*). Lincoln: University of Nebraska Press.

McBride, Lela J. 2000. *Opothleyaholo and the Loyal Muskogee: Their Flight to Kansas in the Civil War*. Jefferson, NC: McFarland and Co.

McDonald, JoAnna M. 1999. *''We Shall Meet Again'': The First Battle of Manassas (Bull Run) July 18–21, 1861*. New York: Oxford University Press.

McGreevy, John T. 2003. *Catholicism and American Freedom*. New York: W. W. Norton and Company.

McLoughlin, William Gerald. 1993. *After the Trail of Tears: The Cherokees Struggle for Sovereignty, 1839–1880*. Chapel Hill: University of North Carolina.

McPherson, James M. 1982. *The Negro's Civil War: How American Negroes Felt and Acted during the War for the Union*. Urbana: University of Illinois Press.

McPherson, James M. 1988. *Battle Cry of Freedom: The Civil War Era*. New York: Ballantine Books.

McPherson, James M. 1992. *Marching Towards Freedom: Blacks in the Civil War, 1861–1865*. New York: Facts on File.

McPherson, James M. 1997. *For Cause and Comrades: Why Men Fought in the Civil War*. New York: Oxford University Press.

McPherson, James M., and William J. Cooper, Jr., eds. 1998. *Writing the Civil War: The Quest to Understand*. Columbia: University of South Carolina Press.

Meagher, Timothy. 2005. *The Columbia Guide to Irish American History*. New York: Columbia University Press.

Micco, Melinda. 2006. *'''Blood and Money': The Case of Seminole Freedmen and Seminole Indians in Oklahoma.'' In *Crossing Waters, Crossing Worlds: The African Diaspora in Indian Country*, edited by Tiya Miles and Sharon P. Holland, 121–144. Durham, NC: Duke University Press.

Miller, Randall M. 1998. ''Catholic Religion, Irish Ethnicity, and the Civil War.'' In *Religion and the American Civil War*, edited by Randall M. Miller, Harry S. Stout, and Charles Reagan Wilson, 261–296. New York: Oxford University Press.

Miller, Randall M., Harry S. Stout, and Charles Reagan Wilson, eds. 1998. *Religion and the American Civil War*. New York: Oxford University Press.

''The Missouri Imbroglio.'' *The Independent*, October 10, 1861, 671.

Mitchell, Reid. 1988. *Civil War Soldiers*. New York: Viking Press.

Mitchell, Reid. 1993. *The Vacant Chair: The Northern Soldier Leaves Home*. New York: Oxford University Press.

Mohr, Clarence L. 1986. *On the Threshold of Freedom: Masters and Slaves in Civil War Georgia*. Athens: University of Georgia Press.

Mohr, Clarence. 2005. ''The Atlanta Campaign and the African American Experience in Civil War Georgia.'' In *Inside the Confederate Nation*, edited by Lesley J. Gordon and John C. Inscoe, 272–294. Baton Rouge: Louisiana State University Press.

Mooney, James. 1900. ''Myths of the Cherokees.'' In *Nineteenth Annual Report of the Bureau of American Ethnology 1897–98, Part I*. Washington, DC: Smithsonian Institution.

Moore, Frank. 1866. *Women of the War: Their Heroism and Self-sacrifice, True Stories of Brave Women in the Civil War*. Hartford, CT: S. S. Scranton.

Morton, Patricia, ed. 1996. *Discovering the Women in Slavery: Emancipating Perspectives of the American Past*. Athens: University of Georgia Press.

Nichols, David A. 1999. *Lincoln and the Indians: Civil War Policy and Politics*. Urbana: University of Illinois Press.

Nichols, Roger L. 2003. *American Indians in U.S. History*. Norman: University of Oklahoma Press.

O'Conner, Thomas H. 1997. *Civil War Boston: Home Front and Battlefield*. Boston, MA: Northeastern University Press.

Oakley, Christopher Arris. 2005. *Keeping the Circle: American Indian Identity in Eastern North Carolina, 1885–2004*. Lincoln: University of Nebraska Press.

Oates, Stephen B. 1994. *A Woman of Valor: Clara Barton and the Civil War*. New York: Free Press.

Oates, Stephen B. 1997. *The Approaching Fury: Voices of the Storm, 1820–1860*. New York: HarperCollins Publishers.

Oates, Stephen B. 1998. *The Whirlwind of War: Voices of the Storm, 1861–1865*. New York: HarperCollins Publishers.

Ochs, Stephen J. 2000. *A Black Patriot and a White Priest: André Cailloux and Claude Paschal Maistre in Civil War New Orleans*. Baton Rouge: Louisiana State University Press.

Ott, Victoria E. 2008. *Confederate Daughters: Coming of Age during the Civil War*. Carbondale: Southern Illinois University Press.

Paine, Albert Bigelow. 1904. *Thomas Nast: His Period and His Pictures*. New York: MacMillan.

Painter, Nell Irvin. 1996. *Sojourner Truth: A Life, a Symbol*. New York: W. W. Norton and Company.

Paludan, Phillip S. 1988. *A People's Contest: The Union and Civil War, 1861–1865*. Lawrence: University Press of Kansas.

Paludan, Phillip Shaw. 1998a. *War and Home: The Civil War Encounter*. Milwaukee, WI: Marquette University Press.

Paludan, Phillip Shaw. 1998b. ''Religion and the American Civil War.'' In *Religion and the American Civil War*, edited by Randall M. Miller, Harry S. Stout, and Charles Reagan Wilson, 21–40. New York: Oxford University Press.

Parker, Arthur C. 1919. *The Life of General Ely S. Parker: Last Grand Sachem of the Iroquois and General Grant's Military Secretary*. Buffalo, NY: Buffalo Historical Society.

Pease, Jane H., and William H. Pease. 1999. *A Family of Women: The Carolina Petigrus in Peace and War*. Chapel Hill: University of North Carolina Press.

Perdue, Theda. 1999. *Cherokee Women: Gender and Culture Change, 1700–1835*. Lincoln: University of Nebraska Press.

Phipps, Sheila. 2004. *Genteel Rebel: The Life of Mary Greenhow Lee*. Baton Rouge: Louisiana State University Press.

Power, J. Tracy. 1998. *Lee's Miserables: Life in the Army of Northern Virginia from the Wilderness to Appomattox*. Chapel Hill: University of North Carolina Press.

Pula, James S. 1963. "Alexander Schimmelfennig: A German-American Campaigner in the Civil War." *Pennsylvania Magazine of History and Biography* 87 (April): 156–181.

Quarles, Benjamin. 1953. *The Negro in the Civil War*. Boston, MA: Little, Brown and Company.

Rable, George C. 1989. *Civil Wars: Women and the Crisis of Southern Nationalism*. Urbana: University of Illinois Press.

Rable, George C. 1992. "'Missing in Action': Women of the Confederacy." In *Divided Houses: Gender and the Civil War*, edited by Catherine Clinton and Nina Silber, 134–146. New York: Oxford University Press.

Rable, George C. 1994. *The Confederate Republic: A Revolution Against Politics*. Chapel Hill: University of North Carolina Press.

Rable, George C. 2002a. *Fredericksburg! Fredericksburg!* Chapel Hill: University of North Carolina Press.

Rable, George C. 2002b. "Hearth, Home, and Family in the Fredericksburg Campaign." In *The War Was You and Me: Civilians in the American Civil War*, edited by Joan E. Cashin, 85–111. Princeton, NJ: Princeton University Press.

Raus, Jr., Edmund J. 2005. *Banners South: A Northern Community at War*. Kent, OH: Kent State University Press.

Reardon, Carol. 1997. *Pickett's Charge in History and Memory*. Chapel Hill: University of North Carolina Press.

Reid, Richard M. 2008. *Freedom for Themselves: North Carolina's Black Soldiers in the Civil War Era*. Chapel Hill: University of North Carolina Press.

Revels, Tracy J. 2004. *Grander in Her Daughters: Florida's Women during the Civil War*. Columbia: University of South Carolina Press.

Richardson, Heather Cox. 1997. *The Greatest Nation on Earth*. Cambridge, MA: Harvard University Press.

Roark, James L. 1977. *Masters Without Slaves: Southern Planters in the Civil War and Reconstruction*. New York: W. W. Norton and Company.

Roark, James L. 1998. "Behind the Lines: Confederate Economy and Society." In *Writing the Civil War: The Quest to Understand*, edited by James M.

McPherson and William J. Cooper, Jr. Columbia: University of South Carolina Press.

Robertson, James I., Jr. 1988. *Soldiers: Blue and Gray*. Columbia: University of South Carolina Press.

Rose, Willie Lee. 1964. *Rehearsal for Reconstruction: The Port Royal Experiment*. Indianapolis, IN: Bobbs-Merrill.

Rosen, Robert N. 2000. *The Jewish Confederates*. Columbia: University of South Carolina Press.

Ross, Kristie. 1992. "Arranging a Doll's House: Refined Women as Union Nurses." In *Divided Houses: Gender and the Civil War*, edited by Catherine Clinton and Nina Silber, 97–113. New York: Oxford University Press.

Royster, Charles. 1993. *The Destructive War: William Tecumseh Sherman, Stonewall Jackson, and the Americans*. New York: Vintage Books.

Rubin, Anne Sarah. 2005. *A Shattered Nation: The Rise and Fall of the Confederacy*. Chapel Hill: University of North Carolina Press.

Sacher, John M. 2003. *A Perfect War of Politics: Parties, Politicians, and Democracy in Louisiana, 1824–1861*. Baton Rouge: Louisiana State University Press.

Sacher, John M. 2007. "'A Very Disagreeable Business': Confederate Conscription in Louisiana." *Civil War History* 53, no. 2 (June): 141–169.

Sarna, Jonathan. 2004. *American Judaism: A History*. New Haven, CT: Yale University Press.

Schultz, Duane. 2002. *The Most Glorious Fourth: Vicksburg and Gettysburg, July 4, 1863*. New York: W. W. Norton and Company.

Schultz, Jane E. 2002. "Seldom Thanked, Never Praised and Scarcely Recognized: Gender and Racism in Civil War Hospitals." *Civil War History* 48 (3): 220–236.

Schultz, Jane E. 2004. *Women at the Front: Hospital Workers in Civil War America*. Chapel Hill: University of North Carolina Press.

Schwalm, Leslie A. 1997. *A Hard Fight for We: Women's Transition from Slavery to Freedom in South Carolina*. Urbana: University of Illinois Press.

Scott, Anne Firor. 1970. *The Southern Lady: From Pedestal to Politics, 1830–1930*. Chicago, IL: University of Chicago Press.

Scranton, Philip. 1983. *Proprietary Capitalism: The Textile Manufacture at Philadelphia, 1800–1885*. New York: Cambridge University Press.

Selby, John G. 2002. *Virginians at War: The Civil War Experiences of Seven Young Confederates*. Wilmington, DE: Scholarly Resources, Inc.

Shannon, Fred A., ed. 1947. *The Civil War Letters of Sergeant Onley Andrus*. Urbana: University of Illinois Press.

Shattuck, Gardiner H. 1987. *A Shield and Hiding Place: The Religious Life of the Civil War Armies*. Macon, GA: Mercer University Press.

Sheehan-Dean, Aaron. 2007. *Why Confederates Fought: Family and Nation in Civil War Virginia*. Chapel Hill: University of North Carolina Press.

Silber, Nina. 2002. "A Compound of Wonderful Potency: Women Teachers of the North in the Civil War South." In *The War Was You and Me: Civilians in the American Civil War*, edited by Joan E. Cashin, 35–59. Princeton, NJ: Princeton University Press.

Silber, Nina. 2005. *Daughters of the Union: Northern Women Fight the Civil War*. Cambridge, MA: Harvard University Press.

Simonhoff, Harry. 1963. *Jewish Participants in the Civil War*. New York: Arco.

"The Sioux War." *Harper's Weekly*, October 31, 1863, 695.

Sizer, Lyde Cullen. 2000. *The Political Work of Northern Women Writers and the Civil War, 1850–1872*. Chapel Hill: University of North Carolina Press.

Smithers, Leslie. 2004. "Profit and Corruption in Civil War Natchez: A Case History of Union Occupation Government." *Journal of Mississippi History* 64 (1): 17–32.

Spence, John C. 1993. *A Diary of the Civil War*. Nashville, TN: Williams Printing Co. for the Rutherford County Historical Society.

Spiegel, Marcus M. 1985. *Your True Marcus: The Civil War Letters of a Jewish Colonel*. Kent, OH: Kent State University Press.

Stevenson, Brenda, ed. 1988. *The Journals of Charlotte Forten Grimke*. New York: Oxford University Press.

Stevenson, Brenda E. 1996. *Life in Black and White: Family and Community in the Slave South*. New York: Oxford University Press.

Storey, Margaret M. 2004. *Loyalty and Loss: Alabama's Unionists in the Civil War and Reconstruction*. Baton Rouge: Louisiana State University Press.

Stowell, Daniel. 1998. *Rebuilding Zion: The Religious Reconstruction of the South, 1863–1877*. New York: Oxford University Press.

Stowell, Daniel W. 2000. "A Family of Women and Children: The Fains of East Tennessee during Wartime." In *Southern Families at War: Loyalty and Conflict in the Civil War South*, edited by Catherine Clinton, 155–173. New York: Oxford University Press.

Sutherland, Daniel. 1995. *Seasons of War: The Ordeal of a Confederate Community, 1861–1865*. New York: Free Press.

Swint, Henry L., ed. 1966. *Dear Ones at Home: Letters from Contraband Camps*. Nashville, TN: Vanderbilt University Press.

Symonds, Craig L. 1998. *Stonewall of the West: Patrick Cleburne and the Civil War*. Kansas City: University Press of Kansas.

Taylor, Amy Murrell. 2005. *The Divided Family in Civil War America*. Chapel Hill: University of North Carolina Press.

Taylor, Lenette S. 2002. "Uncle Sam's Landlord: Quartering the Union Army in Nashville During the Summer of 1863." *Tennessee Historical Quarterly* 61 (4): 242–265.

Taylor, Susie King. 1904/1968. *Reminiscences of My Life in Camp*. New York: Arno Press and *New York Times*.

Taylor-Colbert, Alice. 1997. "Cherokee Women and Cultural Change." In *Women of the American South*, edited by Christie Anne Farnham, 43–55. New York: New York University Press.

Tplzman, Don Heinrich. 2000. "The Friend, a Religious and Literary Journal," May 8, 1863, In *The German-American Experience*. Amherst, NY: Humanity Books.

Trefousse, Hans. 1982. *Carl Schurz: A Biography*. Knoxville: University of Tennessee Press.

Trudeau, Noah Andre. 1998. *Like Men of War: Black Troops in the Civil War, 1862–1865*. Boston, MA: Little, Brown and Company.

Tucker, Phillip Thomas. 1992. *The Confederacy's Fighting Chaplain: Father John B. Bannon*. Tuscaloosa: University of Alabama Press.

Tucker, Philip Thomas. 1993. *The South's Finest: The First Missouri Confederate Brigade from Pea Ridge to Vicksburg*. New York: William Morrow.

Valuska, David L., and Christian B. Keller. 2004. *Damn Dutch: Pennsylvania Germans at Gettysburg*. Mechanicsburg, PA: Stackpole Books.

Varon, Elizabeth R. 1998. *We Mean to Be Counted: White Women and Politics in Antebellum Virginia*. Chapel Hill: University of North Carolina Press.

Varon, Elizabeth R. 2003. *Southern Lady, Yankee Spy: The True Story of Elizabeth Van Lew, A Union Agent in the Heart of the Confederacy*. New York: Oxford University Press.

Venet, Wendy Hamand. 1991. *Neither Ballots nor Bullets: Women Abolitionists and the Civil War*. Charlottesville: University Press of Virginia.

Vinovskis, Maris A. 1990. *Toward a Social History of the American Civil War*. Cambridge, UK: Cambridge University Press.

Vorenberg, Michael. 2004. *Final Freedom: The Civil War, the Abolition of Slavery, and the Thirteenth Amendment*. New York: Cambridge University Press.

Wakeman, Sarah Rosetta. 1995. *An Uncommon Soldier: The Civil War Letters of Sarah Rosetta Wakeman, alias Private Lyons Wakeman, 153rd Regiment, New York State Volunteers*, edited by Lauren Cook Burgess. New York: Oxford University Press.

Wallenstein, Peter, and Bertram Wyatt-Brown, eds. 2005. *Virginia's Civil War*. Charlottesville: University of Virginia Press.

Ward, Andrew. 2005. *River Run Red: The Fort Pillow Massacre in the American Civil War*. New York: Viking Press.

Warde, Mary Jane. 1999. *George Washington Grayson and the Creek Nation, 1843–1920*. Norman: University of Oklahoma Press.

Waugh, Charles G., and Martin H. Greenberg, eds. 1999. *The Women's War in the South: Recollections and Reflections of the American Civil War*. Nashville, TN: Cumberland House.

Weatherford, Doris. 1986. *Foreign and Female: Immigrant Women in America, 1840–1930*. New York: Schocken Books.

Weiner, Marli F. 1998. *Mistresses and Slaves: Plantation Women in South Carolina, 1830–80*. Urbana: University of Illinois Press.

Wells, Cheryl A. 2005. *Civil War Time: Temporality and Identity in America, 1861–1865*. Athens: University of Georgia Press.

Werner, Emmy E. 1998. *Reluctant Witnesses: Children's Voices from the Civil War*. Boulder, CO: Westview Press.

Wetherington, Mark V. 2005. *Plain Folk's Fight: The Civil War and Reconstruction in Piney Woods Georgia*. Chapel Hill: University of North Carolina Press.

White, Christine Schultz. 1996. *Now the Wolf Has Come: The Creek Nation in the Civil War*. College Station: Texas A&M University Press.

White, Ronald C. Jr. 2002. *Lincoln's Greatest Speech: The Second Inaugural*. New York: Simon & Schuster.

Whites, LeeAnn. 1992. "The Civil War as a Crisis in Gender." In *Divided Houses: Gender and the Civil War*, edited by Catherine Clinton and Nina Silber, 3–21. New York: Oxford University Press.

Whites, LeeAnn. 1995. *The Civil War as a Crisis in Gender, Augusta, Georgia, 1860-1890*. Athens: University of Georgia Press.

Whites, LeeAnn. 2005. *Gender Matters: Civil War, Reconstruction, and the Making of the New South*. New York: Palgrave Macmillan.

Wiley, Bell Irvin. 1943/1994. *The Life of Johnny Reb: The Common Soldier of the Confederacy*. Baton Rouge: Louisiana State University Press.

Wiley, Bell Irvin. 1952/1994. *The Life of Billy Yank: The Common Soldier of the Union*. Baton Rouge: Louisiana State University Press.

Wiley, Bell Irvin. 1975/1994. *Confederate Women*. New York: Greenwood Press.

Williams, David. 2005. *A People's History of the Civil War: Struggles for the Meaning of Freedom*. New York: The New Press.

Williams, David. 2008. *Bitterly Divided: The South's Inner Civil War*. New York: The New Press.

Wimmer, Judith Conrad. 1980. "American Catholic Interpretations of the Civil War." PhD diss., Drew University.

Wood, Kirsten E. 2004. *Masterful Women: Slaveholding Widows from the American Revolution through the Civil War*. Chapel Hill: University of North Carolina Press.

Woodworth, Steven E. 2001. *While God Is Marching On: The Religious World of Civil War Soldiers*. Lawrence: University Press of Kansas.

Wyatt-Brown, Bertram. 2001. *The Shaping of Southern Culture: Honor, Grace, and War, 1760s-1880s*. Chapel Hill: University of North Carolina Press.

Young, Mel. 1991. *Where They Lie: The Story of the Jewish Soldiers of the North and South whose deaths—[killed, mortally wounded or died of disease or other causes] occurred during The Civil War, 1861–1865: Someone Should Say Kaddish*. Latham, MD: University Press of America.

Index